DATE			

Rags and Ragtime

Rags and Ragtime

A MUSICAL HISTORY

David A. Jasen & Trebor Jay Tichenor

A Continuum Book
The Seabury Press
New York

The photographs used in this book have been provided from the authors' personal archives, with the following exceptions: the St. Louis parlor in the photo insert section following p. 76, courtesy of Fred and Joe Mazzulla Collection; Rifkin's Joplin rags album cover in the photo insert section following p. 250 © 1970 Nonesuch Records; cover art: Saul Lambert; cover design and art direction: Robert L. Heimall.

1978 *The Seabury Press*
815 Second Avenue New York, New York 10017

Library of Congress Cataloging in Publication Data

Jasen, David A   Rags and ragtime.
(A Continuum book)   Includes index.
1.Ragtime music—History and criticism. I.Tichenor, Trebor Jay, joint author. II.Title.
ML3561.R33J37   781.5'72'09   78–1558   ISBN 0–8164–9342–1

To our wives,
Susan Jasen and Jeanette Tichenor,
and our children, Raymond Jasen
and Virginia and Andrew Tichenor,
for their constant
encouragement and help.

Contents

List of Illustrations

· ix ·

Stark ad
Charles Daniels
Jerome Remick
Ted Snyder
Wild Cherries sheet music
Chatterbox Rag sheet music
Red Pepper sheet music
Minstrel Man sheet music
Heavy on the Catsup (photo of Lewis Muir)
Julia Lee Niebertall
Egbert Van Alstyne
Jean Schwartz
Bunny Hug Rag sheet music
Soup & Fish Rag sheet music
Nat Johnson
Gold Dust Twins sheet music
Julius Lenzberg
Sid Le Protti's shoe shine parlor

FOLLOWING PAGE 250
Circle Label
QRS label of Charley Straight rag
Fred Heltman
Irwin P. Leclere
Luella Anderson Piano Contest story
Ragging the Scale sheet music
Stumbling paraphrase sheet music
Jack Mills
Kitten on the Keys record label
Original *Kitten on the Keys* sheet music
Advertisement of original *Kitten* sheet music
Jack Robbins
Imperial Roll label of Bargy rag
Edythe Baker at piano
Honky Tonk Piano LP cover
Joe "Fingers" Carr, Jasen and Tichenor
Mississippi Valley Ragtime LP cover
Rompin' Stompin' Ragtime LP cover
Slugger Ryan LP cover
Joshua Rifkin's Joplin rags LP cover
The Entertainer LP cover
The Ragtime Review
The Rag Times
The Ragtimer
Eubie Blake and Dave Jasen

Acknowledgments

T his work is the culmination of more than twenty-five years of constant study, research, collecting and performing by both of us, individually. Because, until recently, ragtime was not considered a subject worthy of formal study, libraries and other traditional information sources could not be used. Our personal collections of original artifacts, sheet music, catalogs, trade publications, piano rolls and flat disc recordings formed the basis of this book. It is, therefore, most appropriate to give thanks to those dealers who, over the years, took special pains to provide us with these materials: Helen W. Cole, Bly Corning, Beverly Hamer, Lillian and Dulcina McNeill, William Russell, Michael Schwimmer, Tom Kraeuchi and Les Zeiger.

Throughout the years, interviews with survivors of the period helped to make real the times during which ragtime flourished. We are especially grateful to the late Arthur Marshall, the late Joe Lamb, the late Charles Thompson, the late Zez Confrey, the late Roy Bargy, and the ever-present Eubie Blake.

We should like to thank Rudi Blesh for making available to us the notebooks filled with the information gathered by him and the late Harriet Janis for their pioneering book, *They All Played Ragtime.*

It is our good fortune to have so many great friends in the ragtime world on whom we have drawn for information, artifacts, and stimulating company: Richard Allen, Steve Calt, John "Rusty" David, Sol Goodman, Thornton (Tony) Hagert, Roger Hankins, Joe Lamb, Jr., Max Morath, Dennis Pash, Al Rose, Joe Scotti, Carl Seltzer, Ed Sprankle, Bob Wright, Dick Zimmerman and Bob Darch.

And, finally, our grateful thanks to Mike Montgomery (b. Chicago, Illinois, March 9, 1934), for his generosity in helping to shape the book, in addition to supplying various materials as needed.

❧ 1 ❧

Ragtime as a Form and a Fad

Ragtime is a musical composition for the piano comprising three or four sections containing sixteen measures each which combines a syncopated melody accompanied by an even, steady duple rhythm. If there is one incontestable statement which can be made about ragtime, it is that ragtime is a paradoxical art form with a perplexing history. In an age of rigid racial divisions, ragtime appeared as a racially ambiguous commodity whose earliest composers had no common racial identity, nor the desire to promote their music under an ethnic banner.

Though ragtime constitutes a concrete musical idiom with more tangible structural features than jazz, its distinguishing musical characteristics were lost upon its early promoters and contemporary listening audience, and, thanks to a long tradition of erroneous commentary on the subject, remain muddled to this day. Although ragtime's compositional history must be discerned mostly through musty sheet music scores, it began as a performance medium. Early ragtime leaders viewed such scores as a point of musical departure, if they were able to read them at all. While ragtime's commercial history is inseparable from mainstream American popular music, where it played a prominent role between 1906 and the First World War, the composer who developed ragtime into a profitable commodity —Scott Joplin—seemed curiously innocent of crass commercial impulses, and remote from ragtime's lively tradition as a performing art.

By all rights, ragtime should have enjoyed little popularity, for it was far more complex than the competing pop music of its day and demanded rhythmic techniques that lay beyond the grasp of the amateur pianist for whom sheet music was tailored. Yet it not only became a staple of Tin Pan Alley (the clannish New York publishing houses that monopolized the music industry between 1890 and 1930), but proved so popular that the very word *ragtime* quickly became an indiscriminate label that was used to confer commerciality upon just about any music. But this is yet another paradox, for the original meaning of the word *ragtime* itself remains undiscoverable.*

So, too, are ragtime's pre-sheet music origins, which were lost in an undocumented lower-class tradition of saloon and whorehouse piano-playing, a tradition comprised of talented free-lance itinerants. Because the nineteenth-century saloon was invariably equipped with a piano, it offered ready employment to any roving pianist who could entertain the all-male saloon audiences of the times. Hence, the saloon became ragtime's earliest performance setting.† The typical saloon pianist was hired to provide a pleasant, nondescript background diversion, and was expected to honor requests. It is inconceivable that any of these musicians were restricted to a ragtime repertoire; this would have invited professional suicide. In reality, such now-celebrated "ragtime pianists" as Eubie Blake were all-purpose entertainers. They are not remembered as such now, not because ragtime was their only performing vehicle, but because their other period pieces are less interesting to modern listeners. By the same token, few early composers worked strictly within a ragtime format.

Although early ragtime's detractors made much of its lowly social origins, and even used its presumed racial origins as a means of dismissing the music as an art form, a ragtime that

---

*An early Bert Williams song, *Oh, I Don't Know, You're Not So Warm!*, used the word in 1896, a year before the publication of the first rag. As early as 1899, an etymology of the word appeared in a Boston *Musical Record* article on ragtime (Rupert Hughes' "A Eulogy of Ragtime"): "Negroes call their clog dancing 'ragging' and the dance a 'rag,' a dance largely shuffling." It cannot be demonstrated that this or any other derivation is trustworthy, and by the time *ragtime*—usually printed as "rag-time"—became a recognizable musical form, it had little utility as dance music.
†In early vaudeville, the piano was used only to accompany vocalists and thus offered little opportunity for early ragtime pianists to develop.

had emerged as a polite parlor pastime would have enjoyed little more prestige.* Both its chilly academic reception and the lack of data about ragtime's historical beginnings followed from the fact that it grew in an age when only classical music was considered worthy of serious scrutiny. Most of the written commentary ragtime inspired before its demise as popular music turned solely on the question of ragtime's musical legitimacy, expressing either the writer's individual distaste or, in some instances, enthusiasm for the form.

Ironically, the pompous prejudices that once rejected ragtime largely because it was a pleasurable form of popular entertainment are now responsible for ragtime's current reception as a hallowed art form; the music is now solemnly embraced by classicists precisely because it is construed as something more exalted and serious than mere entertainment. Yet of all ragtime composers, only Scott Joplin had any classical pretensions, and even Joplin was primarily concerned with achieving what he termed a "weird and intoxicating effect" upon the listener.

It was ragtime's relentless syncopation that made the music so striking and unsettling to a public accustomed to a sentimental musical diet of dreary ballads and buffoonish depictions of "darkies." So completely did ragtime mesmerize its turn-of-the-century audience that the word *ragtime* soon acquired a figurative meaning, synonymous with merry or lively.†

As well as creating a new sense of euphoria in American popular music, ragtime represented an unprecedented compositional format. As a musical entity ragtime was, and is, an instrumental work in 2/4 time composed *for the piano* that combines a syncopated series of melodies accompanied by an even, steady rhythm. Despite the fact that ragtime proved to be a

---

*"Ragtime that is different . . . played by the culture of all nations and . . . welcomed in the drawing rooms and boudoirs of good taste," were Classic Rag publisher John Stark's blurbs, obviously aimed at the parlor pianists of polite society. However, outside of St. Louis, it is questionable whether Stark's efforts to establish his publications as ragtime's "crème de la crème" ever superseded his one great success, *Maple Leaf Rag,* sheet music sales of which supported the rest of the catalog.
†A definition of ragtime given in the fifth volume of Farmer and Henley's *Slang and its Analogues* (1902), listed *rag-time girl* as a term for a sweetheart or harlot.

popular recording vehicle for both brass bands and banjos during the first decade of the century, it was seldom conceived for non-piano presentations and was generally ill-suited for it. The most sophisticated solo banjo rendition of a ragtime composition could produce only a one-dimensional melodic rhythm instead of the contrasting melodic and accompaniment rhythms made by the piano. By virtue of the fact that ragtime's *melodies* are too abstract and pianistic to be vocalized or even hummed, and its *syncopations* too elaborate to lend themselves to dancing, ragtime renounces these two basic components of American pop music and black folk music. The customary view of ragtime as a kind of musical hybrid created by someone with a Caucasian cortex and an African central nervous system shortchanges the significance of this renunciation, which Tin Pan Alley sought to obscure by labeling ragtime as dance music.*

A ragtime composition typically contains three or four distinct sections, each consisting of sixteen measures, and each a self-contained entity. In its serial presentation of melody, ragtime resembles the waltz or march rather than classical or jazz music, which give freer play to thematic development and variations. Structurally, the rag most resembles the march, which likewise consists of three or four sections. A march-like rhythm is produced by the left hand of the ragtime pianist, which accents the first and third notes of a measure in contrast with the syncopated right hand. This march-like flavor was undoubtedly a self-conscious device on the part of the earliest ragtime pianists, probably reflecting the fact that marches, such as Sousa's famous *Washington Post* of 1889, were often published for piano, and formed a basic part of the nineteenth-century popular piano repertoire.

The syncopation for which ragtime was chiefly noted, on the other hand, cannot be attributed to any one source. As a musical device, syncopation had an age-old association with black music and had long since been appropriated by minstrel banjoists by the time the first ragtime composition was published

---

*Most frequently, a ragtime composition was called a two-step.

in 1897.* But the syncopated patterns appearing in most subsequent ragtime were of a non-banjoistic character, which is not surprising, considering the fact that the piano had no place within the minstrel show. Moreover, ragtime presented a unique approach to syncopation that was found nowhere in the realm of previously published music, or even in the black folk music that was belatedly recorded in the 1920s. It was not a syncopated treatment of a straight-laced song, but a music whose melodies were *conceived* as fully syncopated. The distinction between ragtime and other styles of music containing syncopated elements was thus qualitative, not quantitative.

The now familiar ordering of ragtime's strains was copied from Joplin's *Maple Leaf Rag* of 1899. In 1906, when *Maple Leaf Rag* had sold nearly a half-million copies, the publication of Charles Leslie Johnson's *Dill Pickles—A New Rag* was destined to inspire the pattern for the hundreds of popular Tin Pan Alley rags. The "new" qualities were a shortened format from four to three sections and the use of the "three-over-four" pattern of syncopation.†

The carefully-wrought framework of *Maple Leaf Rag* was new for its time and brought a measure of stability and precision to a form that had been previously marked by capricious key changes and an unschematic presentation of different sections. It amounted to five parts, with all but the third consisting of a sixteen-measure melody repeated once: AA BB A CC DD. Each part (except the third) was thus given the thirty-two measure value of the typical pop song chorus. The return to the initial strain (A) in the third part derived from familiar dance forms like the polka and the Schottische. This subdominant section (CC) which became a basic ragtime harmonic ingredient, is commonly termed the "trio," after march vocabulary.

Under the homogenizing influence of Tin Pan Alley, ragtime

---

*An anonymously-published instrumental, *The Bonja Song* (1818), contains the earliest documented instance of syncopation in American music.
†Ironically, the "three-over-four" pattern was used in the opening section of one of the first rags, *Roustabout Rag* by Paul Sarabresole of New Orleans. But the idea did not catch on until *Dill Pickles* became successful. Two years later, a similar rag hit, George Botsford's *Black and White Rag*, insured that this pattern would become a favorite device.

was not only given a predictable format but was invariably simplified, particularly in the left hand, to make it accessible to amateur pianists. Had ragtime been a purely compositional medium, its Tin Pan Alley presentation would have had a blighting effect on the form. But only the mediocre ragtime performer, who lacked the capacity to create his own individual flourishes, was ever limited by ragtime sheet music. Even Joplin, who took a strict view of ragtime as an unalterable written form, was willing to add bass embellishments to the seven rags he produced as piano rolls and thus leave his own performance signature for posterity.* His protégé S. Brun Campbell would recall turn-of-the-century ragtime pianists thus: "None of the original pianists played ragtime the way it was written. They played their own style . . . if you knew the player and heard him a block away, you could name him by his ragtime style." A similar observation was offered by Axel Christensen, a Chicagoan who began teaching ragtime to amateurs in 1903 and would author a series of best-selling instruction books on the subject: "In 1902 and 1903 there was no accepted method or system of playing ragtime . . . no two pianists ever played syncopated numbers alike."†

Unfortunately for the music historian, this emphasis on individuality makes it impossible for modern-day ragtime musicians to convincingly re-create the lost styles of legendary ragtime figures; when an artist like Jelly Roll Morton offers pianistic impressions of his idol Tony Jackson, he scarcely suppresses his own distinct musical personality in the process. Because commercial record companies ignored piano ragtime (preferring band and banjo renditions), the true diversity of the form can no longer be fully appreciated.

If Tin Pan Alley tunesmiths and arrangers ultimately con-

---

*All piano rolls which were "hand-played" are open to question as accurate and faithful records of a performance. Unlike phonograph recordings, notes could be added or subtracted to a master roll after the initial performance. However, in 1959 Tichenor played two of the Joplin hand-played rolls for Arthur Marshall (see chapter 3), Joplin's close friend and fellow ragtimer from the Sedalia and early St. Louis days. When his attention was called to the quick octave embellishments in the bass, Marshall responded, "That was his style."

†Cf. Rudi Blesh and Harriet Janis, *They All Played Ragtime*, pp. 137–38.

verted ragtime into a cut-and-dried formula and obliterated much of its performing intricacy, it was nevertheless Tin Pan Alley's very promotion of the form that proved decisive in keeping it before the public. As a continuing vogue, ragtime was almost single-handedly fostered by the largest Tin Pan Alley publishing house, Jerome H. Remick and Company, which issued more ragtime compositions than its next ten competitors combined. The pivotal figure behind this commercial commitment to ragtime was Remick's manager, Charles N. Daniels, a highly successful songwriter whose sponsorship of the form actually preceded its emergence as pop music. While managing the Kansas City publishing firm of Carl Hoffman, Daniels had accepted Scott Joplin's early ragtime manuscript, *Original Rags,* in December of 1898. Upon becoming the head of Remick's predecessor, Whitney-Warner of Detroit, he arranged for the company's acquisition of both *Original Rags* and another previously-published Hoffman rag, the 1901 hit *Peaceful Henry* by E. Harry Kelly. After transferring to Remick, Daniels acquired *Dill Pickles* from Hoffman. Thereupon he seems to have indiscriminately accepted nearly every ragtime composition submitted to him before leaving the company in 1912, and his successor at Remick, Mose Gumble, would follow the same policy over the next five or six years, until ragtime went the way of all fads. Remick issued some five hundred rags, or roughly a sixth of the entire published ragtime output.

Tin Pan Alley's largest output was vocal music, so it was inevitable that rag songs would appear once instrumental ragtime assumed fad-like proportions. The so-called "ragtime song" was a genre whose very name was a contradiction in terms. Like the bona fide ragtime it pretended and was popularly taken to be, the ragtime song enjoyed huge popularity, resulting in such successes as Ted Snyder's *Wild Cherries Rag* of 1908 (which had originally sold nearly a million copies in instrumental form), Percy Wenrich's *Red Rose Rag* (a 1911 composition that could have passed muster as a three-theme ragtime instrumental had it not been vocalized), and such Irving Berlin favorites as *That Mesmerizing Mendelssohn Tune* (a syncopated treatment of Mendelssohn's *Spring Song* appearing in 1909), *The Grizzly Bear* (another work of instrumental origin, co-authored with George Botsford in 1910), *Ragtime Violin* (1911), and *That Mysterious Rag* (1911). Some two thousand such songs were published, two-thirds the number of authentic piano rags. The hack-like, "hokum" nature of the typical ragtime song was not lost upon the composers themselves, as the lyrics of Louis A. Hirsch's *The Bacchanal Rag* (1912) indicate:

> *Take some music,*
> *start to fake some music in a lag time*
> *Then you have some ragtime.*
> *Steal from the masters any classic you see*
> *Rag it a little bit with his melody*
> *Don't try at all to hide*
> *Call it the Gaby Glide**
> *No matter what it may be*
> *Other writers will give brother writers inspiration*
> *Handy op'ra will be dandy just for syncopation.*

Indeed, it was the oversimplified view of ragtime as a musical synonym of syncopation that gave rise to the ragtime song itself and inspired the popular game of "ragging" the classics. Yet the notion that ragtime could be created merely by giving a syncopated bounce to any pre-existent melody had been used as an arranging gimmick by Tin Pan Alley even before the first published ragtime composition appeared in 1897. In 1896 Max Hoffman, an orchestrator for the firm of Witmark and Sons, had furnished the company with what he termed "rag accompaniment" sections for choruses of various then-popular "coon" songs, including Ernest Hogan's *All Coons Look Alike To Me* and W. T. Jefferson's *My Coal Black Lady.* The following year Witmark would issue a Hoffman-arranged *Rag Medley* comprised of six such song choruses and a complete version of Ben Harney's *Mister Johnson, Turn Me Loose,* all rendered as syncopated instrumentals designed for the amateur pianist. A similar Hoffman compilation containing nine songs, *Ragtown*

---

*A reference to a Hirsch hit of the previous year.

Rags, appeared in 1898. *Ben Harney's Ragtime Instructor,* which Sol Bloom of Chicago published in 1897, would carry this notion of syncopated transformations even further by converting a semi-classical tune *(Annie Laurie),* a hymn *(Come Thou Fount),* and a show tune *(The Man That Broke The Bank At Monte Carlo)* into "ragtime."*

It is sometimes supposed that ragtime itself arose through a similar patchwork process of looping together and instrumentalizing various strains of black folk music. But this idea rests largely on an unsupported folk etymology of the word *ragtime,* with its prefix being taken as an analogy to bits of tattered cloth. The only black pianist who is known to have created such a composite was John W. (Blind) Boone (1869–1927), a renowned virtuoso from Columbia, Missouri, whose concert career was built on classical music and Boone's amazing ability to imitate other pianists who played for him. In 1912, however, Boone recorded several hand-played piano rolls for the Q. R. S. Company in Chicago that not only represent the earliest hand-played rolls, but afford one of the earliest glimpses of black folk music as interpreted by a black musician. As Boone was nearly fifty at the time of his Q. R. S. recordings, his playing was probably in the style of the nineteenth century. His treatment of folk material is astonishingly different from his romantic works, like *Woodland Murmurs* and *Sparkling Spring,* as well as Victorian parlor pieces like *When You And I Were Young, Maggie.* It is even more startling that two instrumental adaptations of such material should be offered as ragtime: *Rag Medley #1* (subtitled "Strains From the Alleys") and *Blind Boone's Southern Rag Medley #2* (subtitled "Strains From Flat Branch," invoking a Columbia neighborhood).† Both contained strains that were common to early jazz and blues musicians and remained in the black song tradition well into the 1920s: *I'm Alabama Bound*

---

*In this collection the unsyncopated original was set before its "ragtime" equivalent. In a similar vein, the Detroit composer Fred Stone produced a syncopated waltz, *Silks and Rags* (1901), which began in conventional waltz rhythm.

†The first of these was originally published in 1908 by Boone's manager, Wayne Allen of Columbia.

(which appeared in the "Flat Branch" medley) and *Make Me a Pallet On the Floor* (part of the "Alleys" medley).* While Boone did not syncopate this material in the manner of Max Hoffman's *Rag Medley,* his loose timing and idiosyncratic rhythm techniques give the impression of "ragged time" that some dictionaries see as the semantic source of the word *ragtime.* In one four-measure section of his "Flat Branch" medley, for example, he uses a 5/4 right-hand pattern set against a 4/4 bass. His use of suspension foreshadows a device that was used, though much less extravagantly, by Harlem Stride pianists like James P. Johnson.

Whether Boone's instrumental medleys represent the kind of potpourri approach that eventually blossomed into ragtime or are the products of an eccentric folk artist remains a moot point. Nor is it possible to perceive the direct predecessor of ragtime in isolated nineteenth-century piano compositions such as those of Boone's predecessor, Blind Thomas Greene Bethune, the eccentric slave genius, even though there are noteworthy instances of syncopation, such as Gottschalk's *La Bamboula* (1847), W.K. Batchelder's *Imitation of the Banjo* (1854), Otto Gunnar's *New Coon in Town* (1884), and George Lansing's *Darkies Dream* (1889). With the exception of Gottschalk's work (a depiction of a black festival dance performed in New Orleans to drum accompaniment), these pieces derived their syncopated patterns from minstrel banjo. *Imitation of the Banjo,* a jig-like exercise played cross-handed fashion that was dedicated to the famous minstrel banjoist Tom Briggs, features a marked accent on the second half of the first beat:

New Coon in Town, an instrumental with both folk and classical overtones, has an accent mark on the last after-beat:

*Alabama Bound, which Jelly Roll Morton claimed to have written in 1901–2, appeared in 1909 as the work of another New Orleans composer, Bob Hoffman. W. C. Handy recalled hearing *Pallet on the Floor* as early as 1892.

In *Southern Jollification* by Charles Kunkel (1890), the last after-beat is divided into two sixteenth notes:

Darkies Dream, which became a staple among vaudeville banjoists, mixes a Schottische rhythm with a syncopated pattern:

But in such pieces syncopation is not used as a compositional principle. Rather, it is coyly summoned as a flourish suggesting the imagined quaintness of "darky" music. Lest the parlor pianist failed to appreciate this, the St. Louis publisher of *Southern Jollification* obligingly provided a visual scenario:

> Synopsis: Darkies gathering at twilight after a day of cotton picking in the fields. Uncle Joshua leads off with his favorite song "I'm a happy little Nig" which is responded to by all the darkies in a grand "Hallelujah." Then follow the irresistible "Break Down" and Banjo Solo, while the dusky queens are up and tripping light fantastic step . . .*

In the same spirit of facile and probably far-fetched depiction of Negro life, the "coon" song and the cakewalk were developed in the mid-1890s. In the process, rudimentary syncopation entered mainstream popular music. While it cannot be demonstrated that either of these Tin Pan Alley confections

---

*"Break down" was the conventional nineteenth-century term for a black dancing party.

directly influenced the development of ragtime, their earlier vogues undoubtedly did much to enhance ragtime's commercial prospects.

The "coon" song, the comic counterpart of the 1890s tear-jerker ballad, became a craze with the publication of Ernest Hogan's *All Coons Look Alike To Me* in 1896 and remained standard fare in vaudeville and musical revues throughout the early 1900s. The "ragtime" song was a twentieth-century carry-over of the "coon" song tradition and, had the rag song not acquired more desirable commercial connotations, such "ragtime" favorites as Hughie Cannon's *Bill Bailey, Won't You Please Come Home?* (1902), Irving Berlin's *Alexander's Ragtime Band* (1911), and Shelton Brooks' *Darktown Strutters' Ball* (1917) would have been called "coon" songs. Both genres used lilting melodies and simple syncopation to create a happy-go-lucky quality.

Although the "coon" song lyric was grounded in crude racial stereotypes and portrayed blacks in either a contemptuous or condescending manner, the music that typically accompanied it represented an enlightened rhythmic departure from the straight-laced waltz time of the popular ballad. Most "coon" songs contained slight syncopation in both their vocal and accompaniment, though some (such as the 1894 offering, *Coon from the Moon*) featured no syncopation whatsoever, while others bore either a regularly-accented vocal melody set against a lightly-syncopated accompaniment or a syncopated vocal line set against a straight chordal accompaniment. Some "coon" songs contrasted a syncopated chorus with an unsyncopated verse. A popular "coon" song gimmick, found in such works as *My Coal Black Lady, Good Morning, Carrie,* and *My Lady Hottentot,* was to speed up the tempo in the chorus after a slow, ballad-style beginning.*

The "coon" song's frequent confusion with ragtime is largely attributable to the fanciful self-billing of one of its most gifted composers, Benjamin R. Harney (1871–1938), a Ken-

---

*Some of the early instrumental coon song medleys such as Max Hoffman's *Ragtown Rags* of 1898 indicated a slower tempo for certain tunes with the "C" or "cut-time" marking.

tucky-bred mulatto who promoted himself as "the Originator of Ragtime" while appearing at Tony Pastor's Music Hall (a New York theater that was considered the country's leading vaudeville house) in 1896. Soon afterward, two Harney compositions, *You've Been a Good Old Wagon But You Done Broke Down* (written in 1894) and *Mister Johnson, Turn Me Loose* (1896), were acquired by M. Witmark and Sons from smaller publishing firms and became celebrated hits. Though Harney is even today credited with popularizing ragtime among vaudeville audiences, his known musical portfolio did not include a single authentic ragtime composition. Even the arrangements for his *Ragtime Instructor* were devised by another musician, Theodore Northrup, and probably issued under Harney's banner for reasons of commercial expediency.

If the original impulse that in 1896 led Harney to declare himself the founder of ragtime remains puzzling, it is not difficult to understand why such a pretension was readily accepted: as much of the public (and many commentators on the subject) likewise did, he construed ragtime as a synonym for syncopation per se. While most of Harney's published output did not fall within even this ill-conceived definition of ragtime, the syncopation found in his *Good Old Wagon* (a black folk air that appeared the same year as *Possumala,* by Irving Jones and published by Willis Woodward) far surpassed its "coon" song contemporaries in complexity. Its score alternated between straight rhythm patterns and dotted-note phrasing (with many staccato notes), a mixture reminiscent of both E. B. Hunt's piano instrumental, *The Darky Tickle* (1892), and Les Copeland's *Invitation Rag* (1911). The concluding forty-measure dance segment of the piece, which was divided into three sections and was built on stoptime features, used a sophisticated clash of two syncopated rhythms, one in the bass and one in the treble:

Harney's quasi-instrumental, *The Cake Walk in the Sky* (1899), ended with a syncopated sixteen-measure chorus using interpolated nonsense syllables, but was primarily an exercise in cakewalk rhythm patterns.*

It was the cakewalk that had the distinction of being the first syncopated style of music to become popular in America, and its influence would be felt in some of the earliest published rags. Just as the "coon" song foreshadowed the "ragtime" song, so did the cakewalk anticipate the Tin Pan Alley dance song of the next decade, which was embodied by such hits as *The Cubanola Glide* (1909), *The Grizzly Bear,* and the Irving Berlin turkey trot, *Everybody's Doin' It* (1911). The early convention of labeling ragtime as dance music was probably fostered by the practice of billing cakewalks as two-step pieces.

When not intended for dancing, the cakewalk had a descriptive character, purporting to depict a slow, high-kicking improvisatory black dance (done by couples competing for a prize cake). Though believed to be of plantation origin, the dance became familiar to the general American public through stage representations, beginning with Harrigan and Hart's *Walking For Dat Cake* (1877). Some two decades later it became a vaudeville sensation owing to its Broadway presentation by Bert Williams and George Walker, the country's best-known black entertainers, whose likenesses appear on the first edition of the *Maple Leaf Rag* sheet music. Soon the cakewalk was a high society pastime, both here and abroad. Among blacks it remained less respectable. W. E. B. DuBois, writing in *The Philadelphia Negro,* an 1899 sociological study, relegated it to the bottom third of black society, and remarked of local cakewalk gatherings: "they are accompanied by much drinking, and are attended by white and black prostitutes."

---

*This composition was issued in two versions, both copyrighted in 1899. One version in the key of F arranged by F. W. Meacham is a simplified version of the other in E flat which also has lyrics, including a "chorus in Ragtime—Words ad lib," Harney's famous style of adding syllables to the words (this survives on Gene Greene's recording, *King of the Bungaloos,* Victor 18266, included on "Ragtime Entertainment," Folkways RBF-22. The chorus is the first notation of the notorious Mississippi Valley folk song (known as "Funky-Butt") which became famous as the second section of *St. Louis Tickle* in 1904.

As a Tin Pan Alley product, the cakewalk undoubtedly bore little resemblance to whatever music blacks contrived to accompany their own cakewalks.* In their Tin Pan Alley form, they were 2/4 instrumentals, with occasional vocal trios, founded on a simple march framework and using simple syncopation in a single rhythm pattern. Compositionally, they were unpianistic pieces, involving single-note, easily remembered melody lines one could sketch out on piano with a single finger without disturbing their harmony.† Though cakewalks were often arranged for piano (as were marches), their sheet music covers typically displayed other instruments, like trombones, and they were customarily performed by marching or circus bands, as well as string bands deploying a violin, banjo and string bass. The earliest cakewalk hits were popularized by John Philip Sousa, who was responsible for the cakewalk's European popularity.

The cakewalk's true predecessor was Fred Neddermeyer's *Happy Hottentots* of 1889, a banjo imitation piece that contained scattered syncopation, mixing a Schottische rhythm pattern with conventional accenting. Three years later, Neddermeyer produced the first self-proclaimed cakewalk, *Opelika Cake Walk*, published by Schott of New York. It featured a then-conventional rhythm pattern of two long beats followed by busier phrasing, possibly in emulation of a banjo:

The first truly syncopated cakewalk was *Rastus On Parade*, which was published as a "two-step march" in 1895 by its composer Kerry Mills (1869–1948), a classically-trained violinist. It established what soon became a cakewalk harmonic cliché by beginning in a minor key and moving to the relative

---

*Blacks who published cakewalks, like Fred S. Stone, wrote within the Tin Pan Alley format.
†Recognizing this distinction, John Stark wrote in his ledger: ". . . the truth is that the St. Louis article of ragtime is a distinctive feature of twentieth century creation. It is not a coon song nor a cakewalk."

major, a construction that cakewalk writers later followed with a subdominant section. Mills' cakewalk of 1897, *At a Georgia Camp Meeting*, was likewise self-published, after being rejected by every firm it was submitted to. Its instantaneous success ushered in the cakewalk as a Tin Pan Alley rage. Mills is said to have taken up the cakewalk as a musical protest against the vulgar racial stereotypes projected in the "coon" songs, and his sheet music description of *At a Georgia Camp Meeting* sought to place the music in a genteel, decorous social setting:

> This march was not intended to be part of the Religious Exercises . . . when the young folks got together, they felt as if they needed some amusement. A cake walk was suggested, and held in a quiet place near by—hence this music.

As a sheet music hit, *At a Georgia Camp Meeting* enjoyed a five- or six-year life span, and was still popular at the time of the First World War, when Mills helped ignite a brief cakewalk revival with his *Kerry Mills' Cake Walk* (1915). Other early cakewalk successes included Sadie Koninsky's *Eli Green's Cake Walk* (1898), Abe Holzmann's *Smokey Mokes* (1899), and *Bunch O' Blackberries* (1900), J. Bodewalt Lampe's *Creole Belles* (1900), and Arthur Pryor's *Coon Band Contest* (1900). Pryor, who had produced John Philip Sousa's cakewalk arrangements while working as a trombone soloist in Sousa's band, wrote one of the last cakewalk hits, *Razzazza Mazzazza*, for his own highly successful band in 1906.

The cakewalk craze precipitated by Kerry Mills had only recently erupted when ragtime made its debut in sheet music form. Though some early ragtime composers drew upon cakewalk rhythms, most cakewalk writers never tackled the ragtime form, even after it had replaced their specialty in popularity.* By a process of semantic juggling, however, cakewalks like

---

*Mills wrote a single rag, *Wyoming Prance* (1910), while Lampe, who was the chief arranger for Remick, composed two rags under the pseudonym "Ribe Danmark": *Glad Rag* (1910) and *Turkey Trot-Rag Two Step* (1912).

Sherman Swisher's *King Of Rags* (1908) and Kerry Mills' *Ragtime Dance* (1909) were fobbed off as ragtime to a public that made no real distinctions between the two genres, except to regard the latter as more fashionable. Even before ragtime became popular and the cakewalk passé, the two terms were used capriciously by the music industry. Thus in 1898, a Harry Von Tilzer "coon" song was titled *Rastus Thompson's Rag Time Cake Walk,* while in 1899 Arthur Pryor would publish his *Southern Hospitality Rag Time Cake Walk.* A cakewalk of the same year by the black Detroit songwriter Fred S. Stone was titled *Bos'n Rag.* The first three published "rags," in fact, were cakewalks: William Krell's *Mississippi Rag* (which appeared in January of 1897), William Beebe's *Ragtime March* (published three days afterwards) and R. J. Hamilton's *Ragtime Patrol.* Though Krell's orchestral composition was labeled by its publisher (S. Brainard's Sons of Chicago) as "the first rag-time two step ever written," it presented no departure whatsoever from established cakewalk convention, beginning in the customary minor key and presenting a slightly syncopated, single-note melody. If either the composer or the publisher attached any musical significance to the term *rag-time,* it could only have meant "syncopation." Even as a syncopated two-step, however, *Mississippi Rag* was not novel in any respect, but belonged in the same category as Kerry Mills' *Rastus on Parade.*

It was not until October of 1897 that the first true ragtime composition was published. Like its predecessor "rags," it bore the imprint of a Chicago publishing house.* This was *Louisiana Rag* by Theodore H. Northrup, who worked as an arranger for the firm (Thompson Music Company) which issued the piece. Northrup seemed to have had a special interest in syncopation. His first entry was as early as 1891 with an instrumental, *Two Happy Coons.* In 1897, Thompson published two more: *Night On the Levee,* subtitled "Rag Dance," contrasts

---

*It has been suggested that ragtime's early publishing association with Chicago was a delayed reaction to the Columbian Exposition held there in 1893, which was attended by Ben Harney and Scott Joplin.

cakewalk devices with surprisingly ambitious syncopation; *Plantation Echoes* is similar, but drops most of the cakewalk flavor in favor of more fully textured and pianistic syncopation. Both pieces were steps toward his full-fledged piano rag, *Louisiana Rag.*

Louisiana Rag was a truly unconventional offering even within the context of later ragtime. Though its opening section had a pronounced cakewalk rhythm, it used three different rhythm patterns that removed it from the sphere of dance music. The second section inverted the typical ragtime attack by setting a strong left-hand syncopation against a more steady right hand, a device that was later associated with Harlem Stride pianists. The end of the second section contained an unusual suggestion of Latin rhythm, perhaps reflecting the influence of *Trocha,* a Latin-flavored piece composed the previous year by a West Indian, William Tyers. The basic syncopated patterns of the work were:

Its four sections were unraveled in a pattern later used in Scott Joplin's *The Chrysanthemum* (1904): AABBA/CCDDC. Unlike the latter, however, *Louisiana Rag* closed with a recapitulation of the first section.

Northrup was never recognized as ragtime's earliest composer of record, and his publishers made no historic claims on behalf of the work. Rather, they seemed determined to cash in on the popularity of an 1895 Ernest Hogan "coon" song title by printing the legend "Pas Ma La" on its cover.* Neither this gimmick nor the subsequent appearance of *Louisiana Rag* as a piano roll (issued by the Universal Music Company) rescued it from almost total commercial failure. It was Northrup who provided the syncopated arrangements

---

*The "Pas Ma La" itself was a black dance step which was featured in another song title of the period, Paul Rubens' *Rag-Time Pasmala* (1899).

for Ben Harney's *Ragtime Instructor* of 1897.*

Though a pioneering publication endeavor, *Louisiana Rag* plainly echoed an already established piano tradition that wanted less for composers than promoters. The separate publication of five other rags in 1897 by scattered publishing firms in New Orleans, Cincinnati and St. Louis indicated both the spread of this tradition across the South and Midwest, and its early compositional uncertainties. Were it not for the presence among them of Tom Turpin's relatively elegant *Harlem Rag,* one would be tempted to explain the vagaries of this early ragtime in terms of an unfocused tradition rather than the ineptitude of the typical 1897 composer, who was generally preoccupied with syncopation at the expense of other musical qualities. Two Cincinnati concoctions by Robert S. Roberts, a professional arranger—*Pride of Bucktown* and *A Bundle of Rags* (both published by Philip Kussel)—alternate between cakewalk rhythm patterns and erratic, eccentric syncopated piano figures. Walter Starck's equally ungainly but more engaging *Darktown Capers—An Original Southern Rag* (published by Shattinger Music of St. Louis and later brought out by Scott Joplin's publisher, John Stark) is virtually monothematic, alternating between eight- and sixteen-measure sections in the key of A flat. Besides *Harlem Rag,* the first published product of a black composer, the most compositionally noteworthy of these early entries was Paul Sarebresole's *Roustabout Rag,* published by Gruenewald of New Orleans. It featured the "three-over-four" rhythm pattern that became ragtime's most conspicuous element after 1905: a sequence of three different notes placed within a four-beat measure, which resulted in the accenting of a new note whenever the phrase was repeated.

By 1898 the word *ragtime* had become a sheet music catchphrase, randomly employed in the title or subtitle of over a dozen compositions issued that year by various publishers in New York, Chicago, Detroit, St. Louis, Kansas City and even

---

*In 1898, his *On a Bayou* (a ragtime two-step) was issued by the American Musical Association in Chicago and his name appears as the arranger of a 1901 "coon" song by Brown and Allen, *Every Darkey Had a Raglan On.*

San Francisco. But if the word itself had suddenly acquired sales value in the eyes of music publishers and songwriters (perhaps mindful of Ben Harney's vaudeville success, or merely desperate for novel musical labels), the ragtime form had not. An indication that the music had no commercial status is seen by the fact that the "ragtime instruction" books of Max Hoffman and Ben Harney were actually vehicles to promote "coon" songs. With these publications the technical problems of scoring ragtime syncopation were disposed of. Ragtime composition as such, however, played almost no part in the sheet music of 1898, and had no impact upon the world of popular music until Scott Joplin's masterful *Maple Leaf Rag* appeared the following year. It was Joplin's genius that gave ragtime its self-conscious compositional character and provided a framework that later composers could readily assimilate. Yet for years to come there were numerous ragtime composers who continued to work within the naive, untutored tradition of pre-*Maple Leaf* ragtime, all but oblivious to Joplinesque refinement. These were the so-called "Folk" ragtime composers.

Early Ragtime
1897-1905

T he term "Folk rag" has been applied carelessly in the past (most frequently to designate a later country-music style which loosely adapted some of the principles of ragtime), but there appears to be an actual sub-tradition within the ragtime idiom that should be considered more of the basic folk art. This comprises written rags as well as a body of recordings of performances that is a much more variegated expression than the precise literature of Classic rags. The term indicates the folksy, idiosyncratic character of all the rags which contain a variety of folk qualities. The term is more literal or traditional when applied to the informal recorded ragtime of a Brun Campbell which was never written down—the equivalent of a pure oral folk tradition—but also applies to a finished published rag of a Charles Hunter which reflects a feeling of basic folk roots. Thus the Folk rag refers not to one specific type of rag, but rather a body of performances and compositions which have folk elements of various sorts which are enumerated in the discussion of each individual rag.

The works of Tom Turpin and Charles Hunter conceptually precede the Classic rag, though most are contemporary with the rags of Scott Joplin. In their informal, unpredictable format, and simple, direct use of folk materials, they can be viewed as a link to Classic ragtime composition. However, the Turpin and Hunter rags are also the beginning of a Folk rag tradition that continues throughout the literature of ragtime. Turpin and Hunter are the progenitors, but a Folk rag in an early style might have been published or played at any point in the ragtime era.

All ragtime deals with folk elements, but in varying ways. The early written rags are more direct expressions of the richly varied, frequently unorthodox ragtime playing styles that abounded in the Mississippi Valley as ragtime blossomed. Scott Joplin took these folk elements and formalized them into a new art form—the Classic rag. Later, Tin Pan Alley writers such as Charles L. Johnson and George Botsford formulated the most tantalizing of these elements, and the ragtime cliché was born. Still later, the best writers of Advanced ragtime hybridized the form by adapting newer folk elements. Finally, with the expansion of new harmonies and complex rhythmic patterns of Novelty ragtime, the folk tradition became more stylized and more of an abstraction. But the best ragtime of even this last age—that of Zez Confrey and Roy Bargy—is firmly rooted in the folk tradition, and most of the writers were Midwesterners who began by mastering the older idioms.

Folk rag characteristics determine what is or what is not a Folk rag and it is harder to isolate them than the criteria for a Classic, Tin Pan Alley, or Novelty rag. In general, a Folk rag has an informal, untutored approach. It is frequently a less polished but more spontaneous concept than a Classic or Popular rag, featuring a direct use of folk materials. Some Folk rags are original creations, but others have floating folk strains— not simply folk songs, but favorite instrumental music passages which pop up in many rags. It is not known where they originated or who first used them.

Most Folk rag compositions, particularly those published after the early period (1897–1905), are the products of small-town Midwestern composers, many of whom published their own works. While some of these reveal the influence of some big rag hits, notably Joplin's *Maple Leaf Rag*, most are indigenous to their locale, expressions of rural America. In Kansas City, the prolific Charles L. Johnson influenced the other Folk rag composers in his area with such original devices as those found in *Scandalous Thompson* and *A Black Smoke*. The extraordinary ragtime at Nashville, Tennessee, for instance, could well be called a *school* of Folk rag composition. There is a consistent style here and an ebullient mix of both black folk sources and white Tennessee hill music, a distinctly "southern fried" concoction. The leading composer was blind pianist Charles Hunter. Although there are a few rural black rags, notably in Texas, the small-town Folk rags are mostly by white composers, since most of the black writers sought the larger urban audiences.

As Folk rags became more popular, they were bought up by larger publishers, signaling the end of an era for the small publisher. In this way, Tin Pan Alley began to control the music of America. A good example of an early Folk rag building fame is the printing history of Oskaloosa, Iowa pharmacist Clarence Wiley's *Car-Barlick-Acid,* which Wiley copyrighted in 1901. Wiley then published the work himself in his hometown in 1903. It sold so well that, a year later, the Giles Brothers (of the river towns of Quincey, Illinois and of Hannibal, Missouri) purchased the rights from the composer-publisher. Three years later Jerome H. Remick & Co., Tin Pan Alley's largest publisher, now in New York City, bought it and sold it throughout the country.

Another example is the fine Folk rag by an aspiring doctor, Calvin L. Woolsey, of Braymer, a town near Joplin, Missouri. He helped work his way through medical school by writing and publishing his own rags. His most ambitious use of syncopation, not found in the Classic rags, appears in *Medic Rag,* which Remick also purchased and set on its popular way.

The man responsible for both these purchases and, indeed, all of Remick's vast output of rags was the composer-publisher Charles N. Daniels, who first appeared on the publishing scene when he bought Joplin's *Original Rags* in 1898 and arranged it for the Carl Hoffman Music Company of Kansas City, Missouri.

The important centers of Folk ragtime publications came from Nashville (Frank G. Fite and H. A. French), Memphis (O. K. Houck Piano Company), Kansas City, Missouri (Carl Hoffman Music Co. and J. W. Jenkins' Sons Music Co.), St. Louis (John Stark and Son, Jos. F. Hunleth Music Co., Buck and Lowney, and Placht and Son), Chicago (Will Rossiter, Victor Kremer, and Thompson Music Co.), Cincinnati (Philip Kussel, John Arnold, Joseph Krolage & Co.) and New Orleans (Puderer, Gruenewald, and Hackenjos).

A great part of the Folk ragtime heritage is preserved on

certain gramophone recordings and piano rolls. Most of these were made from ragtime's start in 1897. Many of the recordings were made after the Folk rag period, but the approach to the music is the unifying element.

Folk ragtime on recordings gives us a chance to explore rags, not as composed music, but as music performed by the largely untutored itinerants who wandered from village to town, from saloon to whorehouse.

None of the Folk rags which were recorded, many on the spur of the moment, were ever published. The performances are as varied and diverse as the written and published compositions. The recordings are as definitive as the rag sheets—even more so, because the performer is giving a full interpretation, not a watered-down simplification for the amateur piano players.

Recordings are also important when famous performers reminisce about their musical beginnings. Jelly Roll Morton, for instance, remembered hearing an early rag in St. Louis on his Library of Congress sessions (Classic Jazz Masters CJM-9), and played one strain of *Randall's Rag.* Willie "The Lion" Smith, raised in upper New York state, shared his recollection of *Don't You Hit That Lady Dressed in Green* (Dial 305—10″ LP). The interesting thing about these two stories, in addition to being unusually colorful and informative, is that the strains of both rags are similar to each other. Eubie Blake recalled on the LP, "The Eighty-Six Years of Eubie Blake" (Columbia C2S 847), hearing *Poor Katie Red* and *Jimmy Green* as played by the early ragtime pianists in his home town of Baltimore.

The contrast between Alonzo Yancey playing *Everybody's Rag* and Blind Leroy Garnett doing *Louisiana Glide* (both versions of the same rag and appearing on "Black and White Piano Ragtime," Biograph BLP 12047), is very great, which illustrates vividly the enormous diversity of performed ragtime.

The sophistication of Sugar Underwood playing his own *Dew Drop Alley Stomp* (Victor 21538) sharply contrasts with Will Ezell's rhythmic barrelhouse playing of his *Mixed Up Rag* (Paramount 12688) and the archaic yet lilting sounds of Arnold Wiley performing *Arnold Wiley's Rag* ("Piano Ragtime of the Teens, Twenties & Thirties," Herwin 402). Brun Campbell, discovered to have been Scott Joplin's only white pupil, made only five formal recordings, but also made informal tapes (issued on Euphonic 1201 and 1202), which illustrate his folk roots and how he developed his musical ideas.

Few Folk rag performances of the early Midwestern days were recorded, since recording companies were headquartered in New York. After the First World War, Chicago became a major recording city, but there were few ragtime pioneers around then to record, and the companies didn't want their old-fashioned sounds. Thus, Brun Campbell's recordings are the closest we have to that era. He wasn't a great composer or a flashy vaudeville pianist, but he was the typical itinerant player who roamed the countryside having a good time, listening to all available music, adding ideas remembered from times past and earning enough to sustain this good-natured life. He was an active player in both cheap dives and fancy saloons from 1898 through 1908, when he retired from music to become a barber, a decision forced on him by his wife when they married. He was musically inactive, living in Venice, California until the West Coast Revival of Lu Watters' Yerba Buena Jazz Band focused on ragtime in the early 1940s and Brun was discovered and persuaded to record. These discs show him playing the same way he did in the original era as a Folk ragtime performer. Not all of what Campbell played was simply from his memory, however; he had a trunkful of old sheet music. One in particular, *Rags to Burn* by Frank McFadden, whom he knew and remembered, formed the basis for at least two of his best compositions: *Chestnut Street in the 90s* and *Ginger Snap Rag.* In the Folk style, he put strains together in random fashion, with a stomping, rhythmic playing style. As with the compositions of Charles Hunter, Campbell's ragtime is liberally mixed with traditional Southern hill music.

A further use of floating folk strains is evident in at least two more of his tunes: *Tent Show Rag,* which uses the verse to *Memphis Blues,* and *Barber Shop Rag,* which is based upon the first section of *Muskrat Ramble.*

Will Ezell was one of several Midwestern pianists who featured folk blues and, occasionally, rags. This group includes Charles "Cow Cow" Davenport, Fred Longshaw and Rob

Cooper (all can be heard on "Piano Ragtime of the Teens, Twenties & Thirties," Herwin 402). Throughout the twenties and later, piano solos in the Folk rag tradition were recorded sporadically. Performances tended to include not only the floating folk strains, but favorite sections of published rags (typical was Davenport's treatment of Carey Morgan's 1915 *Trilby Rag,* in both his own *Atlanta Rag* and *Texas Shout*). Ezell's three ragtime solos, for example, are both patchworks: *Mixed Up Rag* is based upon the Original Dixieland Jazz Band's piece, *Sensation Rag* (which isn't a rag); *West Coast Rag* (Paramount 12549), is based on Jay Roberts' 1910 *Entertainer's Rag* and probably other West Coast strains; and *Bucket of Blood* (Paramount 12773), a popular name for saloon-dives, is reminiscent of the B section in Tad Fischer's *Encore Rag.*

Thus, the principle of early Folk ragtime "composition" continues, that of patching tunes together in a medley format. Other examples are *Mr. Crump's Rag* by Jesse Crump (Biograph BLP-12047), *Mr. Freddie's Rag* by J.H. Shayne (Decca 7663 and Circle 1011), *Hobo Rag* by Alonzo Yancey (Session 10-003) and Herve Duerson's *Easy Drag* and *Avenue Strut* (Origin OJL-15).

The improvisatory ragtime school, in particular the Storyville pianists, led by Tony Jackson, were recalled by Jelly Roll Morton in his Library of Congress sessions (Classic Jazz Masters CJM-2-9), all of whom performed rags, blues and pop songs. In *Storyville, New Orleans* by Al Rose (University of Alabama Press, 1974), an ex-prostitute fondly recalled the blues playing of Buddy Carter. Jelly Roll played a sample of how Carter played ragtime. Other legendary figures during the earliest years of this century were conjured up by Jelly Roll, including Alfred Wilson, Sammy Davis and Kid Ross.

The basic principles of Folk ragtime, and much of the folk material on sheet music, rolls and recordings, are still viable, as evidenced in the recent Folk-flavored rags of Tom Shea and Trebor Jay Tichenor. Because ragtime is piano music, written for and performed on an instrument of fixed diatonic tonality, the primary ragtime impulse was toward a set form, with a sense of established, formal musical disciplines. Some of the earliest and finest Folk rag scores—those of Turpin, Hunter and Northrup—have a finished quality. Many problems of early scoring were solved by the professional arrangers hired by the Tin Pan Alley publishers, namely D. S. DeLisle, Charles N. Daniels, Theodore Northrup, Max Hoffman, Ben Jerome and Robert S. Roberts.

In this sense, then, the earliest Folk rags are something of a compromise, though a glance at some of the less polished scores—Walter Starck's December 15, 1897 *Darktown Capers* and Fred Neddermeyer's October 7, 1898 *In Colored Circles*— shows that the schooled arrangers added a much-needed sense of order to a world of improvisatory, unpredictable, patchwork conceptions. Lacking the vital manuscripts and documentary recordings of the pioneers, it is impossible for us to assess, for example, D. S. DeLisle's work on Turpin's rags. As most later rags written by the schooled musicians, such as Joplin, follow much the same basic patterns and principles of these fine early Folk rags, it can be assumed that these early arrangers had a constructive effect on the published music. Some of the irregular idiosyncrasies can be heard in those folk performances recorded on 78s and piano rolls, where undoubtedly a few playing characteristics were lost (probably in the way of bass patterns), but the rag was destined to become more formalized, a disciplined form of broader and more varied expression.

THOMAS M. J. TURPIN
Born: Savannah, Georgia, 1873
Died: St. Louis, Missouri, August 13,
    1922

Pioneer ragtime pianist and composer whose first saloon was at 9 Targee Street, a notorious area recalled by W. C. Handy when he passed through St. Louis in 1893 as "so crowded it was a luxury to sit down in one of the many pool halls there." Before he ran his own saloon, Tom played piano at Babe Connors' world-renowned Castle Club in St. Louis, where several popular songs of the 1890s originated in versions later expurgated for polite society—*Hot Time in the Old Town, Ta-Ra-Ra-Boom-Der-A* and *Bully of the Town*. All were introduced by the famous New Orleans octoroon entertainer, Mama Lou, and a chorus line of girls who wore only skirts and danced on a mirrored floor. In 1900 Tom opened at 2220 Market Street in the heart of the St. Louis District, then growing up around Union Station, the new train depot. This area, centering around Market and Chestnut Streets, became known as "Chestnut Valley," but was referred to by the clergy as "Death Valley." Most outraged was Father Koffee who tried to get a law passed in 1893 removing the pianos from the wine rooms. Turpin's Saloon became the Rosebud Bar, the mecca for all underground ragtime musicians. Tom is referred to in the black newspaper of the time, *The St. Louis Palladium,* as "President of the Rosebud Club," a group of ragtime pianists. He and his brother Charlie controlled the Booker T. Washington Theatre where music was composed and arranged at various times by Tom, Joe Jordan and Artie Matthews. The brothers were the first black politicians in town and ran gambling houses, dance halls and sporting houses. Tom was so heavy that his piano was raised on blocks so that he could play it standing up, his stomach getting in the way when seated.

The Turpin rags are vibrant, energetic rags, stamped with a distinct personality and have the spontaneity of a creative performance. They are mostly linear and always in one of the following keys: C, F or G. They have what was called a "jumpy," urban flavor mixed with a Mississippi Valley folk-roots flavor, and are intensely pianistic overall. They are creative transformations of folk backgrounds into early idiomatic rag scores for piano—not very bucolic, as with many small-town Folk rags, but rather with a restlessness and gaiety of Old St. Louis, itself evolving from a countrified atmosphere to a metropolitan center.

Harlem Rag. December 17, 1897.* Robt. De Yong & Co., St. Louis.

Recordings: Wally Rose, Good Time Jazz 51, July, 1951. Trebor Tichenor, "King of Folk Ragtime," Dirty Shame 2001, 1973. Dave Jasen, "Rompin Stompin Ragtime," Blue Goose 3002, 1974.

Structure: A BB_1 CC_1 DD_1 A

This is a pioneering Folk rag masterpiece, one of the earliest rags deliberately written for the piano. The A section is a busy melodic line—a Turpin hallmark. He always included one such strain for contrast. The rest of the rag is constructed of three sections and their variations. Beyond the older tradition of syncopating an unsyncopated melody, here the B, C and D sections are written with simple syncopation followed by more involved syncopated variations of them (B_1, C_1 and D_1). In addition, it further illustrates the older tradition of performing themes with variations by writing them out, thereby giving us insights as to how the pioneer ragtime pianists thought. The Father of St. Louis ragtime here demonstrates in his own personal style how original rag strains were developed. At the same time, this is a rare documentation of the improvisatory

---

*Date refers to date of copyright.

performer-oriented side of ragtime, the same impulse that
spawned jazz. There are two different De Yong editions, both
arranged by D. S. DeLisle, bearing identical copyright but with
completely different c sections. In 1899, Jos. W. Stern & Co.
purchased the rights and published an arrangement by their
chief arranger, William H. Tyers, which eliminated the first
section and is generally simplified. The Wally Rose version
listed above follows the first printed edition. The original c
section is the first published example of what became the folk
ragtime staple—ragging a basic circle-of-fifths. The D section
has a march-like character and its folk-song flavor indicates an
adaptation. The following are the rhythmic patterns in each
section of the melodies:

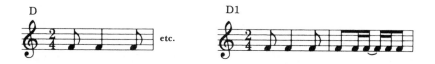

Bowery Buck. March 6, 1899. Robt. De Yong & Co., St. Louis.
Recording: Trebor Jay Tichenor, "Mississippi Valley Ragtime,"
    Scroll LSCR 102, 1966.
Roll: Universal 8355 (65 note).
Structure: AA BB CC
A typical Folk rag, especially in form and use of tonality, sometimes described as linear or additive. Such a rag simply states
a section, repeats it, and moves onto the next. It also stays in
the same key throughout. Here the repeats of B and C are
written out, with added treble notes in the B repeat, filling out
the texture. This became a standard scoring device much later
in the Popular rags. As with *Harlem Rag,* the A section is a busy
one with a syncopated single-note line with an emphasis on a
flatted ninth. Section B breaks away in strutting fashion, but the
highlight is C. According to St. Louis ragtime pianist, Charles
Thompson, Turpin adapted it from a street-organ melody
heard often in Chestnut Valley (see *Georgia Grind* in chapter 5).
Sparked by a triplet "rip" in the bass, it is an unusual concept
that avoids the oom-pah bass and causes a brief but very notable suspension in which the beat must be inferred—quite a
sophisticated device for such an early rag. De Yong sold this
piece the same year to Rossiter, who at first used the original
plates, but who later made a new set to conform to the familiar
Rossiter style. The music is identical in all editions, with the
addition of an "ff" in the final Rossiter one. All editions were
"Dedicated to my friend, E. J. Morgan," but the interesting "N.
B., 'The Most Original Rag-Time Two Step Ever Written'"
was not on the original De Yong issue.

A Ragtime Nightmare. April 13, 1900. Robt. De Yong & Co.,
    St. Louis.
Roll: QRS 3789 (65 note).
Structure: INTRO A B C B
"A Ragtime Nightmare" was used as a subtitle for Ben Har-

ney's *Cakewalk in the Sky* of 1899, but here Turpin is effecting a musical contrast most widely popularized in a banjo instrumental recorded by Vess L. Ossman and Fred Van Eps. The performance is based on a very popular pre-rag character piece, *Darkies Dream,* by George Lansing, one of several whimsical compositions that achieve a rustic sound through the use of the old Schottische rhythm. However, a later version by the banjoists included a second part in fast march style called *Darkies Awakening,* contrasting to the slow dream opening. Here in *Nightmare* Turpin condenses the idea, opening with an 8-measure Schottische introduction which changes suddenly to the even rhythm of the A strain as the real *Ragtime Nightmare* begins. This was the last of the Turpin De Yongs that went almost immediately to Rossiter. The A section is spiced with a chromatic run, a bit of Turpin's dramatic pianistics, and one that Classic rag composer James Scott would use ten years later in the same context *(Ophelia Rag).* C is the busy single-note line here, a tradition that harks back to virtuoso fiddle and banjo playing.

St. Louis Rag. November 2, 1903. Sol Bloom, New York.
Recordings: Arthur Pryor's Band, Victor 2783, March, 1904. St. Louis Ragtimers, "Volume 5," Audiophile AP-122 March, 1977.
Roll: Chase & Baker 2150-J (65 note).
Structure: INTRO AA BB CC DD
This was written to celebrate the Louisiana Purchase Exposition, better known as the St. Louis World's Fair, scheduled originally for 1903, but realized a year later. This is the most orthodox of the Turpins, with the usual Classic rag key change to the subdominant at section C, which is a typical melodic trio. However, A does not return after B in the most frequent Classic rag pattern. It features typical Turpin fireworks, beginning with a beautifully syncopated and very pianistic A section. There are breaks in both B and C sections (another pioneering feature in ragtime by the composer). D is the final display, sparked with a blaze of ascending chromatic runs, a fitting overture to "that splendid summer" in St. Louis. This is the first Turpin rag without D. S. DeLisle indicated as arranger.

The Buffalo Rag. November 2, 1904. Will Rossiter, Chicago.
Recording: Vess L. Ossman w/Orch, Columbia A-218, December, 1905.
Structure: INTRO AA BB C D INTRO
This is the only other Turpin rag with no indicated arranger, and its idiosyncrasies may give the best clues as to how he sounded as a performer. It is all in one key in a linear format, closing with the introduction as coda. Of all of his rags, this one seems to be the most folk-rooted in flavor: there are banjoistic ideas as the ascending figure in B and in the quick 32nd-note bass descents in D. The entire composition has a capricious air: the treble texture is punctuated with quick chords and abrupt phrasing, contrasted with longer, lyrical single-note melody lines. The Turpin flair for contrast, surprise, and creativity was never better displayed, as C evolves beautifully from B. The title may reflect Turpin's hunting days and his Western adventures, but most probably refers to "The Benevolent Order of Buffaloes," a St. Louis lodge in which he was very active.

Pan-Am Rag. June 8, 1914. *They All Played Ragtime,* Oak Publications, New York, 1966, third edition.
Recording: John Arpin, "They All Play Ragtime," Jazzology JCE-52.
Structure: INTRO AA INTERLUDE BB C D B
Arranged by Classic rag composer-pianist Arthur Marshall, who worked for Turpin at his Eureka Saloon. It has an eccentric format, highlighted by typical Turpin pianistics in section B in the form of quick arpeggios alternating between bass and treble. Written for the Pan-American Exposition of 1914, most of the rag has an implied Latin-American tango rhythm and feeling.

CHARLES HUNTER
Born: Columbia, Tennessee, May 16,
 1876
Died: St. Louis, Missouri, January 23,
 1906

Hunter attended the School for the Blind in Nashville, where he was taught the trade of piano tuning. He worked for the Jesse French Piano Company in Nashville, where he taught himself to play the piano and had his rags published. He was transferred to the St. Louis branch of the French company, which he soon left for the easy life of the District. He contracted tuberculosis and died before reaching thirty. He was buried by the Knights of Pythias.

Though Turpin and Hunter both wrote in a Folk rag style and are the most important early rag composers, there are basic differences in approach. There is more of an orthodox march-cakewalk feeling in the Hunter rags that is almost completely absent from the eccentric, twisting and turning pianistics of Turpin. Form for Hunter was a more complex matter. Whereas Turpin approached the standard Classic rag format (inspired by the *Maple Leaf Rag*) only once (in *St. Louis Rag*), Hunter uses a familiar Folk rag emphasis on pentatonic melodies. These he mixes with an ambitious use of non-chord tones, a feature which reveals a decided influence of white folk music, presumably that which the composer heard in the Tennessee hills where he grew up. Though black rags generally make use of non-chord tones, they do so in a much more limited fashion and are usually overwhelmingly pentatonic, whereas the flair for non-chord tones pervades all Caucasian rags to a great extent. In contrast, the Hunter rags are less restless and more bucolic than Turpin's. Hunter preferred the more deeply flatted keys of A flat and D flat in his writing. This is a characteristic of much Mississippi Valley Folk rag writing, and many writers in this genre preferred to work in these keys.

Tickled to Death. May 11, 1901 (first appeared in 1899). Frank
    G. Fite, Nashville, Tenn.
Recordings: Prince's Band, Columbia A-972, December, 1910.
    John Arpin, "Concert in Ragtime," Scroll LSCR-101, September, 1965.
Roll: W. Arlington. Connorized 20349.
Structure: INTRO AA B C INTERLUDE C

A joyous, stomping debut. It is a typical Nashville rag in that it combines very ambitious syncopation:

with simpler cakewalk figures:

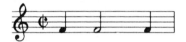

This became a popular and standard rag, and remained available on piano roll into the twenties. The c section is scored as 32 measures in the tradition of a march. The 32-bar strain, whether derived from the pop song or the march, persisted in ragtime through the Novelty rags of the twenties. Usually the section could be scored as 16 measures with two different endings of four measures each. In early rags, the 32-bar strain is almost never repeated until after an interlude is played. In later ragtime it was repeated immediately. Some of these double-16-measure sections have different ideas in each of their last 8 measures. In two of the Hunter rags, in fact, they are even more asymmetrical in phrasing, as well as in the total concepts. In these, the basic concept overall is indeed 32 measures.

'Possum and 'Taters, A Ragtime Feast. April 20, 1900. Henry
    A. French, Nashville.
Recording: Trebor Jay Tichenor, "Mississippi Valley Ragtime,"
    Scroll LSCR 102, 1966.
Roll: QRS 3465 (65 note).
Structure: INTRO AA BB CC A B
The score is prefaced by a setting of the scene: "Just after the
first severe frost in the Fall . . . the persimmons are full ripe and
the possums are all fat . . . possum hunts are of nightly occur-
rence . . . sweet potatoes are an invariable . . . accompaniment
to a possum feast . . . always an occasion for a general gathering
and great rejoicing. The title was suggested by the composer's
having been a witness at one of these joyful occasions" (the
term "witness" here, unless applied carelessly, may indicate
that the composer was not totally blind). This is Hunter's most
moving rag; it is carefully marked with dynamics. The joyous
c section has surprising and beautiful harmonies. At the end
of the last c, there is what will become a characteristic pause
(last note is dotted half-note in cut time) which he was to use
between strains or midway into one. This idiosyncrasy marks
a separation between sections indicating a contrast and usually
implies a change of dynamics.

A Tennessee Tantalizer. November 19, 1900. Henry A.
    French, Nashville.
Roll: Connorized 4091 (65 note).
Structure: INTRO A BB C A B
Most of the syncopation is effected by delayed entrance of the
right hand:

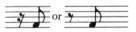

extended to the bass in quick one measure comments or an-
swers to the treble. The c section is a true 32-measure musical
thought. It does not split into parallel 8-measure periods. The
last 16 measures of c, however, split into 4 measures plus 12,
and are further spiced with a blue seventh.

Cotton Bolls. June 7, 1901. Frank G. Fite, Nashville.
Roll: Kimball B-5405 (65 note).
Structure: INTRO AA BB A CC A
One of his prettiest and more unorthodox rags. All sections are in the key of D flat except section B which is in A flat. The highpoint is C, which alternates a raggy pattern in the treble with syncopated bass breaks.

Queen of Love—Two-Step. June 21, 1901. Henry A. French.
    Nashville.
Roll: QRS 3419.
Structure: INTRO A BB CC A B
Note the designation "two-step" instead of "rag." This is actually a lightly syncopated cakewalk-march, somewhat reminiscent of *Tickled to Death.* Sections A and C are 32-measure strains each.

Just Ask Me. April 5, 1902. Frank G. Fite, Nashville.
Recording: Trebor Jay Tichenor, "King of Folk Ragtime," Dirty
    Shame 2001, 1973.
Roll: QRS X3093.
Structure: INTRO AA B CC D
A is in the key of C major. Section B begins abruptly in the key of A flat, and repeats 8 measures. C contains the usual 16 measures, also in A flat, and is somewhat reminiscent of *'Possum and 'Taters.* D is a 32-measure march-like section. The change from the key of C to A flat is a startling one but very effective. Joplin extended this idea in *Breeze From Alabama,* published later the same year (see chapter 3). It is based on the use of the lowered sixth chord (a change, for example, in the key of C, from C to A flat). This is a staple in Folk rags, which became a feature in later pop music.

Why We Smile. September 28, 1903. Frank G. Fite, Nashville.
Structure: INTRO AA BB CC A
The title may have been taken from the original caption of an advertisement used on the cover of *Tickled to Death* of three happy children smiling.

Back to Life. November 18, 1905. Charles K. Harris, New York.

Structure: INTRO A B A C INTRO-2 DD A

One of the most curious rags ever published. While the form appears typical enough for a Folk rag, the use of keys is not. The rag begins on a G minor chord which is the II chord, the supertonic, of the A section's tonic, F. The B section moves abruptly to D flat, after which A is repeated. C is also in the key of F. D moves up a fourth to B flat. Finally A returns to end the rag. Without section B, the tune is fairly orthodox, but as it is it has the overall effect of a medley, with the A strain barely holding it together.

CHARLES LESLIE JOHNSON

Born: Kansas City, Kansas, December 3, 1876

Died: Kansas City, Missouri, December 28, 1950

By the time he was six, he was pounding away on his neighbor's piano, composing and creating music. The neighbor, Mrs. Cree, gave him his first piano lessons. When he was nine, his parents bought him his own piano. He continued to play the popular music of the day while taking classical lessons. After three years, he suddenly quit when his teacher, Mr. Kreiser, complained about his playing ragtime. At sixteen he studied harmony and theory. He had a fine ear and taught himself to play several stringed instruments. He became proficient on the violin, banjo, guitar and mandolin. Mandolin and guitar clubs were fashionable, and Charlie joined several. His earliest published tunes were written for the various groups he played with. He got to be well known in the twin cities by organizing several string orchestras which played in theaters, hotels, restaurants and dance halls. During the day, he demonstrated songs and pianos for the large J. W. Jenkins & Sons Music Company, which published his first rag in May 1899. He married Sylvia Hoskins in 1901 and they had a daughter, Frances. Shortly after, he entered a partnership in the Central Music Publishing Company which published his Indian song hit, *Iola.* Interestingly, both this one and Daniels' earlier *Hiawatha* were named after towns in Kansas and not Indians. The lyrics to both songs were added after they had become successful as instrumental numbers. (*Iola* didn't become a big hit until Charles N. Daniels bought it for Whitney-Warner and exploited it nationally.) Coincidentally, Charlie Johnson was working for Daniels' old firm, Carl Hoffman Music Company, at the time of the purchase. It was at that same time that Charlie was working over a new rag late one Saturday afternoon when the bookkeeper came in and asked him what the name of it was. The man was carrying a carton of dill pickles for his dinner and Charlie looked at them and said, "I'll call it *Dill Pickles Rag.*" Of his more than thirty rags, it remained his favorite. When he first joined Hoffman's, he arranged Harry Kelly's only hit, *Peaceful Henry,* named after the Hoffman janitor. Fun-loving, practical joker though he was—and his music reflects his good humor and zest for living—he composed steadily in all areas of popular music throughout his life and made a good living as an arranger for publication of the works of others. After Remick bought *Dill Pickles* in 1907 (having been published by Hoffman the year before), Charlie started his own publishing house which was finally sold to Harold Rossiter in 1911 with the stipulation that Johnson not enter the business again for one year. This didn't stop him from being published by other firms (notably by Remick, Vandersloot, Sam Fox, Forster and Will Rossiter). His biggest money maker was *Sweet and Low,* for which he earned thirty thousand dollars. He was so prolific as a composer that he had to use pseudonyms. In addition to writing rags under his own name, he also wrote as Raymond Birch, Fannie B. Woods and Ethel Earnist. His ragtime output is impressive and abounds in Midwestern folk roots. He married a second time during the twenties, to Mrs. Eva Johnson, who survived him.

Johnson's ragtime compositions really fall into two categories: Folk ragtime and Popular ragtime. Johnson's early work reveals a creative folk talent and a skill at composition which heightens the style. Though his rags became more predictable after *Dill Pickles,* he maintained a respectable level of folk inspiration in his work. He, in turn, became the inspiration for several other rag composers in Kansas City. Unlike other successful Tin Pan Alley writers, Johnson elected to stay in his hometown. Most of the Kansas City Folk rags were published by Hoffman and Jenkins, as well as by Johnson's own company. The Kansas City rags are mostly simple folksy tunes, lyrical melodies voiced in thin textures of single notes and triads, more often than octaves. Almost all are three-sectioned rags in the keys of C, F, G and B flat. They have an affinity with the older marches and cakewalks in their simplicity and directness, but are more clearly the product of the ragtime era than transition pieces. Other composers of this genre include Ed Kuhn, E. Harry Kelly, Irene Cozad, Maude Gilmore and Mamie Williams.

Scandalous Thompson. May 27, 1899. J. W. Jenkins' Sons, Kansas City, Mo.
Recording: John W. "Knocky" Parker, "Golden Treasury of Ragtime," Audiophile AP-89.
Roll: Aeolian 8169 (65 note).
Structure: INTRO AA BB A CC INTERLUDE-C INTERLUDE-C
A marvelously polished and original rag concept for 1899. The A strain was quoted ten years later by Classic rag composer James Scott in his A section of *Great Scott Rag.* C is the most clever use of stop-time in a piano rag, making it difficult for the ear to perceive just where C begins and ends, thus the CC part of the rag one hears as a seamless continuum. The overall structure was in the march-cakewalk tradition which was not frequently used in rags, probably because it is rather lengthy.

A Black Smoke. Not copyrighted but published 1902. Carl Hoffman, Kansas City, Mo.
Recording: Terry Waldo, "Snookums Rag," Dirty Shame 1237, 1974.

Roll: Chase & Baker 1036-J.

Structure: INTRO VAMP AA BB CC DD INTRO VAMP A

An imaginative Folk rag essay all in one key, but one which achieves surprising variety. The introduction and vamp are extended ideas which leave no doubt that the home key is G. Section A has syncopation crossing the bar line, a rarity in early rags, and has a rather complex stop-time ending. B, by contrast, uses a different syncopation and shorter phrasing. C is a buck-dance executed with careful dynamics in the call-and-response pattern. D has the cleverest harmonies, bringing in the relative minor.

Dill Pickles Rag. Not originally copyrighted but published 1906. Carl Hoffman, Kansas City, Mo. September 16, 1907, Jerome H. Remick & Co., Detroit.

Recordings: Chris Chapman, Victor 5560 & 16678, July, 1908. Ralph Sutton, Circle 1053, January, 1949. Pee Wee Hunt Orch, Capitol 57–773, January, 1949.

Roll: U.S. Music 61356-B.

Structure: INTRO AA B A CC B

Syncopation is marked in the music to point up the "three-over-four" idea. Left hand in the B section suggests a trombone used in the military bands. C is the most lyrical section.

Sneeky Peet. January 10, 1907. J.W. Jenkins' Sons Music Co., Kansas City, Mo.

Structure: INTRO AA BB A CC BB

Eubie Blake used the B section in his song, *You're Lucky To Me.*

Southern Beauties. October 12, 1907. Jerome H. Remick & Co., Detroit.

Recordings: Arthur Pryor's Band, Victor 16073, September, 1908. The Etcetera String Band, "The Harvest Hop," Moon 200, 1975.

Roll: Melographic 9365.

Structure: INTRO AA BB A CC INTERLUDE-C INTERLUDE-C

Harks back to the cakewalk and uses common syncopated figures. However, the B section was used by Luckey Roberts for his A section in *Shy and Sly.*

All The Money (as Raymond Birch). March 13, 1908. Charles
L. Johnson & Co., Kansas City, Mo.
Roll: Connorized 4439.
Structure: INTRO AA BB A CC AA

Powder Rag (as Raymond Birch). August 20, 1908. Chas. L.
Johnson & Co., Kansas City, Mo.
Recording: Black Diamonds Band, (E) Zonophone 1016, No-
vember, 1912.
Roll: Angelus 25655 (65 note).
Structure: INTRO AA BB A CC INTERLUDE AA
A popular hit scored in 4/4 instead of the usual 2/4. Thickly
textured using octaves instead of single notes. Favorite with
bands for its strutting, folksy nature. In his happiest vein.

Beedle-Um-Bo (as Raymond Birch). December 17, 1908.
Chas. L. Johnson & Co., Kansas City, Mo.
Structure: AA BB A CC A

Silver King Rag. April 5, 1909. Thompson Music Co., Chi-
cago.
Roll: U.S. Music 62354.
Structure: INTRO AA BB A CC AA C

Apple Jack, Some Rag. April 7, 1909. Vandersloot Music Pub-
lishing Company, Williamsport, Pa.
Recording: Red Nichols & the Five Pennies, "Blues and Old-
Time Rags," Capitol ST-2065, 1965.
Roll: QRS 30924.
Structure: INTRO AA BB A CC BB
An inspired A section leads to a most lyrical B section, a high
point in his rags.

Pansy Blossoms. June 28, 1909. American Music Publishing
Co., Chicago.
Structure: INTRO AA BB A CC INTRO-2 A

Pigeon Wing Rag. July 26, 1909. Will Rossiter, Chicago.
Structure: INTRO AA BB CC BB

Porcupine Rag. September 15, 1909. M. Witmark & Sons, New York.
Recordings: Prince's Band, Columbia A-901, November, 1909. Harry Roy's Band, (E) Parlophone F-388, January, 1936.
Roll: QRS 30756.
Structure: INTRO AA BB A CC BB
One of his most popular, lyrical and lightly syncopated.

Kissing Bug. Not copyrighted but published 1909. Keith Music Co., Louisville.
Structure: INTRO AA BB A CC BB

Lady Slippers (as Raymond Birch). May 26, 1910. Chas. L. Johnson & Co., Kansas City, Mo.
Structure: INTRO AA BB A CC INTERLUDE AA

Golden Spider. November 3, 1910. Vandersloot Music Publishing Co., Williamsport, Pa.
Roll: QRS 30929.
Structure: INTRO AA BB A CC BB

Cloud Kisser (as Raymond Birch). January 3, 1911. Johnson Publishing Co., Kansas City, Mo.
Roll: U.S. Music 470 (in medley).
Structure: INTRO AA BB A CC BB

Melody Rag (as Raymond Birch). January 3, 1911. Johnson Publishing Co., Kansas City, Mo.
Roll: U.S. Music 64808.
Structure: INTRO AA B A CC INTRO A
Ragging the classics, based on Rubinstein's *Melody in F.*

Tar Babies. January 3, 1911. Johnson Publishing Co., Kansas City, Mo.
Roll: QRS 31233.
Structure: INTRO AA BB A CC INTERLUDE-A INTERLUDE-A

The Barber Pole Rag. April 1911. Hal G. Nichols Co., Denver.
Structure: INTRO AA BB A CC INTERLUDE-B INTERLUDE-B

Peanuts, a Nutty Rag (as Ethel Earnist). July 20, 1911. Johnson Publishing Co., Kansas City, Mo.
Structure: INTRO AA BB A CC A

Cum-Bac. December 22, 1911. Jerome H. Remick & Co., Detroit.
Recording: Charlie Rasch, "Ragtime Down the Line," Ragtime Society RSR-4, January 8, 1966.
Roll: Connorized 2215.
Structure: INTRO AA BB A CC BB
One of his best. A section features unusual bass. A bouncy, happy rag. Fun to play.

Hen Cackle Rag. January 31, 1912. J.W. Jenkins' Sons Music Co., Kansas City, Mo.
Structure: INTRO A B 1/3A TRIO-INTRO C D C A CODA

Swanee Rag. March 18, 1912. Sam Fox Pub. Co., Cleveland.
Roll: Kimball B-7075.
Structure: INTRO AA BB A C INTERLUDE-C INTERLUDE-C

Sweetness (as Fannie B. Woods). June 14, 1912. Forster Music Publisher, Chicago.
Recording: London Orchestra, (E) Cinch 5068, May, 1913.
Roll: U.S. Music 65449-B.
Structure: INTRO AA BB A CC B

Crazy Bone Rag. March 29, 1913. Forster Music Publisher, Chicago.
Recording: U.S. Marine Band, Victor 35380, March, 1914.
Rolls: U.S. Music 65903. Ernest Stephens, Artempo 976.
Structure: INTRO AA BB A CC BB
A section is the reverse of the A section to *Dill Pickles.*

Pink Poodle. May 6, 1914. Forster Music Publisher, Chicago.
Structure: INTRO AA BB A CC A
One of his more ambitious rags. The first two sections alter-

nate between the keys of C and A flat. Section B is a tango, first suggested in section A, and also recalled in the imaginative 24-measure trio (in the key of F).

Peek-A-Boo Rag. September 28, 1914. Forster Music Publisher, Chicago.
Roll: Supertone 869364.
Structure: INTRO AA BB A CC BB
A most lyrical rag, but one which stays in one key throughout (A flat). The C section is, nevertheless, marked "trio" and alternates a straight rhythm with a dotted-note pattern more typical of fox-trot writing, which began in 1914.

Alabama Slide. July 21, 1915. Forster Music Publisher, Chicago.
Roll: Universal 6315.
Structure: INTRO AA BB A CC AA

Blue Goose Rag (as Raymond Birch). January 3, 1916. Forster Music Publisher, Chicago.
Recordings: Melodograph Dance Band, Melodograph 217. Dave Jasen, "Rompin', Stompin' Ragtime," Blue Goose 3002, 1974.
Roll: Kimball B-7009.
Structure: INTRO AA BB A CC BB
Unusual C section which is not written in syncopation.

Teasing the Cat. August 19, 1916. Forster Music Publisher, Chicago.
Recording: Van Eps Trio, Victor 18226, December, 1916.
Roll: Felix Arndt, Uni-Record 203019.
Structure: INTRO AA BB A C BB
A later-style rag, almost entirely in dotted rhythm.

Snookums. February 9, 1918. Forster Music Publisher, Chicago.
Recording: Terry Waldo, "Snookums Rag," Dirty Shame 1237, 1974.
Structure: INTRO AA BB A C INTERLUDE C

A beautiful finale to the Johnson rags, this one is more in the style of his older rags, with imaginative harmonies in the A section, a very country-sounding B, and a trio that is in the late-teens one-step pattern.

THERON CATLEN BENNETT

Born: Pierce City, Missouri, July 9, 1879
Died: Los Angeles, California, April 6, 1937

Local pianist who went to work for the Victor Kremer Co., Bennett later became a music publisher, purchasing W. C. Handy's first success, *Memphis Blues*. Afterward he owned a chain of music stores in New York City, Chicago, Omaha, St. Louis, Memphis and Denver. Finally, he settled in Denver, where he operated the famous Dutch Mill Cafe, rendezvous for musicians and artists. His big hit was *Around Her Neck She Wore a Yellow Ribbon*.

Pickaninny Capers. March 16, 1903. Cornelius J. Shea, Springfield, Mo.

Satisfied. January 2, 1904. Victor Kremer Co., Chicago.
Roll: QRS X-3041.
Structure: INTRO AA BB INTRO-2 CC B_1B_1
Originally published in Pierce City by Bennett-Kreyer Music Co. under the alias of Bruce Raymond. This is a combination of ragtime and cakewalk song features. Instead of ending with a simple repeat of B, Bennett created a fine variation to finish it.

St. Louis Tickle (credited to Barney & Seymore). August 20, 1904. Victor Kremer Co., Chicago.
Recordings: Vess L. Ossman & Orch, Columbia A-937, September, 1909 ("Kings of the Ragtime Banjo," Yazoo L-1044). Van Eps Trio, Victor 16092, September, 1920. St. Louis Ragtimers, "Volume 5," Audiophile AP-122 March, 1977.
Roll: Universal 80747.
Structure: INTRO AA BB CC DD INTRO-2 B D
This was probably written by Bennett, as a note in the Pierce City newspaper of late 1903 reports him going to Chicago and wowing them with his tunes, including *The Tickle.* Kremer published much music in commemoration of the St. Louis World's Fair of 1904. This was a hit at the fair and became one of the most beloved rags of all time. The tune is a natural for strings (Bennett had a mandolin orchestra). Several of his other tunes have similar strains, especially *Pudnin' Tame.* Its second section was a notorious bit of musical low-life. One old timer remembered getting his face slapped as a kid for whistling it. Another reported that in small Missouri towns you could be jailed for whistling it. Another remembered the original set of lyrics which began, "Been to the East, Been to the West, I found my honey can do it the best." It is generally credited to New Orleans cornetist Buddy Bolden, but it appears in several early rags, and was well known in Missouri as *Funky Butt.* More polite words were written for the song version, brought out by Kremer in 1905. The phrase "take it away" survived in the O'Dea version from the original bawdy lyrics.

Sweet Pickles (credited to George E. Florence). October 23, 1907. Victor Kremer Co., Chicago.
Roll: Chase & Baker 3867.
Structure: INTRO VAMP A BB CC D EE D
The first printing and the copyright stated the author as appears above. On subsequent editions Bennett has been given sole credit. This is his most original folk-inspired rag. Section A is 8 measures repeated, and also serves as the last half of B, a regular 16-measure section. This idea was used in a few other Folk rags (e.g. *Cotton Patch*), and the principle was adapted to the Classic rag form by Joplin in his use of the same 4-measure

ending for two different sections in the same rag (e.g. *Easy Winners* and *Sugar Cane*). Another highlight is the sense of tonality which is an ambivalent C minor/E flat feeling from section C to the final D. The ending of C has a surprising descent of consecutive fourths, in a sequence pattern, much like later Novelty rag patterns, while section E develops the sequence idea in phrases of 2 measures in C minor, modulating to E flat at the end. D consists of a busy, brisk and winding melody in single notes with an unexpected 1-measure break.

Pork and Beans. January 26, 1909. Victor Kremer Co., Chicago.
Roll: U.S. Music 61321-B.
Structure: INTRO AA BB A C A
A more conventional rag in three sections which combines the "three-over-four" pattern with a melodic cakewalk style of construction. The more rambunctious A and B sections contrast with the more genteel trio, marked *cantabile,* which seems ideally suited for a mellow string band treatment.

Pudnin' Tame. March 25, 1909. Jerome H. Remick & Co., New York City.
Structure: INTRO AA BB A C INTERLUDE C

Sycamore Saplin'. April 9, 1910. Jerome H. Remick & Co., New York.
Structure: INTRO AA BB A CC DD C_1
One of his most inspired, and certainly one of his most folksy rags. The overall construction is rarely used (identical to Joplin's *Chrysanthemum*), wherein C becomes the featured strain in the last half, and the D in relative minor has the effect of an interlude. The final C section has a different and more varied bass structure, a development from an idea set forth in section A.

Chills And Fever. August 27, 1912. Sam Fox Pub. Co., Cleveland.
Structure: INTRO AA BB A C B
His most conventional rag, with a bucolic-sounding device

which was used in those Tin Pan Alley rags called "Barnyard rags." B uses clichés, almost identical with Wenrich's last section of *Peaches and Cream*. The 32-measure trio features a dynamic (mf-pp) call-and-response pattern.

Some Blues, for You All. January 8, 1916. Joe Morris Music
     Co., New York.
Roll: Diamond 18493.
Structure: INTRO A BB CC DD
One of the most fascinating of the rag-blues mixtures of the teens. A fitting compositional end as the A section recalls the opener of his earlier small masterwork, *Sweet Pickles*. A comparison between the two reveals the evolution in musical styles (see chapter 5 for full discussion of the rag-blues tunes). In *Sweet Pickles* the first phrase featured, ironically, is a flatted third—a true blue note. Here, the melodic emphasis is on sixths and ninths, with the blues effect on a flatted sixth. A more idiomatic, down-home blues develops in the last half of the tune.

EUDAY LOUIS BOWMAN
Born: Fort Worth, Texas, November 9, 1887
Died: New York, New York, May 26, 1949

Composer of the most famous and biggest-selling rag in sheet music and recordings, it is surprising to find much of Bowman's life shrouded in obscurity. He was a light-skinned black who passed for white when needed, but his home was in the black area of Fort Worth. From the turn of this century through the depression he was an itinerant pianist, typical of his time, wandering throughout the Midwest and South. After Pee Wee Hunt made his sensationally best-selling recording of *12th Street Rag* (over three million copies sold), Bowman de-

cided to cash in on that popularity by recording it himself on
his own label, using the piano on which he originally wrote it.
He came to New York City to promote the sale of his record
and died there. A product of the districts, his ragtime compositions reflect this atmosphere. The numbered streets, 6th-12th,
cut across Calhoun Street in Fort Worth, which was the heart
of the District, while Petticoat Lane was in the "red light"
district in Kansas City (where his major publisher was located).
Of his other compositions, mostly blues numbers, *Kansas City
Blues, Colorado Blues, Fort Worth Blues* and *Tipperary Blues* are the
most idiomatic Midwestern blues ever scored—real blues tunes
with ragtime flavor in the traditional soulful style.

Twelfth Street Rag. January 30, 1914; August 24, 1914; Janu-
ary 2, 1915. Euday L. Bowman, Fort Worth.
Recordings: Pee Wee Hunt & Orch, Capitol 15105, May, 1948.
Euday L. Bowman, Bowman 11748, ("Piano Ragtime of
the Forties," Herwin 403).
Roll: W. Arlington. Connorized 20374.
Structure: INTRO A A₁ INTRO-2 A₂
This rag, except for its 16-measure introduction (see also
Maple Leaf Rag), is a scored 32-measure theme and variations.
Written variations are not common (e.g. Turpin's *Harlem Rag*
and James E. C. Kelly's *Bully Rag*), but there is no other example of a written rag which has one section with variations
throughout. A magnificent example also of what has become
the major standard musical cliché in ragtime—the "three-over-
four" pattern. The first edition and his own recording confirm
that this rag was written on the order of the Folk school of
improvisatory playing.

Sixth Street Rag. November 11, 1914. Unpublished.

Tenth Street Rag. November 11, 1914. Unpublished.

Petticoat Lane. June 1, 1915. unpublished. August 14, 1915,
transferred to J.W. Jenkins' Sons, Kansas City, Mo.
Roll: U.S. Music 7484.
Structure: INTRO A INTRO-2 B C TRIO-INTRO D INTRO-3 EE

This is the composer's most ambitious rag, which combines his feeling for blues with a lyricism not present in his other rags. This is in the key of C and seems to allow a bit more freedom of movement. The thick treble chords are relieved by lighter, single-note lines. The rag ends triumphantly with a blazing, insistent motive in the right hand.

Shamrock Rag. January 21, 1916. Euday L. Bowman, Fort Worth.

Structure: INTRO A B C D E

As is the case with most of his rags, this one is in the key of E flat. The introduction and A section total 18 measures combined, giving the piece an asymetrical feeling. Though each section makes use of the "three-over-four" pattern made famous in *12th Street Rag,* he mixes it with several others, adding a welcome variety to the rag. Each section is a fresh idea, sustaining interest while keeping the entire piece in the same key.

Eleventh Street Rag. November 16, 1917. Unpublished. July 15, 1918, Bowman & Ward, Gary, Ind.

Structure: INTRO A B C

It is a loose collection of very funky ragtime phrases. The introduction is modified from the one used in *12th St Rag.* Each section has the same ending. The rag builds intensity through the use of slurs ending in a rip-roaring style rarely preserved on paper. A musical kissing-cousin to *12th Street Rag.*

Chromatic Chords. February 12, 1926. Unpublished.

SANFORD BRUNSON CAMPBELL

Born: Oberlin, Kansas, March 26, 1884

Died: Venice, California, November 23, 1952

Born with a natural interest in music, he was given piano lessons at ten, ran away from home to Oklahoma City when he was fifteen to attend a celebration, and earned pocket money playing at the Armstrong-Byrd Music Company where Joplin's friend and colleague Otis Saunders asked Brun to play from the manuscript of the *Maple Leaf Rag*. Shortly thereafter he went to Sedalia where he then met Joplin, who taught him his four earliest rags. He traveled over the Midwest and South, playing in honky tonks, barrelhouses, pool halls, roadhouses, confectionery stores, theaters, hotels, steamboats, nautch houses, restaurants and saloons. He retired from active playing in 1908 when he married and became a barber. His writings about ragtime and recordings date from the mid-1940s and early fifties.

Unlike most composers, especially the Classic rag pioneers, Brun does not use secondary-chord relationships such as relative minor or minor of the dominant, but sticks close to the basic I-IV-V harmony, with heavy use of the basic circle-of-fifths. In Folk ragtime, the minor tonality is touched on lightly, usually as a regular II chord, or brief use of the relative minor. It is rarely prolonged, as in some Joplin rags, except where it is a carry-over from the A section cakewalk tradition of beginning in a minor key—descriptive of an exotic setting of dancers preparing for the competition. Campbell's avoidance of minors and especially his recurring use of the circle-of-fifths is reminiscent of Charles Hunter's rags (however, Hunter did make skillful use of minor keys, briefly, for a change of color), and early country string band music. Campbell's playing is in the typical Folk rag style of the earliest ragtime performers, placing strains of diverse or similar feelings in a random fashion. In several of his works you can hear a blues-rag mixture of slurs, flatted thirds and sevenths in a 12-measure form. There is a great deal of improvisation in his playing—part of the transformation of syncopating folk tunes, marches, popular songs and classical material. It is most dramatically demonstrated on his two different recordings of *Essay in Ragtime.* The patchwork of using floating folk music within an original conception is evident in his playing. Some of the idiosyncrasies of the earliest scoring of Folk rags appear in these performances, such as adding extra beats to a measure *(Barber Shop Rag),* and placing harmonic changes in unexpected places *(Campbell Cakewalk).*

Barber Shop Rag. Not copyrighted and unpublished.
Recording: Brun Campbell, "The Professors, Vol. 1," Euphonic
    ESR 1201.
The c strain is an asymetrical 15½ measures. The most striking, however, is the 8-measure B section which is identical to the first half of *Muskrat Ramble.* Perhaps this was a floating folk strain, as it is very pianistic.

Blue Rag. Not copyrighted or published.
Recording: Brun Campbell, "The Professors, Vol. 1," Euphonic
    ESR 1201.
The blue quality is the melodic flavor. Structurally, it has three sections of 16, 8 and 32 measures respectively.

Campbell Cakewalk. Not copyrighted or published.
Recording: Brun Campbell, "The Professors, Vol. 2," Euphonic
    ESR 1202.
This is his most eccentric, unorthodox solo. Only the B and c sections contain 16 measures. A has 28 (in a form of 20 plus 8), while D is almost formless—14½ measures with chords and harmonies changing at unexpected places. Folk ragtime in the rough.

Chestnut Street in the 90s. Not copyrighted or published.
Recording: Brun Campbell, West Coast 113, December, 1946.
Structure: INTRO VAMP A B CC D E F G
The title is a reference to the Chestnut Valley sporting district
in St. Louis which centered around Union Station on Market
and Chestnut Streets. Generally, Market had the saloons and
Chestnut the "houses." In the late 90s, Brun was following
Joplin and Saunders around, from Sedalia to St. Louis. This
solo, in his Folk rag style, is his best, drawing substantially from
an 1899 Kansas City published Folk rag medley, *Rags to Burn*
by an acquaintance, Frank X. McFadden. (Listen to Wally
Rose's performance on "Whippin the Keys," Blackbird C-
12010.) It is a composite of Brun's favorite phrases, and a rare
example of early Midwestern ragtime performance at its best.
It is in one key (B flat) until the F section (a circle-of-fifths)
which leads to the exquisite final section in D flat. The E blues
section was once described by Brun as copying "Chauvin's
barrelhouse style." In an interview, Charles Thompson
confirmed that Chauvin also played the blues.

Essay in Ragtime. Not copyrighted or published.
Recordings: Brun Campbell, West Coast 114, August, 1946.
    Brun Campbell, "The Professors, Vol. 1," Euphonic ESR
    1201.
Structure: INTRO A B B_1 B_2 CC
Both solos start with slightly different introductions. The
"essay" idea is the middle part of the performance, the B section followed by two variations. C is a 12-bar blues. The Euphonic solo is Brun's most rollicking, with a strong, self-
assured rhythmic drive.

Ginger Snap Rag. Not copyrighted or published.
Recording: Brun Campbell, "The Professors, Vol. 2," Euphonic
    ESR 1202.
Another patchwork solo, beginning with the introduction of
Peaceful Henry, proceeding to a familiar "Salty Dog" circle-of-
fifths, while sections B and C once again draw on *Rags to Burn.*

Grandpa Stomps. Not copyrighted or published.
Recording: Brun Campbell, Echoes 1.
In the style of several Folk rags, the last half of section B quotes the last half of section A (also see Bennett's *Sweet Pickles*). C section modulates to the subdominant and forms a trio in the regular rag style of construction.

Rendezvous Rag. Not copyrighted or published.
Recording: Brun Campbell, "The Professors, Vol. 2," Euphonic ESR 1202.
A reworking of *Chestnut Street in the 90s.*

Tent Show Rag. Not copyrighted or published.
Recording: Brun Campbell, "The Professors, Vol. 2," Euphonic ESR 1202.
This is Brun's version of the last part of the verse of *Memphis Blues.* The title commemorates the Turpin brothers' Tent Shows in St. Louis, which came before their Booker T. Washington Theatre was built.

LESLIE C. COPELAND
Born: Wichita, Kansas, June 4, 1887
Died: San Francisco, California,
    March 3, 1942

An anomaly among eccentrics, Copeland started out in minstrelsy, playing with the famous minstrel troop of Lew Dockstader and appearing before the King of England and other European royalty. He then graduated into vaudeville, making piano rolls in the early teens. He composed in the archaic style of the original itinerants of fifteen years earlier, but was published by Remick, the largest commercial publisher of popular music.

He is usually categorized as a Tin Pan Alley writer because of the time in which he wrote and because of his publisher. However, his style is decidedly of the earliest in ragtime's history. He was, moreover, a contemporary of Brun Campbell, who recalled that both he and Copeland were auditioning for the Dockstader job and Brun lost out only when he demanded more money. Copeland uses only three sections and usually ends with a repeat of an earlier section. Harking back to the Turpin era, *Race Track Blues, Invitation Rag* and *Bees and Honey* stay in the same key for all three sections. *Dockstader Rag* and *French Pastry Rag* have 32-measure sections, recalling the march influence, à la Hunter. *Race Track Blues* and *Rocky Mountain Fox* contain strong blues-rag mixtures, a hallmark of the Midwestern players. The use of floating folk strains which occurs in the B section of *French Pastry* and in *Dockstader Rag,* which features what is probably the most popular recurring folk strain in ragtime. The markings on the sheet music of *Invitation Rag* are identical with Harney's *Good Old Wagon*—a dotted pattern alternating with a straight, even one. Many notes are also marked staccato. His piano roll performances indicate a loose, rhythmic feeling, and perhaps the dotted notes represent an attempt to notate it. He also uses a 4-note crash chord which Jelly Roll Morton remembered as being used by "piano sharks with a four-fingered bass."

Cabbage Leaf Rag. November 2, 1909. Marsh & Needles, Wichita.
Structure: INTRO AA BB C B

Invitation Rag. December 20, 1911. Jerome H. Remick & Co., New York.
Roll: QRS 31120.
Structure: A BB C B
Section A is a development from the B section of *Cabbage Leaf*

Rag. B begins with incipient Novelty rag phrasing using a ⅜ figure. C reflects Copeland's best approach to the down-home feelings by using treble slurs.

The Dockstader Rag. November 29, 1912. Jerome H. Remick & Co., New York.
Roll: Universal 99995.
Structure: A B C B
Section B emerges with an odd harmonic progression: B flat/Gm/F/Dm/E flat/B flat. The final B flat resolution is spiced with a characteristic treble slur that is best described as "funky." It is one of the most successful stylistic features of the Copeland rags—a direct carry-over from performance practices. Section C is apparently a floating folk strain, as it bears a close relationship with Morton's *The Naked Dance,* both melodically and harmonically. Even the minor of the subdominant is used here at the end, consistent with the Morton performance (see chapter 8).

38th Street Rag (Les Copeland's Rag). January 17, 1913. Waterson, Berlin & Snyder, New York.
Recording: Band, Little Wonder 293.
Roll: Les Copeland, Metro Art 200296.
Structure: A B A CC
The composer's most popular rag, though one of his less interesting efforts.

42nd Street Rag (with Jack Smith). December 2, 1913. Waterson, Berlin & Snyder, New York.

French Pastry Rag. September 1, 1914. Jerome H. Remick & Co., New York.
Roll: Les Copeland, Metro Art 202652.
Structure: AA B A CC
A melodic rag with an extended C section of 36 measures. Section B was recently discovered to be a floating folk strain. Claude "Chauff" Williams, once an itinerant ragtime pianist, included it as part of his *Williams' Rag.* He announced it to a festival audience as "one of the rags we all played."

Bees and Honey Rag. Not copyrighted or published.
Roll: Les Copeland, Universal 202759.
Structure: AA B A CC A
This is one of several that stay in one key, recalling the Turpin approach. However, the "three-over-four" device in the A section is an accretion of Popular rag writing which betrays its later date. These last four rags were done exclusively as piano roll performances and were never written down.

Race Track Blues. Not copyrighted or published.
Roll: Les Copeland, Universal 202753.
Structure: A BB CC A
Though Copeland later wrote at least one Midwestern-style blues in a 12-bar format (*Texas Blues* in 1919), this solo contains three sections of 16 measures each of blues influence, all in one key (E flat). Here, rag and blues elements are mixed with the true vigor of a gifted Folk rags artist, outdistancing the more hybridized blues-rags Tin Pan Alley was turning out during the teens.

Rocky Mountain Fox. Not copyrighted or published.
Roll: Les Copeland, Universal 202725.
Structure: AA INTRO-B B CC B CODA
A stomping Folk rag which begins with a tinge of the blues but evolves into a more typical rag after the introduction to section B.

Twist and Twirl. Not copyrighted or published.
Roll: Les Copeland, Universal 202755, 1917.
Structure: AA BB CC
Perhaps Copeland's finest and most original rag, presented in a simple linear format. Section A recalls *38th Street Rag* and features slurs in the right hand. B is the most melodic of the three. C is a tour de force, a high point in Folk rag performance wherein Copeland executes a quick bass descent in straight octaves which melt suddenly into a more funky *broken* octave bass, an inspired bit of good humor.

JOE JORDAN

Born: Cincinnati, Ohio, February 11, 1882

Died: Tacoma, Washington, September 9, 1971

Jordan grew up in St. Louis where he heard the early greats of ragtime. He studied music formally at the Lincoln Institute at Jefferson, Missouri, became an orchestra leader in Chicago, then wrote and arranged revues in New York City. Back in Chicago, he became musical director, arranger and composer for the Pekin Theatre. Later he wrote pop songs (*Lovie Joe* gave Fannie Brice her start in show business). He dropped out of music, and became a millionaire four times during a lengthy career in real estate and business. He wrote commemorative tunes in his final years.

Jordan's rags are structured with remarkable consistency. With one exception, all contain three sections, modulating to the subdominant at the trio, and ending with this c section. His use of the trio follows professional popular songwriting patterns where it was added to a verse-chorus song to create the instrumental version. In this case, the trio always moved to the subdominant, and this was probably the basic function of a trio. Most often, this is a very melodic strain.

Double Fudge. December 20, 1902. Jos. F. Hunleth Music Co., St. Louis.

Structure: A BB A CC

A fascinating concept which sounds as though it were written in the Rosebud Bar with Tom Turpin looking over the composer's shoulder. It opens with an odd minor strain that weaves a genteel romantic aura rather more involved than a simple cakewalk minor strain. B moves to the relative major smoothly by opening on the regular II chord and features a call-and-response pattern. C has the strongest Turpin flavor, only suggested in B and returns to the quick triplets used in A.

Nappy Lee. December 15, 1903. James E. Agnew, Des Moines.
Recording: Lois Delano, "The Music of Joe Jordan," Arpeggio 1205.
Structure: INTRO AA BB A CC
Named after a trombonist associate who was notorious for his unkempt hair. B opens with part of the chromatic descent that became famous in Chauvin's *Heliotrope Bouquet* of 1907. The C section recalls Tom Turpin in his use of bass triplets (see *Bowery Buck*) and in the general melodic style.

Pekin Rag. September 24, 1904. Jordan & Motts Pekin Pub. Co., Chicago.
Recording: New Orleans Ragtime Orchestra, Vanguard VSD 69–70, 1974.
Structure: INTRO AA BB A CC
The remarkable feature of this 1904 rag is the C section where Jordan applies anticipatory syncopation in an extended pattern throughout the entire section, giving the right hand a forward-moving, horizontal feeling, independent of the basic pulse—a texture usually associated with Advanced rags. The C section was later used as the chorus for his *Sweetie Dear.*

J. J. J. Rag. April 17, 1905. Pekin Publishing Co., Chicago.
Recording: Lois Delano, "The Music of Joe Jordan," Arpeggio 1205.
Structure: INTRO AA BB A CC
A section preserves a rag idea floating around St. Louis which Charlie Thompson used in *Delmar Rag.* The trio is a typical bit of Jordan's eccentric Folk ragtime, characterized here by unusually wide jumps in the melodic line.

That Teasin' Rag. December 24, 1909. Jos. W. Stern & Co., New York.

Roll: QRS 40795.
Structure: INTRO A BB A TRIO-INTRO CC
Section c contains 32 measures and is by far the best-known of all trios. This was due to the Original Dixieland Jass Band using it as their trio in *The Original Dixieland One Step.*

Darkey Todalo, A Raggety Rag. November 15, 1910. Harry Von Tilzer Music Pub. Co. New York.
Recording: John W. "Knocky" Parker, "Golden Treasury of Ragtime," Audiophile AP-91.
Roll: Metrostyle 100531.
Structure: INTRO AA B CC A DD
Though "Todalo" signifies a dance tune, this is more of an involved piano rag. Section A has a descending melodic figure out of the folkways (see *Wild Cherries Rag*). The overall structure then becomes unusual as section B takes on the character of an interlude leading to the folk-like call-and-response of section c. The trio is then delayed by a return to section A. In this sense, the trio acts like a melodic section at the end and is not the usual third section of a rag. This final section has the St. Louis Rosebud Bar flavor which Jordan's music recalled.

CALVIN LEE WOOLSEY
Born: Tinney's Point, Missouri, December 26, 1884
Died: Braymer, Missouri, November 12, 1946

Woolsey was a small-town physician who served in the First World War. He did his post-graduate work at Harvard University's Medical School, specializing in mental hygiene. He was also an accomplished gourmet cook, carpenter and builder of radios. He played ragtime piano and published his own rags, which reflect his own playing style, with many elements found in the Folk rags of the turn of the century, when these were probably first written.

Funny Bones. July 17, 1909. Jerome H. Remick & Co., New York.
Structure: INTRO AA BB TRIO-INTRO CC DD
Section D contains full treble octaves and chords after a C full of busy sixteenth notes. The phrasing is one measure repeated, reminiscent of James Scott, who usually went an octave higher for the repeated measure.

Medic Rag. April 13, 1910. Jerome H. Remick & Co., New York.
Roll: Universal 92525.
Structure: INTRO AA BB CC INTERLUDE C_1 B
His most inspired piece and his most commercially successful. It is a memorable, thickly-textured Folk rag in A flat and D flat. The trio contains his most complex use of syncopations, rarely encountered in the scores, but sometimes found in the highly articulate and sophisticated ragtime performances of the Harlem Stride school. This figure:

is extended over a 4-measure pattern. It is an ingenious touch as Woolsey prepares us for this rhythm by using the more conventional:

achieving a subtle developmental feeling in the complexity of the rag's syncopation.

Poison Rag. May 3, 1910. C. L. Woolsey, Braymer, Mo.
Roll: QRS 31101.

Structure: INTRO AA BB A TRIO-INTRO C A
Interesting device in section A which states a phrase and then
echoes it in minor.

Peroxide Rag. May 3, 1910. C. L. Woolsey, Braymer, Mo.
Roll: QRS 31100.
Structure: INTRO AA BB A C INTERLUDE C B
A melodious rag with a varied bass pattern in the folksy B
section. The cover shows the following prescription: "For Miss
Peroxide Blonde—Hydrogen Peroxide . . . apply morning and
night. . . . Dr. Funny Bones."

Mashed Potatoes. August 12, 1911. C. L. Woolsey, Braymer,
   Mo.
Roll: QRS 31118.
Structure: AA B C B C INTERLUDE ½ C
One of the most idiomatic Folk rag scores. Section A has ascending bass octaves scored with the middle note, a characteristic of folk playing, and much in evidence on early hand-played
piano rolls. The middle note (the fifth of the chord) stays the
same as the octaves ascend, which is a more harmonically cor-
rect way of using a funky bass pattern—usually with the middle
note moving as well as the octave, thereby creating a dissonance, the sound associated with both Folk rag and blues players. C is built on an octave interchange in both hands that was
apparently popular with pianists, encountered as early as 1907
in *That Rag* by Ted Browne. Section D is sparsely syncopated
in the style of a straight march, a contrasting touch used in rag
composition (also found in Chas. L. Johnson's *Blue Goose
Rag*). Apparently "mashed potatoes" referred to playing ragtime; on another Woolsey tune he is advertised as "The 'Guy'
that 'Mashed Potatoes' à la Piano."

Lover's Lane Glide. October 5, 1914. C. L. Woolsey, St. Joseph, Mo.
Structure: AA BB TRIO-INTRO CC C$_1$
Certainly the most folksy glide ever published. The A section
somewhat resembles the 1909 dance hit, *The Cubanola Glide,*
but overall, contains more ragtime elements than dance tune.

Section B is a magnificent example of well-scored Folk rag circle-of-fifths with a touch of bass syncopation. The trio is a collection of the composer's idiosyncratic licks, with the characteristic *Mashed Potatoes* bass. The fine variation of the trio is spiced with startling bass octave grace notes.

OTHER IMPORTANT RAGS

African Pas'. Maurice Kirwin. December 29, 1902. John Stark & Son, St. Louis.
Recording: John Maddox, "Authentic Ragtime," Dot 102 (10").
Roll: Connorized 6045.
Structure: INTRO AA B A C D C
"Pas' " means "step" in the sense of African dance. This is the rag Stark advertised for aspiring ragtime pianists as "easy and brilliant—good to catch the ragtime swing." Section A, marked *pianissimo,* gets the rag rolling gently and interestingly uses the lowered sixth chord (E flat$_7$ in the key of G).

All the Grapes. James Fahy. July 1, 1908. James Fahy, Springfield, Mo.
Structure: INTRO AA BB A CC INTRO A

Amazon Rag. Teddy Hahn, February 11, 1904. John Arnold & Co., Cincinnati.
Roll: Chase & Baker 1904-J.
Structure: A B A CC DD
The most advanced of the rags published by this firm, noted for their adventurous rags. Section A is the most pianistic with a descending broken-chord C minor pattern much like later Novelty rags. B is an unexpected interlude in G minor. C has a startling harmonic change and D is a dramatic through-composed section in the manner of Lamb's *Dynamite Rag.*

Apple Sass. Harry Belding. Not copyrighted but published 1914. Buck & Lowney, St. Louis.
Roll: W. Arlington, Connorized 20377.
Structure: INTRO AA BB TRIO-INTRO CC DD

A Black Bawl. Harry C. Thompson. June 16, 1905. W.C. Polla Co., Chicago.
Roll: QRS X-3426.
Structure: INTRO AA BB CC DD INTRO-2 A B
Sections c and d bear a strong resemblance to parts of McFadden's medley, *Rags to Burn* (see also Brun Campbell).

Brain-Storm Rag. Bud Manchester. June 3, 1907. Stark Music Co., New York.
Structure: INTRO AA BB CC D
Manchester was an alias used by E. J. Stark. Section d is only 8 measures long.

Bric-A-Brac Rag. Maurice Porcelain. Not copyrighted but published 1906. Vinton Music Co., Boston.
Structure: INTRO A B C INTERLUDE D E
Rambling, ebullient rag which appears to consist of a series of improvisations. The interlude has a written break "on board," or in front of the keys. The cover illustrates a broken willow-ware plate, once the most popular chinaware in America.

Cannon Ball. Jos. C. Northup. April 17, 1905. Victor Kremer Co., Chicago.
Recording: Roy Spangler, Rex 5024, c. 1917.
Roll: William Axtmann, Connorized 10341.
Structure: INTRO A B CC A CODA
One of the most popular of the early rags written by a still unknown (who is not to be confused with Theo. Northrup), and arranged by Thomas R. Confare, who collaborated on a follow-up entitled *Bombshell Rag* (see chapter 4). Section a is a floating folk theme, as it appears in Mullen's *Levee Rag* of 1902 and in Tournade's *Easy Money* of 1904. b is blazingly pianistic which starts with a dramatic circle-of-fifths and climaxes in a fast, downward run of treble triads.

Car-Barlick-Acid Rag-Time. Clarence C. Wiley. August 9, 1901. C. C. Wiley, Oskaloosa, Iowa.
Recording: Robert Darch. "Ragtime Piano," United Artists UAL-3120.
Roll: Universal 77299 (65 note).
Structure: INTRO AA BB C B CODA
Though copyrighted in 1901, the earliest known copies bear a 1903 copyright date published by the composer. Sold to Giles Bros. in 1904 and then to Jerome H. Remick & Co. in 1907. The cover states, "something new in Rag-time . . . an excellent piano piece for rag-time lovers." Indeed, for once the blurb is right; it is one of the most rollicking Folk rags ever written.

Chicken Chowder. Irene Giblin. April 12, 1905. Jerome H. Remick & Co., Detroit.
Recordings: Victor Orch, Victor 4715, 16091, July, 1906. Ossman-Dudley Trio, Columbia 3591, A-220, January, 1907.
Roll: Kimball B-5092.
Structure: INTRO AA BB A TRIO-INTRO CC A
Her first popular hit rag and a favorite with string groups because of the chromatic runs.

Cole Smoak. Clarence H. St. John. December 28, 1906. John Stark & Sons, St. Louis.
Roll: Connorized 1387.
Structure: INTRO AA BB A CC DD
Noted in a surviving ledger of John Stark, "St. John is the king of present-day ragtime invention . . . [he] seems to be crowding Joplin off the perch." These comments are somewhat hyperbolic, but this is a first-rate rag.

A Cotton Patch. Chas. A. Tyler. July 31, 1902. J. W. Jenkins' Sons, Kansas City, Mo.
Roll: Aeolian 8491.
Structure: INTRO AA B CC DD A B
A melodious Folk rag with an unusual structural feature characteristic of several Folk rags: the D section closes with the last half of the previous section (see also Bennett's *Sweet Pickles*). B

is a fine stoptime buck-and-wing, contrasting with the flowing melodies of A and C.

Cotton Time. Charles Neil Daniels. September 26, 1910. Jerome H. Remick & Co. Detroit.
Recording: Dawn of the Century Ragtime Orchestra, "Silks and Rags," Archane 602. 1972.
Roll: QRS 03360 (65 note).
Structure: INTRO AA INTRO-2 BB CC B
An infectious folk-inspired rag by one of the most influential men in ragtime publishing who, curiously, wrote few rags. It was also issued as a vocal piece the same year.

Dixie Queen, A Southern Ragtime. Robert Hoffman. Not copyrighted but published 1906. Victor Kremer Co., Chicago.
Structure: INTRO AA BB A C
As in his *I'm Alabama Bound,* Hoffman used a floating folk strain here recalled years later by Jelly Roll Morton in his recording of *Mama's Got a Baby, Tee-Nah-Nah.* It was also used as a song by J. Russel Robinson, who had then recently visited New Orleans *(Te Na Na).*

Down Home Rag. Wilbur C. S. Sweatman. September 18, 1911. Will Rossiter, Chicago.
Recording: Earl Fuller Rector Novelty Orch., Columbia A-2547.
Roll: Steve Williams, Artempo 1305.
Structure: INTRO A B A TRIO-INTRO C D ½C
A most apropos title for perhaps the most basic bucolic rag essay of all time. The composer had a vaudeville act that featured his playing three clarinets at the same time.

Eatin' Time Rag. Irene Cozad. April 27, 1913. J. W. Jenkins' Sons, Kansas City, Mo.
Structure: INTRO AA BB A CC

Florida Rag. George L. Lowry. September 25, 1905. Jos. W. Stern & Co., New York.

Recording: Van Eps Trio, Victor 17308, July, 1912.
Roll: Universal 72559 (65 note).
Structure: INTRO AA BB A C INTRO B (Note: Second intro is the same as the first, only transposed.)
Highlight is the trio with barbershop-style harmonics: F-E$_7$-F.

Freckles. Larry Buck. November 25, 1905. W. C. Polla Co., Chicago.
Roll: QRS 30484.
Structure: INTRO AA BB CC DD EE
Ambitious Folk rag woven skillfully together by repeating motives and using the same ending in sections A, B and D.

Fried Chicken Rag. Ella Hudson Day. February 27, 1912. Thos. Goggan & Bros., Galveston.
Structure: AA B A C AA B A
This publisher had branches in five Texas cities. This has an interesting A section which uses an ambitious and seldom-encountered syncopation (but see *Lion Tamer Rag*).

Funny Folks. W.C. Powell (Polla). February 25, 1904. W.C. Polla Co., Chicago.
Roll: Chase & Baker 1854.
Structure: INTRO AA BB A CC DD
The title is a reference to foreign visitors at the St. Louis World's Fair of 1904.

Good Gravy Rag (A Musical Relish). Harry Belding. January 18, 1913. Buck & Lowney, St. Louis.
Recordings: Paul Lingle, "Vintage Piano," Euphonic ESR-1203. Dave Jasen, "Rompin', Stompin' Ragtime," Blue Goose 3002, April, 1974.
Roll: U.S. Music 65979.
Structure: INTRO AA BB A C DD
Great Folk rag which became a hit and a regular feature by its vaudevillian composer.

Holy Moses. Cy Seymour. April 26, 1906. Arnett-Delonais Co., Chicago.

Roll: QRS 30570.
Structure: INTRO AA BB A TRIO-INTRO CC DD C

I'm Alabama Bound. Robert Hoffman. September 28, 1909.
Robert Ebberman, New Orleans.
Recording: Prince's Band, Columbia A-901, November, 1909.
Roll: U.S. Music 65338.
Structure: INTRO A B A CC A
Section A was one of the best-known folk songs of the Southern
Mississippi Valley, recalled in later years by Jelly Roll Morton.
It is also part of Blind Boone's *Southern Rag Medley #2,* published the same year.

Jungle Time. Eric Philip Severin. February 23, 1905. Severin
Music Co., Moline, Ill.
Roll: Connorized 4206.
Structure: INTRO AA BB A C BB C
A rollicking rag by the trombonist-publisher. A has an octave
interchange between the hands in sixteenths so that the left
seems to be chasing the right. Section B uses the popular broken-chord figure of the *Maple Leaf Rag* B section, but is a more
extended idea, running to 20 measures. C, also 20 measures
long, is a lyrical trio.

Kalamity Kid. Ferdinand Alexander Guttenberger. Not copyrighted but published 1909. Ferd Guttenberger, Macon.
Recording: Dave Jasen, "Rip Roarin' Ragtime," Folkways FG-3561, June, 1977.
Roll: QRS X 3886 (65 note)
Structure: INTRO AA BB A C INTERLUDE C
Unusual placement of sections with an imaginative use of harmonies characterize this fine Folk rag.

Lazy Luke. George J. Philpot. December 10, 1904. Walter
Jacobs, Boston.
Structure: AA BB C INTERLUDE C
Sections A and B seem to be a rehash of Kelly's *Peaceful Henry,*
but it is the delightful and unforgetable C section which makes
this rag outstanding.

Louisiana Rag. Theodore Northrup. October 20, 1897.
Thompson Music Co., Chicago.
Roll: Universal 88995.
Structure: INTRO AA BB AA CC D C INTRO AA BB AA
The first published ragtime composition done expressly for the
piano (Krell's *Mississippi Rag* was done as an orchestral cakewalk.) Northrup is one of the important yet overlooked professional arrangers who not only helped codify syncopations, but
also made excellent contributions to the genre of rags. In this
he is unique among the earliest arrangers. Section A weaves the
aura of the lost South so prevalent in many early "characteristic" instrumentals. The bass movement here is extraordinary
for such an early rag and C is most heavily syncopated.

Mandy's Broadway Stroll. Thomas E. Broady. Not copyrighted but published 1898. H. A. French, Nashville.
Structure: INTRO AA BB C INTERLUDE C A B
His first published tune occurred in 1896 in his hometown of
Springfield, Illinois. This, the first Nashville rag in print, is one
of the most melodious and forthright ragtime marches ever
done. Basic cakewalk syncopations are beautifully combined
with more sophisticated patterns such as this one found in the
A section:

Old Virginia Rag. Clyde Douglass. December 19, 1907. W. C.
Parker Music Co., New York.
Roll: QRS 30631.
Structure: INTRO A B TRIO-INTRO C D C
As scored, one of the great throwaways of ragtime, as only the
trio is repeated.

One O' Them Things! James Chapman & Leroy Smith. Not
copyrighted but published 1904. Jos. Placht & Son, St.
Louis.
Structure: INTRO AA BB CC INTRO-2 AA
The most fascinating of all St. Louis rags published by small

firms. Section A is the first scored 12-bar blues found to date. B and C melodically and harmonically have an air of Joplin, which isn't surprising as both Joplin and Stark were known to Chapman. The latter published his march, *Military Parade,* for which Joplin did the orchestration. In one of his ledgers, Stark commented, "Its composer was a real genius but sad to say died suddenly while the piece was in press. This march was his idol but like many another he never saw the fruition of his hope." This last comment was probably a reflection on the many talents wasted in the sporting world. This rag was kept alive by its co-composer, Leroy Smith, who is listed as having performed it at a birthday party, as chronicled in the May 25, 1907 issue of the *St. Louis Palladium.*

Panama Rag. Cy Seymour. August 15, 1904. Albright Music Co., Chicago.
Roll: Aeolian 68287.
Structure: INTRO AA BB A CC B
This is the composer's most popular rag. Measures 5–8 in section B come from the ragtime folkways, as they turn up in an obscure Florence, Alabama rag of 1913 by D. W. Batsell, *Sweety, Won't You Be Kind To Me.*

Peaceful Henry. Edward Harry Kelly. Not copyrighted but published 1901. Carl Hoffman Music Co., Kansas City, Mo.
Recording: Vess L. Ossman, Columbia 1620, ("King of the Ragtime Banjo," Yazoo L-1044).
Roll: Chase & Baker 915-J (65 note).
Structure: INTRO AA BB CC D C B
An all-time favorite, it is a most richly folk-inspired Missouri rag with a fine cakewalk flavor. It was later purchased and published by Jerome H. Remick & Co.

Pickles and Peppers. Adaline Shepherd. November 7, 1906. Jos. Flanner, Milwaukee.
Recording: Pryor's Band, Victor 5713, March, 1909.
Roll: Universal 75449 (65 note).
Structure: INTRO AA BB C INTERLUDE C_1 INTERLUDE-2 C_1

One of the most beloved rags, it defines a creative Folk rag. The most important feature, the key to its success as a popular Folk rag, is its developmental c to c_1 idea which turns a straight cakewalk theme into a stomping syncopation.

Pride of the Smoky Row (Q Rag). J. M. Wilcockson. February 5, 1911. J. M. Wilcockson Music Co., Hammond, Ind.
Recording: Bill Mitchell, "Ragtime Recycled," Ethelyn ER-1750, 1972.
Roll: U.S. Music 64799.
Structure: INTRO AA BB A C DD C
A less familiar structure which ends the rag with a lyrical trio rather than the more rhythmic D, a great folk strain in the circle-of-fifths pattern. The subtitle is still a mystery but may be a reference to "Bar-B-Que."

Rag Picker's Rag. Robert J. O'Brien. October 19, 1901. Union Music Co., Cincinnati.
Roll: QRS X 3886 (65 note).
Structure: INTRO AA BB A C
Section C best illustrates restlessness through syncopation; it begins as a straight march, then for contrast ends with a riotously syncopated 16 measures.

Ragtime Chimes. Egbert Van Alstyne. October 16, 1900. Will Rossiter, Chicago.
Structure: INTRO AA B A C INTERLUDE C
The first rag published to use the chimes effect which subsequently became a popular device. Van Alstyne later became a famous popular composer (see chapter 4), best known for his songs.

The Shovel Fish. Harry L. Cook. October 4, 1907. H. L. Cook, Louisville.
Roll: QRS 30156.
Structure: INTRO AA BB A CC INTERLUDE C DD EE D FF (Note: C, D and E are 8 measures each.)
Cook was a professional clown who later worked with the Six Brown Brothers, a popular vaudeville saxophone group who

recorded for the Victor Talking Machine Co. He manages to create a unified work from six sections that avoids the feeling of a medley.

Snowball. Nellie M. Stokes. February 23, 1907. Jerome H. Remick & Co., Detroit.
Roll: Aeolian 74707.
Structure: INTRO A BB A CC BB

Splinters. Maude Gilmore. May 21, 1909. Chas. Johnson & Co., Kansas City, Mo.
Structure: INTRO AA BB A CC AA
This was also issued by Johnson as *Slivers* the same year, with the same artwork on the cover.

Teddy in the Jungle. Edward J. Freeberg. February 8, 1910, Rinker Music Co., Lafayette, Ind.
Roll: QRS 03242.
Structure: INTRO A BB TRIO-INTRO CC
The title is a reference to Theodore Roosevelt's hunting days which section A describes by using the minor tonality and numerous grace notes, suggesting the exotic jungle atmosphere.

Ten Penny Rag. Clarence E. Brandon & Billy Smythe. December 6, 1911. Brandon & Smythe, St. Louis.
Structure: A BB CC B
A heavily textured rag voiced almost entirely in treble octaves over an Octave-Chord-Chord-Octave bass. John Stark later took over this rag. Both active musicians in St. Louis, Brandon wrote the first *I Ain't Got Nobody,* which he published in 1911, years before the Warfield-Williams hit to which it bears some similarity.

A Tennessee Jubilee. Thomas E. Broady. Not copyrighted but published 1899. H. A. French, Nashville.
Recording: Trebor Tichenor, "King of Folk Ragtime," Dirty Shame 2001, 1973.
Roll: QRS 3483 (65 note).
Structure: INTRO A B CC DD

This is a good study of a conventional cakewalk developing into a full-fledged piano rag.

Texas Rag. Callis Welborn Jackson. June 5, 1905. C. W. Jackson, Dallas.
Roll: Aeolian 69055.
Structure: A B C DD C
This is a study in contrasting syncopations. A and B are constructed of typical broken-octave syncopation, but while A features an anticipatory syncopation crossing the bar line

B has this pattern:

C enters on the sub-dominant and is a complete change of pace: it is march-like with the bass written in two quarter-note octaves instead of the usual four eighth-note pattern. Section D moves up another fourth and combines features of all the previous sections in a masterful, beautifully melodic inspiration. This section returns to the regular 2/4 pattern of four eighth notes in the bass. The rag ends with a return to section C twice, written out as a 32-measure section.

That Rag. Ted Browne. April 6, 1907. Thiebes-Stierlin Music Co., St. Louis.
Recording: Pryor's Band. Victor 16043. September, 1908.
Roll: Connorized 4384 (65 note).
Structure: AA BB C DD E
"Dedicated to the lovers of ragtime." This entire piece may well be a collection of floating folk strains: the B section has an interesting octave interchange between the hands which forms part of a section in Woolsey's *Mashed Potatoes*. C has an eccentric idea in dotted rhythm. The 32-measure E section was the best remembered. Marked "Chicago Slow Drag," it is a pure

ragtime delight, and remained popular enough to be included in Gene Rodemich's 1920s band recording of *St. Louis Tickle* as an interlude.

Whittling Remus. Thomas E. Broady. April 20, 1900. H. A. French, Nashville.
Roll: Perforated D-522.
Structure: INTRO A BB C INTERLUDE last-half-A
Broady's best, with a fine melodious A section, a rousing B and capped with a trio which is a highpoint of Nashville ragtime (of which there are eighteen rags known to have been published here).

Who Let The Cows Out, a Bully Rag. Charles Humfeld. March 10, 1910. Howard & Browne Music Co., St. Louis.
Structure: INTRO AA BB A TRIO-INTRO C INTERLUDE C_1
A whimsical rag by a prominent St. Louis pianist who called himself "Humpy" and also "the Musical Architect." A 1-measure break challenges the pianist to "make a noise like a cow."

Whoa You Heifer. Al Verges. October 13, 1904. F. C. Schmidt, New Orleans.
Recording: Columbia Orch., Columbia A-165, ("Ragtime Entertainment," Folkways RBF-22).
Roll: Connorized 1438.
Structure: INTRO AA BB C INTRO A

X. L. Rag. L. Edgar Settle. December 21, 1903. A. W. Perry & Sons Music Co., Sedalia, Mo.
Recording: Trebor Jay Tichenor, "Mississippi Valley Ragtime," Scroll LSCR-102, March, 1966.
Structure: INTRO AA BB A TRIO-INTRO CC
A rare jewel of Folk ragtime, "Respectfully dedicated to the X. L. Club of New Franklin, Mo."

Yankee Land. Max Hoffman. August 31, 1904. Rogers Bros. Music Publishing Co., New York.
Recording: Vess L. Ossman. Columbia 3155, A-230, April, 1905 ("Kings of the Ragtime Banjo," Yazoo L-1044).

Roll: Connorized 4210 (65 note).

Structure: INTRO AA BB A TRIO-INTRO CC INTERLUDE-C
INTERLUDE-C

Most of his early original work such as that contained in the Witmark "Pioneer Ragtime Folio" is mediocre—restless syncopes that ignore the need for some measure of lyricism and melody. This one, however, is a sturdy composition with a trio that became more famous as the chorus of Del Wood's *Ragtime Melody,* and the reverse of the trio of Botsford's *Black and White Rag.*

Max Hoffman,
early ragtime arranger

Taking the title literally

Other popular songs advertised on back of Hoffman's 1897 hit, *Rag Medley*

Earliest song with ragtime accompaniment

Mr. TOM TURPIN

A ROSEBUD NOVELTY
"An Electric Christmas Tree."

The above is a perfect likeness of Mr. Tom Turpin, proprietor of the "Rosebud Bar," who, in addition to the new features (which have been recently installed), has decided to remember his many friends and customers by placing an electric "Christmas tree" in his saloon, at No. 2220 and 2222 Market street, upon which he will place presents for all.

The "Palladium" man visited the above-mentioned resort one day this week and was surprised at the completeness and beauty of the arrangement of the tree, as well as the most decided novelty of having a "Christmas tree" in a saloon for its patrons.

Appreciating the fact that providence has not dealt unkindly with him, and desiring to, in a measure, share his prosperity with his friends and customers, Mr. Turpin will expend upwards of $250 or $300 for presents, and the list embraces everything from a miniature bottle of Applegate's Famous Rosebud whisky (which has been made especially for the Rosebud Bar) to a diamond stud. The tree is beautifully illuminated by scores of electric lights in all colors.

By this one can readily see that all arrangements have been made to comfortably accommodate all patrons of the Rosebud. At a time like Christmas, when there are so many calls upon one's purse, a gift such as will be given on this occasion should be more than highly appreciated, and Mr. Turpin should be highly commended for his extreme largeness of heart.

One of the most pleasing events of the evening is that everybody in attendance Sunday, December 25, (Christmas night) will receive a present.

THIS MEANS YOU.

Taken from *The Palladium*, St. Louis

A DUEL TO THE DEATH.

Desperate Fight With Revolvers at Short Range.

BOTH MEN IN A WINEROOM.

SHOT AFTER SHOT FIRED AND NEITHER TRIED TO ESCAPE THE LEADEN HAIL.

ONE BROUGHT DOWN AT LAST.

Abe Keeler Dying at the City Hospital and Thomas Turpin Behind the Bars—The Latter's Father Also a Prisoner.

Thomas Turpin and Abe Keeler, negroes, fought a duel with pistols, 3 o'clock Tuesday morning in a wineroom at Jack Turpin's saloon, Nineteenth and Chestnut streets.

A dozen or more shots were exchanged and Keeler is dying at the City Hospital.

Turpin, who escaped injury, is in the Central District holdover. His father, Jack Turpin, saloon proprietor, is also behind the bars charged with complicity.

The negroes met in the wineroom at Turpin's place, shortly after midnight, and for an hour or more they indulged in revelry. The conversation turned to dusky belles and cake walks, and a heated argument as to the relative merits of negro women followed. When it became apparent that trouble was coming, the other revelers fled, leaving Turpin and Keeler alone.

Inflamed by liquor, each drew a pistol and dared the other to shoot. Turpin carried a Smith & Wesson, Keeler a Colt's. Each fired simultaneously. The first shots sped at random. Other shots followed in rapid succession, as the desperate negroes scrambled about the stuffy little wineroom, hoping for advantage of position.

It was a battle to death and both of the black men exhibited nerve and bulldog tenacity. Neither tried to escape, although in the scuffle the door was pushed open.

One of Keeler's shots grazed the hair on Turpin's head and in return he received a bullet in the abdomen. He reeled, but clutching at a chair, regained his feet and resumed pressure on the trigger of his gun. His aim was unsteady and Turpin successfully dodged. Then came a bullet that prostrated Keeler. It entered his left side and he sank to the floor.

Turpin gazed upon the scene a moment and walked to a hydrant to wash his hands. Just then a squad of policemen entered and arrested Turpin. His father, Jack Turpin, was also taken. He is charged with firing one shot.

Keeler, the dying negro, is 32 years old, married and has a home at 804 Market street, in the rear. Tom Turpin, the saloon keeper's son, is 26 years old.

FATAL FALL TO THE FLOOR.

William Fogarty Dying From Hemorrhage of the Brain.

From the *St. Louis Post-Dispatch,* February, 1898

Charles Hunter and girls in a St. Louis parlor in 1900

Tom Turpin standing in front of his Rosebud

Headquarters for Colored Professionals.

The Rosebud Bar,

TURPIN, Prop.

Pool Room
in connection.

a first-class cafe in
. Open all night and
All Prices. Pri-
Dining-room.

220-22 Market St.,   St. Louis, M

Two former "districts" in more recent times

The House of Lords on top of drugstore in Joplin, Missouri with Trebor Tichenor on left

Down the line on Chestnut Street, near Market in St. Louis

The first rag ever published

Representative Folk rag from
Nashville, Tennessee

The original "vegetable" rag
published by Hoffman in 1906

Another "animal" rag by the
prolific composer-publisher

Most successful ragtime recording—over three million sold

This piano roll is this rag's only existence.

The famous rag as originally published by the composer

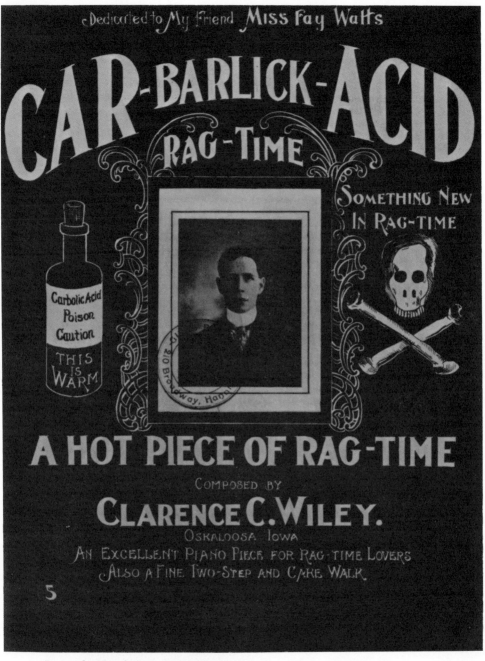

Iowa pharmacist's 1901 masterpiece

St. Louis vaudevillian
composer of *Good Gravy Rag*

John Stark, famous publisher of rags
by Joplin, Scott and Lamb

THE MASTERPIECE
GRAND
CONCERT RAG

GRAND
CONCERT RAG

KEY of G and C
Songsheet and Orchestra Key

ERIC SEVERIN

British Copyright Secured   Copyright MCMVIII by E. P. Severin, Moline, Ill.   All Rights Reserved

This is the greatest number I have ever written, even surpassing my famous "Jungle Time" Rag.

ERIC SEVERIN.

THE MUSICAL WONDER OF MODERN TIMES

THIS NUMBER has won the favor of great musicians and critics everywhere, who say it is the greatest number in its line ever written, and one destined to take its place along side the great classics and live on and on for all time, as it is not merely a great Rag—it is a *Rag Classic of the highest order*. ¶ Learn to play this Rag which is fairly boiling over with new and original ideas, and you will be envied by all who hear you, your reputation as a rag-time player will be made over night. It has that great *masterful sound*, giving the hearer the impression that it is very, very difficult. Yet any one with a fair knowledge of piano who can play popular songs at all, can easily master it by following these instructions: Play slowly over and over each period (*four bars*) at the time, playing each figure twenty or more times if necessary until you understand it thoroughly. Do this through the whole number; then connect all the parts you have learned, going slowly, making sure you can play every thing perfectly as you go along, and you will be surprised to find you have learned to play the world's greatest Rag. ¶ Are you one of the many who have longed to be able to sit down to a piano and play for your friends a good standard Rag. Something that would distinguish you from the average *popular song thumper*, and yet when you see a *good Rag* give up before you even try, and say: "My! I can't play that," or else rattle over it in a hurry and not even beginning to actually play any part of it—just simply grating the ears of those who hear you as well as discouraging yourself. No one can play a *hard Rag* in that way, but follow simple instructions above and you can play any and all the *great Rags* on the market. ¶ Get your copy of Concert Rag to-day. It will pay you to learn it as it will be played long years after the *popular songs on the music counters* of to-day are entirely forgotten, and it should be in every *pianist's repertoire*.

AT ALL MUSIC COUNTERS OR SENT POSTPAID, FOR 30 CENTS

E. P. SEVERIN   MUSIC PUBLISHER   MOLINE, ILL.

Article of Agreement.

This agreement entered into this 10th day of August in the year of our Lord 1899 by and between John Stark and son party of the first part and Scott Joplin party of the second part both of the City of Sedalia and County of Pettis and State of Missouri.

Witnesseth: That whereas Scott Joplin has composed a certain piece of music entitled Maple Leaf Rag and has not funds sufficient to publish same it is hereby agreed with above parties of the first part that John Stark and son shall publish said piece of music and shall pay for all plates and for copy right and printing and whatevr may be necessary to publish said piece of music

It is further agreed by and between the parties hereto that John Stark an son shall have the exclusive right to said piece of music to publish and s sell and handle the same as they may seem fit and proper to their interest

It is further agreed by and between the parties hereto that Scott Joplins name shall appear in print on each and every piece of music as composer and John Stark and son as publishers.

It is further agreed by and between the parties hereto that Scott Joplin shall have free of charge ten copies of said piece of music as soon as published.

It is further agreed by and between said parties that Scott Joplin the composer of said music shall have and recieve a royalty of one cent per copy on each copy of said piece of musi sold by said Stark and son.

It is further agreed by and between said parties that the said Scott Joplin shall be allowed to purchase and the said Stark and son agrees to sell to the said Joplin all the copies of said music he may want at the price of Five cents per copy ~~be sold for less than Twent-five cents per~~ said copies shall not copy~~by said Joplin. It is further agreed that John Stark & son~~

Witness our hands and seals the day and year first above written.

will not retail for less than Twenty five cents per copy.

John Stark & son

Scott Joplin

Signed in presence of

R A Higdon

Historic agreement giving a royalty to the composer for the first time

⚈ 3 ⚈

The Joplin Tradition

The term "Classic rag" has been as misused, abused and misunderstood as the very word *ragtime* itself. A basic definition of "classic" is "best of its type." Ragtime publisher John Stark was the first to coin the phrase and he used the term as an advertising gimmick to include every rag he published: only he published the "Classic rags"! Other writers on ragtime have been equally absurd in using it to describe rags they liked and approved of. It is now clear that the term "classic ragtime" refers to those compositions in the Joplin tradition of ragtime writing—a form with the style of musical composition which was created and developed by Scott Joplin, combining the folk music of the Missouri and Mississippi Valleys with the European tradition in classical music of the nineteenth century.

Although ragtime derived from the performance tradition of improvised styles, Joplin's idea was to develop the rag as a composed music with thoroughly worked-out harmonies, voice leadings and other rhythmic considerations as equal partners with and frequently in contrast to the necessary syncopation. W. P. Stark had an interesting comment along these lines in a 1909 *St. Louis Post-Dispatch* article: "In ragtime of the past syncopation was carried to an extreme in which it overshadowed everything else. Rhythm was everything; melody of little importance. But many of the writers have made money enough to study harmony and counterpoint, and have themselves been affected by the spread of musical culture all over the country. . . . Many of the recent compositions of ragtime writers plainly show an effort firmly to subdue the once masterful rhythm to its proper place, and to make it a means, instead of an end." It was to be played essentially as written to preserve the composer's detailed conception. It is this basic premise which characterizes Classic rags and sets them apart from all other rags.

We know (through recordings of such pioneers as Brun Campbell and through early hand-played rolls) that the creative performers like Louis Chauvin, who couldn't read music, used many melodic and rhythmic embellishments as they played. Joplin made seven hand-played rolls that were issued and, while he was a mediocre pianist, most of the rolls contain embellishments in the bass. When these rolls were played for Joplin's protégé Arthur Marshall, he verified this bass work as being part of Joplin's performing style—which was, of course, a departure from the printed admonition to play as written. The entire question of interpretation, though, rests with the individual nature of the composition. Those which are of simpler conceptions (most Popular rags), lend themselves to embellishments, more than the more musically polished and fine constructed Classic rags.

If Scott Joplin was the creator of the Classic rag, then John Stark was its greatest fan and promoter. It was Stark who became involved with Joplin by publishing the *Maple Leaf Rag* (there are conflicting anecdotes about how that happened), giving Joplin fifty dollars for it and a royalty of one cent for every copy sold (an unheard of thing at that time). The initial printing, done by the firm of Westover in St. Louis, we are told, was five thousand copies, and by the end of 1909, according to Stark's personal ledger, *Maple Leaf Rag* had sold a total of half a million copies.

John Stillwell Stark was born on April 11, 1841 in Shelby County, Kentucky, but grew up on a farm in Gosport, Indiana. He joined the 1st Regiment of the Indiana Heavy Artillery Volunteers, in which he was bugler during the Civil War. While stationed in New Orleans, he met and married Sarah Ann Casey. They settled with their growing family on a farm near Maysville, Missouri. A little later, he gave up the farm and moved the family to Cameron, where he pioneered in the new business of making ice cream. To stimulate trade, he traveled around the countryside selling it from his Conestoga wagon. He soon outgrew Cameron and moved to Chillicothe, where he engaged in the piano and organ business. Looking for a more prosperous town, he finally moved to the railroad center of Sedalia around 1885, where he established his firm of John Stark & Son at 516 Ohio Street. His general music store was one of three, and about ten years later he bought out one of his competitors, J. W. Truxel, and with it the seven copyrights he owned. That was Stark's beginning as a publisher.

With the success of *Maple Leaf Rag,* Stark moved his family and business in 1900 once again to St. Louis, where he purchased a printing plant at 210 Olive Street. He later moved to larger premises at 3804 Laclede Avenue. In August, 1905 he set up editorial offices at 127 East 23rd Street in New York City while maintaining his printing plant in St. Louis. On August 15 he printed the following statement in trade journals: "We are here with the goods. We left our sombrero in St. Louis—and we have had our hair cut—and even now there is not one person in five who turns to take a second look at us when we have met them on the street. And more, we will soon be able to describe our prints in the native vernacular. We should shrink from the firing line were it not for the fact that our rag section is *different.*" His son William ran the plant while Stark concentrated on selling and publicizing his music. And publicize he certainly did. He invented the term "Classic rag" to distinguish his music from that of the other publishers and helped to perpetuate the myth that these selections were the source and inspiration for all other ragtime; in his hyperbolic ads he insisted that the Stark rags were the "Simon-pure," and that everything else was a "pale imitation." The label "Classic rag" was an appropriate choice to proclaim the rags of Joplin, Scott, Lamb, et al. as truly immortal works. But the Classic rag *form* was also just one way of organizing folk materials and writing ragtime. From 1897 on, there were publishers all over the country who, like Stark, published the ragtime they believed in. Composers and performers everywhere were producing excellent ragtime, and much of it was more syncopated, more raggy, than the formal Classic rag. The ragtime world outside the Classic school was extremely variegated and, with the exception of *Maple Leaf Rag,* most people were unfamiliar with the Stark catalogue. While Tin Pan Alley was opening new branches in the larger cities, small publishers, both rural and urban, were exercising the last vestige of pioneer initiative in publishing fine works of local talent.

When Sarah Stark died late in 1910, John closed his Manhattan office and went back to St. Louis to live and work. He continued publishing the rags of James Scott and Joseph Lamb as well as other, lesser-known composers until 1922. He lived to see Lottie Joplin renew the copyright on *Maple Leaf Rag* and sign it over to him on November 26, 1926. Retired from active business, John Stark died in St. Louis on November 20, 1927 at age eighty-six.

No greater champion of the Classic rag existed, and it is to Stark's credit that his faith in Joplin's creation never faltered and that he continued to publish and publicize that ideal as expressed by Hayden, Marshall, Chauvin, Scott and Lamb.

One of the few surviving pianists of the ragtime era was W. N. H. Harding, who plied his trade in ragtime's heyday from 1908 through 1914. Communicating in 1964 with the Ragtime Society, whose aim is "dedicated to the preservation of classical ragtime," he wrote a fascinating letter responding to what had previously been published and how differently he remembered the musical life. Part of his letter follows:

> . . . your efforts to give an interesting picture of an attempt to revive what may be termed the Sedalia or St. Louis style of ragtime, for as Brunson Campbell points out, there were many styles of playing and this particular style seemed to have had a slow growth, and was largely of local interest. Ragtime certainly didn't reach Chicago, New York or vaudeville in that form. I speak from experience for in my youthful days I played in our big night spots.
>
> One summer season I played the opposite twenty minute shift to Mike Bernard, who was then admitted best performer in the country. He played rag solos and I played for the singers. In Chicago in those days, if you could only play what was printed you had little chance of a future. Rags as printed may have been used as the basis for the coloured boys who had to learn by ear and who were usually referred to as having a weak left hand. I heard many of them, and I think they played the *Maple Leaf Rag* more as Joplin wanted, than the rest of us did. Most Chica-

goans, in fact most large city listeners, liked the brilliant verve that Mike put into his playing, and most piano players attempted to imitate him. In my day our big restaurants seated many hundreds, so in a special appearance with only a few minutes to make a showing, it was necessary to put on a sparkling performance. In the smaller places, the slow drags, bucks, and ragtime played largely as printed as possible, but I do not think that Joplin's "Not Too Fast" meant "To Be Played Slowly."

In playing for the coon shouters, it was customary on the second chorus to rag up the number to a climax so the singer would get a good hand. For the ballad singers and others, everything was played straight. When Mike went back to New York, I took his place and played rags as well for the singers, while a twenty piece orchestra played the classics.

I knew Percy Wenrich quite well before he went to New York. He was a fine piano player and his style of playing his numerous rags was hard to beat. I occasionally visited the Pekin Restaurant where Joe Jordan had a band, and their playing of ragtime was a long way from the Sedalia style. Jordan wrote a *Pekin Rag* in 1904 and it is strictly in Chicago style. In those days in the vaudeville houses there would usually be a ragtime player on the weekly bill, mostly white boys who featured their own stuff and who would never have dared to play in the more confined and restricted manner of Stark's arrangements. You may have noticed that Joplin's numbers issued by other publishers are very differently arranged. Even Stark's music in the 1910–16 period gives more latitude to the left hand.

I don't recall hearing any rags by Lamb or Scott in those days and of Joplin, aside from the *Maple Leaf Rag* there were few that attained popularity. I played his *Pine Apple, Cascades* and a few others, but for the most part, it was the rags of Wenrich, Bernard, Snyder and similar composers that were used, and all our local boys had special numbers of their own.

SCOTT JOPLIN
Born: Bowie County, Texas, November 24, 1868
Died: New York, New York, April 1, 1917

Joplin came from a musical family where his ex-slave father Giles played the violin for plantation parties in North Carolina. His mother was freeborn, Florence Givens of Kentucky, who sang and played the banjo. One of six children (the others were Monroe, Robert, William, Myrtle and Ossie), Scott showed musical ability, so his mother, who was by now raising the family alone, let him take music lessons. For financial reasons these were sketchy, but they helped to provide enough background for him to make his way as a roving pianist throughout the Mississippi Valley. In 1885 he was working at "Honest John" Turpin's Silver Dollar Saloon in St. Louis. In 1893 he went, along with thousands of other itinerant musicians, to Chicago for the World's Fair. He then went for the first time to Sedalia, Missouri, where he became the second cornetist in their Queen City Concert Band. Then he organized the Texas Medley Quartette, which sang its way to upstate New York and back to Sedalia, where Joplin played at the Williams Brothers' saloon, whose social club was named the Maple Leaf Club. At this time he attended the George R. Smith College and studied theory, harmony and composition. While studying, he was befriended by Marie Walker, who owned a music store in Hannibal, and she helped him write his songs. During his studies, in 1897, he started writing rags; it is more than likely that Mrs. Walker also helped with these. After the successful publication by John Stark of the *Maple Leaf Rag,* Joplin married Belle Hayden, a young widow who was Scott Hayden's sister-in-law. The young couple moved to St. Louis when Stark established his printing company there. Thanks to a royalty arrangement on *Maple Leaf,* Joplin gave up playing for the more enjoyable pursuits of teaching and composing ragtime. After the death of their two-month-old girl, the Joplins became estranged and Belle died in 1906. At loose ends, he wandered around Chicago, visited family in Texarkana, then came to New York City in 1907, where Stark had set up his editorial office. He met Lottie Stokes, whom he married in 1909. She provided him with the comfort, love and understanding he needed to further inspire his musical ideas. It was at this time that he expended most of his energy working on *Treemonisha,* the folk opera which was to occupy his thoughts for the rest of his life. Joplin's life is a lesson on how a black artist could rise above the district life. He opposed the life chosen by Chauvin and Hunter on basic principle and rejected the attendant performer dimensions of a ragtime life. It is a bitter irony that, in the end, the district life caught up with him —he died of complications arising from syphilis.

Scott Joplin was the most influential ragtime composer of all time, mainly because he wrote the first popular ragtime hit— *Maple Leaf Rag.* Except for the small-town Folk rag composers, all other writers emulated the formula of this great rag. As for influencing others, only a few were aware of being so influenced. That two of them turned out to be among the finest ragtime composers is indeed a tribute to Joplin. He combined the traditions of Afro-American folk music with nineteenth-century European romanticism; he collected the black Midwestern Folk rag ideas as raw material for the creation of original strains. Thus, his rags are the most heavily pentatonic, with liberal use of blue notes and other outstanding features that characterize black folk music. In this creative synthesis, the syncopated folk art was wedded with formal principles of European composition; the traditional march became the dominant form, and the result was a new art form, the Classic rag—a unique conception which paradoxically both forged the way for early serious ragtime composition, and, at the same time, developed along insular lines, away from most other ragtime playing and composing. He infused early Folk ragtime with a

moving, bittersweet quality and made the rag a more sophisticated and complex expression. His work can be divided into
three periods. The first is the early Sedalia/St. Louis phase
(from *Original Rags* to *The Favorite*), which is colored with a
bright optimism, a spring-like freshness. There is a developing
emotional subtlety, fed by a growing self-consciousness as a
ragtime classicist: Scott Joplin as "the King of Ragtime Writers," the slogan Stark used as early as 1900. This feeling was
certainly boosted by the accolade Joplin received the following
year from the prestigious Alfred Ernst of the St. Louis Choral
Symphony Society who, in a February 1901 *Post-Dispatch* article, declared Joplin "an extraordinary genius as a composer of
ragtime music." Ernst planned to take Joplin's rags to Germany and was enthusiastic to the point of wanting to actually
take Joplin to Europe with him, a venture described as "the
dream of his life" for Joplin. After 1900 the idiomatic syncopations become more subdued, more implicit rather than explicit
in the composer's rags. By 1901 he had already created a new
masterpiece in a distinctly different style from his *Maple Leaf
Rag,* which culminated in the great riches of the very early
explosive rag playing of black Midwestern pioneers. In contrast, *Easy Winners* is in a flowing legato style that was to become one of his compositional characteristics. By 1904 and *The
Cascades,* Joplin displays a bolder use of the piano's total resources and his rags become more thickly textured (compare
the *Easy Winners* A section with the C section of *Cascades*—
similar changes but very differently executed). This second
phase (from *The Sycamore* to *Pine Apple Rag*), produced mature
works by an assured Joplin who wrote chromatically and used
the minor tonality distinctively. He expressed deeply-felt emotions in his rags, but more importantly, he expressed several
varying moods within one rag. In this he was unique. For all
other writers one emotion per rag was sufficient. A peak is
reached with *Fig Leaf Rag,* a quintessential Joplin masterpiece
of majestic melodies and possessing a deep, reflective quality.
His third and experimental period (from *Wall Street Rag* to
Magnetic Rag) is a moving and autobiographical one which has
a non-consistent development. This phase includes some of
the most probative work in the idiom, epitomized by the ex-

panded harmonics of *Euphonic Sounds*. His *Scott Joplin's New Rag*, however, has older stylistic ideas combined with a stark melancholy, a marriage that is more successfully achieved in his most intense and personal ragtime essay, *Magnetic Rag*, probably his last rag, certainly his most affecting. Joplin was steeped in nineteenth-century romanticism, especially in his use of minor tonality to effect a melancholy mood. All other rag composers used it merely for a change of color in a simpler, happier vein. But the Joplin hallmark was actually juxtaposing different deeply-felt emotions in one rag, which he accomplished with attention to subtle details. He had a classical approach to composition, much as Beethoven and Chopin had, and also a skill in handling both folk material and his own clearly developed musical ideas. The way in which he developed was highly individualistic, outside the mainstream of ragtime composition. In this sense he was much like Jelly Roll Morton (see chapter 8). There is a nether-world aura in Joplin's bittersweet music, an esoteric fantasy, a nostalgia that evokes imagery of the Old South, replete with Spanish moss and plantation oaks. But where the black Broadway musicals of Williams and Walker were spoofing plantation life, Joplin, in *Treemonisha*, was trying to convey a serious message set on that same plantation. Joplin's early ragtime influence, his great friend and companion, the legendary Otis Saunders of Springfield, Missouri, undoubtedly encouraged him in his organization of folk elements (he claimed to have helped Joplin write the *Maple Leaf Rag* and *The Favorite*, as well as Turpin his *St. Louis Rag*). But it was Joplin's formal training at Smith College which allowed him to write down his ideas in detail. Whereas the rags before, during and after Joplin were simplified by schooled arrangers, Joplin's rags were published the way he conceived them. This was true not only because he could express himself accurately on paper, but because Tin Pan Alley respected success, and Joplin's *Maple Leaf Rag* was the unquestioned success throughout his lifetime. Joplin was a constant experimenter with the form, exploring it emotionally more than any other writer. The original impetus toward composition away from the piano, rather than the usual writing down of what was being played, stemmed from the fact that Joplin was not a good performer.

And, although he stopped performing, he recognized and appreciated superior players. In a letter, Joe Lamb recalled Joplin telling him that he, Joplin, had little hope for the success of his *School of Ragtime* exercises, recognizing that some players had a greater feel for playing ragtime than others. From interviews with fellow musicians who knew and heard him, the reports were all the same. Composer-conductor-arranger Will Vodery said, "Joplin was nervous, not literate. Made his music sort of academic, tried to be concert, strictly his own style. He felt he was above entertainment type of music." Sam Patterson, friend and colleague remembered, "Joplin never played well. He couldn't play continuously." And Artie Matthews (see chapter 5) recalled, "All the players could beat Joplin in playing. All took delight in cutting him." So, Joplin devoted his life in making ragtime a classic in form and content. Truly, "the King of Ragtime Writers."

Note: The definition of ragtime formulated by the authors precludes consideration of certain works which fall outside this definition. Some of these, especially in the case of Joplin, are among his most revered pieces. These include the syncopated waltzes *Bethena, Pleasant Moments,* the "Afro-American Intermezzo" *Chrysanthemum,* and the syncopated tango, *Solace.* The syncopated waltzes are basically adaptations to ragtime of an older idiom and this is true also of the "tango-rags" which also do not have an "even, steady duple rhythm."

Original Rags (arr. Charles N. Daniels). March 15, 1899. Carl Hoffman, Kansas City, Mo.
Recordings: Wally Rose, West Coast 112, February, 1947. Jelly Roll Morton, General 4001, December, 1939. ("Black & White Piano Ragtime," Biograph BLP 12047).
Roll: Chase & Baker Special Music 147-J (65 note), "Scott Joplin Ragtime," Biograph BLP 1010Q.
Structure: INTRO AA BB CC ½ INTRO A DD EE
A bewitching, irresistible rag that illustrates his genius with folk materials. Until this time, most "rag" medleys consisted of popular "coon" songs arranged for piano. He transformed this format in his debut publication from a "coon" song medley to

a real piano ragtime medley, clearly establishing his higher musical ideals of syncopated composition. The A section has a decided cakewalk feeling mingled with the minstrel banjo pickings. The D section is remarkable for its harmonic similarity to H. O. Wheeler's *A Virginny Frolic* (A section), by a strange coincidence published in 1898 by Hoffman. Could Daniels have taken it and syncopated it or did Joplin?

Maple Leaf Rag. September 18, 1899. John Stark & Son, Sedalia, Mo.
Recording: "They All Played the Maple Leaf Rag," Herwin 401.
Roll: Scott Joplin, Connorized 10265 (Biograph BLP 1006Q).
Structure: AA BB A CC DD
The A section has always seemed to one of the authors to be an elongated introduction with the B section as the actual beginning of the rag. Joplin has used the A section in *Cascades, Sycamore, Leola, Gladiolus* and *Sugar Cane.* As if to demonstrate the validity of the statement that the A section is really an introduction, Joplin, in extended form, took the A section for his prelude to Act Three of his folk opera, *Treemonisha.* The B section contains the pianistic syncopated pattern that was the most influential part of the rag and established the first ragtime cliché (e.g. B section of Scott's *Frog Legs Rag* and the B section of Lamb's *Contentment Rag*). Section C has a thicker texture and uses a counter bass line of descending octaves, accentuating the more idiomatic syncopation of this section. The phrasing and syncopated figures in the D section (measures 3, 5, and 11) recall the B section of *Original Rags.* It is with this D section that Joplin conceptually is most involved, with alternating bass patterns which enrich the complexity of this great final section. The transition from the trio (in the key of D flat) back to the home key for the final section is done smoothly by opening with a D flat harmony, which then becomes the subdominant of the home key of A flat. Joplin had done a similar change in *Original Rags,* opening its E section on a D_7 (coming from a section in the key of D). In this rag, however, the D_7 becomes the dominant seventh of the last section (for this example in the key of G). With this rag, Joplin begins using his triumphant endings. Surely, this one is his greatest.

Peacherine Rag. March 18, 1901. John Stark & Son., St. Louis.
Recording: Dave Jasen, "Fingerbustin' Ragtime," Blue Goose
   3001.
Roll: Connorized 6047 (65 note).
Structure: INTRO AA BB A CC DD
A totally different composition from *Maple Leaf Rag,* it is
nonetheless excitingly original. The fresh spring-like sounds of
wonderment unfold reaching the apex in the c section (which
Wenrich took wholesale for his c section in *The Smiler*). The
most exotic effect in the c section comes at the 32nd-note
triplets which have the effect of bluesy slurs. And, instead of
capitalizing on his whirlwind climactic endings, this one shows
a rare degree of musical sophistication in its conclusion of the
development, and the piece comes to a logical and firm end.

The Easy Winners. October 10, 1901. Scott Joplin, St. Louis.
Recording: Wally Rose, West Coast 113, February, 1947.
Roll: QRS 3749.
Structure: INTRO AA BB A INTERLUDE CC DD
Continuing in his advanced and mature use of instrumental
folk materials, this piece vividly illustrates Joplin's develop-
ment as the leading ragtime composer. In the Stark Ledger,
there is a comment that if one could play this rag as well as
Joplin, one could borrow five dollars from anyone present.
After Shattinger Music Co. of St. Louis bought the piece (issuing a simplified edition which apparently was not successful),
Stark finally published it from Joplin's original plates, with the
blurb that it was "Joplin's favorite." The a section is a beautiful
adaptation of an improvisatory folk ragtime pattern that lies
well in the right hand in the key of A flat, and is best done in
Jelly's *Naked Dance.* It is the first instance of an idea that eventually became one of the most popular ragtime clichés (also see
comment on *Paragon Rag*). The b section is outstanding in its
thorough realization of a syncopated chromatic melody line.
An interesting device used to unify the composition is in using
the same ending for both c and d sections. The strong echo-
like effect in the d section was a favorite device later exploited
with great success by his leading disciples, James Scott and
Joseph Lamb.

A Breeze From Alabama. December 29, 1902. John Stark & Son, St. Louis.

Recording: The Southland Stingers, "Palm Leaf Rag," Angel S-36074.

Structure: INTRO AA BB CC INTRO-2 DD INTRO-3 BB

Advertised by Stark as "a story in transitions," this is an ambitious experiment in tonality, far ahead of any other rag writer of the day. After two sections in the key of C, the composer begins the C section abruptly in the key of A flat (this is a favorite harmonic change in Folk ragtime, but more thoroughly explored here). Within this C section, Joplin modulates to E natural, and back again to A flat, telescoping the effect of the previous C-A flat change. Then he moves to F and finally ends in the key of C.

Elite Syncopations. December 29, 1902. John Stark & Son, St. Louis.

Recordings: Dave Jasen, "Fingerbustin' Ragtime," Blue Goose 3001, March, 1972. Mary Lou Williams, "An Evening With Scott Joplin," Nonesuch NYPL-SJ. October, 1971.

Structure: INTRO AA BB A CC DD

An excellent example combining Joplin's use of folk strains with a lyrical melodic line. The A and D sections use folk materials where sections B and C are effectively contrasted with flowing melodies. The juxtaposing of differing musical ideas was a favorite compositional device first used by Joplin. The A section beautifully incorporates one of the earliest ragtime clichés, usually overdone for the effect of hands chasing each other. The D section features an especially strong finish.

The Entertainer. December 29, 1902. John Stark & Son, St. Louis.

Recording: Marvin Hamlisch and Orch, "The Sting," MCA 390.

Roll: QRS 30358.

Structure: INTRO AA BB A CC INTRO-2 DD

This was the number one song on the "top ten" popular song charts during 1974—a phenomenal occurance seventy-two years after it was published. Section A features an advanced use of a pianistic call-and-response pattern with dynamic markings indicated by the composer. In section B, the third and fourth measures act as a fill-in between the first two and the fifth and sixth, similar to arrangements of pieces for string orchestra. In the rare two-mandolin-and-guitar arrangement issued by Stark, the string concept is clearly realized especially in the trio. It was even dedicated to "James Brown and His Mandolin Club." Just six months after it appeared on sheet music counters, Monroe H. Rosenfeld, a prominent Tin Pan Alley lyricist-composer, wrote about Joplin in the *St. Louis Globe-Democrat* of June 7, 1903: "Probably the best and most euphonious of his latter day compositions is *The Entertainer.* It is a jingling work of a very original character, embracing various strains of a retentive character which set the foot in spontaneous action and leave an indelible imprint on the tympanum."

The Strenuous Life. Not copyrighted but published 1902. John Stark & Son, St. Louis.
Recording: The Southland Stingers, "Magnetic Rag," Angel S-36078, 1974.
Roll: QRS X3625 (65 note), ("Scott Joplin Ragtime Vol. 2," Biograph BLP 1008Q).
Structure: INTRO AA BB A TRIO-INTRO CC DD
Very march-like, it echoes President Theodore Roosevelt's advocacy of a strenuous life. A section is similar in feeling to its counterpart in the *Easy Winners.* C section features an unusual bass rhythm of Octave-Chord-Chord-Octave instead of the usual Octave-Chord-Octave-Chord. However, the final section is a strong one maintaining the martial feeling created at the beginning.

Weeping Willow. June 6, 1903. Val A. Reis Music Co., St. Louis.
Recordings: Swingle II, "Rags and All That Jazz," Columbia PC-34194. Trebor Tichenor, "King of Folk Ragtime," Dirty Shame 2001.
Roll: Scott Joplin. Connorized 10277 ("Scott Joplin-1916," Biograph BLP 1006Q).
Structure: INTRO AA BB A CC DD
The first two sections seem like a happy, carefree romp during

a lazy, sunny afternoon down South. Beautifully melodic and with clever use of syncopation it evokes different images—just what Joplin intended. A wonderfully constructed rag whose various sections bring out differing emotions. Section c begins with a favorite black folk strain, best remembered in *'Tain't Nobody's Business If I Do.*

Palm Leaf Rag. November 14, 1903. Victor Kremer Co., Chicago.

Recording: The Southland Stingers, "Palm Leaf Rag," Angel S-36074.

Roll: Kimball B5824.

Structure: INTRO AA BB CC INTRO-2 AA

A fitting companion to *Weeping Willow,* this one shares a grace and elegance along with a sophisticated use of anticipatory syncopation (most noticeable in the c section). Asymmetrical phrasing (not only found in the A section here but also in the D section of *Weeping Willow*) contributes to the darker emotions expressed here and contrasts nicely with the lighter content in the B and c sections.

The Favorite. June 23, 1904. A. W. Perry & Sons' Music Co., Sedalia, Mo.

Recordings: Trebor Jay Tichenor, "Mississippi Valley Ragtime," Scroll LSCR-102. The Southland Stingers, "Palm Leaf Rag," Angel S-36074.

Roll: QRS X3345 (65 note).

Structure: INTRO AA BB A CC DD

Although published in 1904, it was written in 1900. In fact, the B section with its minor tonality (G minor) going to its relative major (B flat) is similar to the writing of the *Ragtime Dance,* probably written at the same time. D section harks back to the A section, very march-like.

The Sycamore. July 18, 1904. Will Rossiter, Chicago.

Recording: Canadian Brass, "Rag-Ma-Tazz," Boot BMC-3004.

Roll: QRS X3283 (65 note), ("Scott Joplin Ragtime Vol. 2," Biograph BLP 1008Q).

Structure: INTRO AA BB CC DD

The most notable development is the treatment Joplin gives his A section, which is a breakthrough in *Maple Leaf*'s A section. The C section is a foretaste of a song in *Treemonisha*. The D section is unusual for its time with its changing harmonies and use of a diminished chord within such a happy framework. Joplin experiments with textures of sound here and will develop it in later rags.

The Cascades. August 22, 1904. John Stark & Son, St. Louis.
Recordings: Ralph Sutton, Down Home 10, November, 1949. Joe Glover & Cotton Pickers, "That Ragtime Sound," Epic LN-3581. The St. Louis Ragtimers, Audiophile AP-122, 1977.
Roll: QRS 30088 ("Scott Joplin Ragtime, Vol. 2," Biograph BLP 1008Q).
Structure: INTRO AA BB TRIO-INTRO CC DD
Inspired by the spectacular water display which became the symbol of the St. Louis World's Fair of 1904, this masterpiece of syncopation displays ragtime's grace and majesty. Section C is a highpoint in ragtime literature, with a thick, complex texture of fast moving octaves in both hands which, when properly executed, reveals a new, wider command of the piano's resources by the composer. D section is a full and grand movement with a more profound ending, rather than the flamboyant ones used earlier.

Leola. Not copyrighted but published 1905. American Music Syndicate, St. Louis.
Recording: Dick Hyman, "Scott Joplin, The Complete Works for Piano," RCA CRL5-1106, 1975.
Structure: AA BB A CC DD
A graceful reworking of *Maple Leaf Rag*. A foretaste of *Gladiolus*.

Eugenia. February 26, 1906. Will Rossiter, Chicago.
Recording: Hank Jones, "This Is Ragtime Now!" ABC-Paramount 496.
Structure: INTRO AA BB A C INTERLUDE C INTERLUDE C
An incredibly lovely work showing a growing maturity in dealing with beautiful melodic lines in each section. For the first

time, Joplin extends a musical bridge between sections to the entire length of a section. However, this interlude-c interlude-c is among the oldest cakewalk patterns. The fast bass octaves in sixteenths midway in the A and C sections, as well as in the first ending of A, are similar to the embellishments in the hand-played rolls Joplin made. This stylistic feature occurs in some of the earliest of Joplin's rags, including the trios for *Swipesy* and *Sunflower Slow Drag* (see also Marshall's remarks). In an unprecedented blurb, Rossiter advertised this rag as "rather difficult." The title was undoubtedly suggested by Eugenia Street, behind the Rosebud in the St. Louis district.

The Ragtime Dance. December 21, 1906. John Stark & Son, St. Louis.
Recordings: Neville Dickie, "Rags & Tatters," (E) Contour 2870–190. The New England Conservatory Ragtime Ensemble, "Scott Joplin: The Red Back Book," Angel S-36060, 1973.
Roll: QRS X3626 (65 note).
Structure: INTRO AA BB CC D E F
Originally written as a folk ballet with lyrics, it was performed at Wood's Opera House in Sedalia before the turn of this century. Published in this form by Stark in 1902, it was a commercial failure. In an effort to recoup his losses, he issued this instrumental version which eliminated a 32-measure verse. This is a joyous work and, in keeping with his other rags written in Sedalia, a most beautiful ragtime number.

Search Light Rag. August 12, 1907. Jos. W. Stern & Co., New York.
Recording: Marvin Ash, "Piano Ragtime of the Fifties," Herwin 404.
Roll: QRS X3866 (65 note), ("Scott Joplin Ragtime, Vol. 2," Biograph BLP 1008Q).
Structure: INTRO AA BB A CC DD
Optimistic and strutting, the A section looks forward to the brilliant *Pine Apple Rag.* The C section is unusual for Joplin as he switches the syncopation from right to left and back to the right hand. The D section is in the old socko finish tradition

with which he ended his earliest works and which becomes a feature of all the 1907–8 rags.

Gladiolus Rag. September 24, 1907. Jos. W. Stern & Co., New York.
Recording: Wally Rose, "Ragtime Classics," Good Time Jazz M-12034.
Roll: QRS 30162 ("Scott Joplin Ragtime, Vol. 2," Biograph BLP 1008Q).
Structure: AA BB A CC DD
This closely follows the sound of the *Maple Leaf Rag*, especially in the A and B sections. A comparison of the two reveals the change in Joplin's writing style. It has a grand air about it. Section C produces most unusual harmonies which enlarge the scope of this fine work. As in *Search Light Rag*, this D section harks back to the ebullient ending.

Rose Leaf Rag. November 15, 1907. Jos. M. Daly Music Publishing Co., Boston.
Recording: Dick Hyman, "Scott Joplin, the Complete Works for Piano," RCA CRL5–1106, 1975.
Roll: Connorized 4473 ("Scott Joplin Ragtime, Vol. 2," Biograph BLP 1008Q).
Structure: INTRO AA BB A CC DD
Section A is a study in contrary motion in ragtime. Section B shows a highly developed syncopation pattern for the piano. C section works in the folk idiom with sophisticated harmonies. D section follows the other 1907 rags with a strong and happy finish.

Nonpareil. Not copyrighted but published 1907. Stark Music Co., St. Louis.
Recording: Richard Zimmerman, "Scott Joplin, His Complete Works," Murray Hill 931079, 1974.
Roll: Connorized 4401 (65 note), ("Scott Joplin Ragtime, Vol. 2," Biograph BLP 1008Q).
Structure: INTRO AA BB CC DD
The A section is surprisingly gentle and flows into the B section which contains a very busy left hand, interspersing rapid 16th

notes between the conventional Octave-Chord-Octave-Chord approach. In an effort to unify this rag, Joplin used the same endings in both the B and D sections. Section D has a marvelously pretty melody and an infectious rhythm.

Fig Leaf Rag. February 24, 1908. Stark Music Co., St. Louis.
Recordings: Dick Wellstood, "Alone." Jazzology JCE-73. Dave Jasen, "Rip-Roarin' Ragtime," Folkways FG-3561, June, 1977.
Roll: QRS 30141 ("Scott Joplin Ragtime, Vol. 2," Biograph BLP 1008Q).
Structure: INTRO AA BB A CC DD
A masterpiece, Joplin's genius is evident everywhere, from the expansive conception, through the exploring C section, to the jubilant D section. Its subtitle, "A High Class Rag" is certainly apt. The unexpected harmonies in the majestic D section may be described as chromatic writing, but it sounds more as if the whole idea was dictated by the extraordinary harmonic concept. In general, Joplin was more of a pentatonic writer and used less chromaticism than his disciple Joe Lamb.

Sugar Cane. April 21, 1908. Seminary Music Co., New York.
Recordings: The New England Conservatory Ragtime Ensemble, "Scott Joplin: The Red Back Book," Angel S-36060, 1973. James Levine, "Music of Scott Joplin, RCA ARL1–2243, 1977.
Roll: Connorized 4421.
Structure: AA BB A CC DD
John Stark objected to Joplin's re-use of the *Maple Leaf Rag* format, as expressed in his personal ledger. These remarks were probably intended for advertising blurbs or for use in his *Intermezzo* magazine: "No one will perhaps ever surpass Joplin's *Maple Leaf, Sunflower* or *Cascades* but alas like all composers do sooner or later, Joplin is verging to the sear and yellow leaf. His muse seems to have been pumped into inocuous (sic) desuetude, and his labored efforts are but a rehash of *Maple Leaf* or some of his first numbers that no self respecting publisher would print. Joplin's case is pitiful. When he hawks a manuscript around and finally sells it for a few dollars—the next

publisher he strikes tells him, 'Why I would have given you $500 for that'—this keeps Joplin miserable and thinking that his last publisher is cheating him. We have several Joplin manuscripts that were written before the spring of inspiration had run dry which we will bring out from time to time." A most interesting variation of *Maple Leaf Rag* which contrasts nicely with *Gladiolus* but even more illustrates just how fine an improvisor Joplin was. To tie the sections together, as in *Nonpareil,* he uses the same ending for B and D. The point about the A section in *Maple Leaf* is here amply demonstrated. In the C section, the device in the third measure was borrowed by Lamb for his *Ragtime Nightingale.* The D section, as in the last few rags, has a cheery and vital ending.

Pine Apple Rag. October 12, 1908. Seminary Music Co., New York.
Recording: Wally Rose, West Coast 110, June, 1946.
Roll: Rag Medley No. 6, Universal 92715 ("Scott Joplin Ragtime, Vol. 3," Biograph BLP 1010Q).
Structure: INTRO AA BB A CC DD
This is among the very finest rags ever written. An advanced way of handling folk material, the A section is one of his happiest and brightest. The B section is extremely pianistic with a solid use of rhythm as the major focal point of this section. The C section changes the emotional level to one of introspection. In keeping with this, note the use of the minor seventh in the trio which is the only time Joplin used such an intense blues coloration. Changing moods once again for the last section, Joplin cleverly integrated the former mood while offering a more optimistic outlook. In the last two sections (C and D) the harmonies and use of bass lines are extremely adventurous. In a detailed analysis of ragtime composition, one characteristic becomes evident: the intermingling of pentatonicism, chromaticism, formal European traditions and black folk-materials produces moments of the richest beauty which sometimes defy a one-way analysis of what we hear. This ambiguity arises from the strength of incorporated traditions, a synthesis of both black and white sources, and is at the same time one of the joys of ragtime's art. For example, the most moving idea

in Joplin's trio of *Pine Apple Rag* comes with the melodic and harmonic coloration in the third measure which can be heard three different ways. A jazz-oriented listener would hear this idea as a blue seventh on the subdominant. If the melody line alone is heard, one hears it as a flatted third. It can also appear as an enharmonically-spelled German six-chord (see also the commentary on Marshall's *The Peach*).

Wall Street Rag. February 23, 1909. Seminary Music Co. New York.
Recording: William Bolcom, "Heliotrope Bouquet," Nonesuch H-71257, 1971.
Roll: Master Record 653 ("Scott Joplin Ragtime, Vol. 3," Biograph BLP 1010Q).
Structure: INTRO AA BB CC DD
This begins Joplin's experimental period and an attempt to continue his programmatic music which he began with *The Cascades.* He labeled each section, intimating a musical description: A section is entitled, "Panic in Wall Street, Brokers Feeling Melancholy." B section is called, "Good Times Coming." C section (the most happily syncopated in the entire rag) is titled, "Good Times Have Come." D section is in the fine tradition of having a splendid and victorious ending, utilizing tone clusters and deliberately creating a Folk rag atmosphere for its "Listening to the Strains of Genuine Negro Ragtime, Brokers Forget Their Cares." There is a gentle, lullaby quality to the A section, and the whole rag is of such sensitivity and character that we may infer a new contentment by the composer in the year of his successful second marriage, and the time of his settling permanently in New York City.

Country Club. October 30, 1909. Seminary Music Co., New York.
Recording: Dick Hyman, "Scott Joplin, the Complete Works for Piano," RCA CRL5-1106, 1975.
Structure: INTRO AA BB A CC DD
Seemingly like earlier works, this is an advanced working out of syncopated marches contrasted with long-flowing ballad-like melodies. Much of the treble voicing is in thirds (especially

the B section). Section D contains an early example of a written "break." The "break" is a musical interruption which separates musical ideas within a phrase and which jazz bands featured as a performance trick rather than as a compositional device. The major ragtime composer to utilize the break as an integral part of the composition was, of course, Jelly Roll Morton.

Euphonic Sounds. October 30, 1909. Seminary Music Co., New York.

Recordings: James P. Johnson, "The Original James P. Johnson," Folkways FJ-2850. Dick Hyman, "Scott Joplin, the Complete Works for Piano," RCA CRL5–1106, 1975.

Roll: Universal 92715 (in medley) ("Scott Joplin Ragtime, Vol. 3," Biograph BLP 1010Q).

Structure: INTRO AA BB A CC A CODA

More of a musical exercise, it is one of Joplin's most ambitious creations. The entire conception illustrates his heaviest leanings toward European romanticism. The A and B sections have eliminated the standard left hand of ragtime (Octave-Chord, Octave-Chord). Interestingly, the ending of section A is similar to the comparable ending of A in *Pine Apple Rag.* B section is one of his most high-reaching ragtime selections. The use of the minor tonality combined with diminished chords and the usual major tonality, gives this rag a wide variety of expression, creating several moods.

Paragon Rag. October 30, 1909. Seminary Music Co., New York.

Recordings: Joshua Rifkin, "Piano Rags by Scott Joplin, Vol. 2," Nonesuch H-71264. James Levine, "Music of Scott Joplin," RCA ARL1–2243, 1977.

Roll: U.S. Music 75378 (in medley).

Structure: INTRO AA BB A CC DD

The A section harks back to the A section of *Weeping Willow Rag,* reminiscent of the plantation era. Section B carries us on to the Sedalia ragtime days, adding a break in measures 3 and 4 which foreshadows a device used by the Novelty rag composers (see Confrey's *Kitten on the Keys*). C section is interesting not only for its block-chorded left hand (similar to measures 9–16 of the A

section of *Maple Leaf Rag*), but for using melodies called for in
Treemonisha. Section D combines the flag-waving of the older
days with a sophistication found from 1907 onward—a re-
strained but grandly triumphal ending.

Stoptime Rag. June 4, 1910. Jos. W. Stern & Co., New York.
Recording: Marvin Hamlisch, "The Entertainer," MCA 2115.
Roll: QRS 30786, ("Scott Joplin Ragtime, Vol. 2," Biograph
   BLP 1008Q).
Structure: AA BB A CC DD EE DD FF GG
This appears in one sense to be a throwback to the earlier
Ragtime Dance in which musical breaks are provided so the
dancers' stomping feet could be heard. The stop effects are
indicated in the scores of both numbers. Another unusual feature is that there are seven different melodies of 8 measures
each, rather than the usual three or four sections containing 16
measures each. Truly an experiment—one which worked. The
C section is used as a contrast with long lyrical melody lines in
the traditional 16-measure section. Once again Joplin combines the major and minor tonalities in one piece. And, for
once, the performer is permitted to play "fast or slow."

Scott Joplin's New Rag. May 1, 1912. Jos. W. Stern & Co.,
   New York.
Recordings: Wally Rose, "Ragtime Piano Masterpieces," Co-
   lumbia CL 6260 (10"). London Festival Ballet Orchestra,
   "Scott Joplin: The Entertainer Ballet," Columbia
   M-33185.
Roll: QRS 31282.
Structure: INTRO AA BB A CC INTRO-2 INTERLUDE A CODA
A magnificent rag combining the sparkling effervescence of his
youth with the understanding and maturity gained from his
experiments. An extended interlude of minor and diminished
chords leading to a repeat of the A section is quite out of
character for this rag, but would be appropriate, for example,
in *Euphonic Sounds.*

Silver Swan Rag. Not copyrighted but published 1971. Maple
   Leaf Club, Los Angeles.

Recording: Richard Zimmerman, "Scott Joplin, His Complete Works," Murray Hill 931079, 1974.

Roll: Master Record 1239, ("Scott Joplin Ragtime, Vol. 3," Biograph BLP 1010Q).

Structure: INTRO AA BB A CC INTRO A

Found on a piano roll in 1970, *Silver Swan* was issued both by QRS and National in 1914. Dick Zimmerman and Donna McCluer then transcribed it and had it published. It is a serious work, definitely done in his last working period. The C section sounds as though it consists of three fragments put together, with the third a folksy rhythmic idea usually done at the beginning of a section—its use here at the end gives the effect of a seamless 32-measure section.

Magnetic Rag. July 21, 1914. Scott Joplin Music Publishing Co., New York.

Recording: The Southland Stingers, "Magnetic Rag," Angel S-36078.

Roll: Scott Joplin, Connorized 10266, ("Scott Joplin 1916," Biograph BLP 1006Q).

Structure: INTRO AA BB CC VAMP DD AA CODA

The final rag in the most distinguished series of rags by a single composer. Experimenting to the end, he begins with a section that combines the joyous Folk rag style with a bittersweet quality and follows with a B section in the relative minor which changes the rag to a melancholy mood. The 24-measure C section is one of Joplin's most moving, incorporating down-home blues elements with much syncopation. The D section in the parallel minor of A (B flat minor), is the most somber in all of Joplin's rags. Joplin sensed that the rag couldn't end that way, so he repeated the A section twice. As if loath to say farewell to ragtime, he added a joyful coda with which to be remembered. In all, this is Joplin's most autobiographical rag and certainly one of the most moving in all of ragtime.

Reflection Rag. December 4, 1917. Stark Music Co., St. Louis.

Recording: Richard Zimmerman, "Scott Joplin, His Complete Works," Murray Hill 931079, 1974.

Structure: INTRO AA BB CC DD EE

Posthumous publication of a work Stark had bought before 1908. In a blurb when this was issued, Stark mentioned two more unpublished Joplin manuscripts owned by him. These were destroyed during the 1930s when the family moved their plant. *Reflection* is a pleasant rag with a characteristic final section which winds up Joplin's ragtime with a strong, optimistic feeling.

LOUIS CHAUVIN
Born: St. Louis, Missouri, March 13, 1881
Died: Chicago, Illinois, March 26, 1908

A shadowy figure from ragtime's obscure past, this towering genius, heralded as the "King of Ragtime Players," and easily the finest pianist in the early years of this century in and around St. Louis, was also of tremendous importance to the musical development of Scott Joplin. The haunting, bittersweet quality much admired in Joplin's later work was due to the influence of this musically inventive performer who couldn't read music and didn't care to have his compositions preserved in writing. Charles Thompson recalled him as "strictly an ear player," and ranked him the best of St. Louis pianists. He also remembered that Chauvin played an entire musical show score from memory after hearing it only once. During the St. Louis World's Fair of 1904, when the best pianists from around the country came there to earn fame and fortune, Louis won the most important ragtime contest from among the finest in the land. After flirting with vaudeville and enjoying the wandering life in show business as part of vocal quartets and duos (singing and playing piano), he settled down to the life of a "professor" in the district of St. Louis. At the end of his life, in Chicago's district, he died of multiple sclerosis.

Note: In the recently discovered *Palladium,* a black Republican newspaper published in St. Louis from 1893–1907, the following article appeared in the February 27, 1904 issue concerning a pre-World's Fair ragtime piano contest sponsored by the Rose Bud Club on February 22, 1904:

On Tuesday last the Rose Bud club gave its third annual ball and piano contest at the New Douglass hall, corner Beaumont and Lawton avenue (formerly Chestnut Street), and it was one of the largest, finest and best conducted affairs of the kind ever held in St. Louis. The hall was packed and jammed, many well-dressed, good-looking and orderly people, from all classes of society. A great many of the best people in town were present, among them being *The Palladium* man, to enjoy the festivities and witness the great piano contest.

Mr. Tom Turpin presented an elegant gold medal to the successful contestant, Mr. Louis Chauvin. Messrs. Joe Jordan and Charles Warfield were a tie for second place, Mr. Mann Reynolds, Mr. Conroy Casey and Mr. Ed Williams were all close up in the contest, and were well received by the crowd. Music was furnished by the matchless World's Fair band. Mr. Tom Turpin was general manager, ably assisted by Messrs. Tom Watkins, John H. Clark, George Isabell, Lonnie Johnson, Charles Warfield, Sam Patterson, Willie North, Alonzo Brooks, Howard Anderson, Dick Curry, Louis Chauvin, Richard Kent, George Kinsey, Mr. Helms, E. J. Bruner, and several others. The bar was presided over by Messrs. Charles Turpin, Charles Weinstock, Ed Isabell, Walter Nevels, Dave Young, Henry Taylor and "Fatima." Messrs. Ike Commodore and "Nubba" Watson sold tickets. The union waiters promised to do better next time. The club desires to thank their many friends for their very gracious support, and promise on the occasion of their next annual ball to see to it that every piano player of note in the United States enters, and will give an elegant diamond medal to the winner, and hold the contest at the Exposition coliseum, where there will be plenty of room, and all can hear and see to the very best advantage.

Mr. Samuel Patterson came from Chicago just to attend

the Turpin ball. Clarence Goins danced with every girl that would look pleasant at him. He went out of his cravat, but still held on to his half-smoked cigar.

Heliotrope Bouquet (with Scott Joplin). December 23, 1907. Stark Music Co., New York.

Recordings: Lee Stafford, Castle 10, January, 1950. David A. Jasen, "Creative Ragtime," Euphonic 1206, July, 1966. William Bolcom, "Heliotrope Bouquet," Nonesuch H-71257, 1971. Dick Hyman, "Scott Joplin, the Complete Works for Piano," RCA CRL5–1106, 1975.

Roll: U.S. Music

Structure: INTRO A BB A CC DD

The first two sections (A and B) of this rag are by Chauvin and the last two (C and D) are by Joplin. The first half of this exquisite masterwork (advertised by Stark as "the audible poetry of motion"), has stylistic idiosyncrasies not found in other rags by Joplin, features he took great care to notate, giving us the sole example of Chauvin's ragtime style. The structure of A is a most effective variation on the usual pattern: here the last 4 measures are detached from the idea of the first 12, forming a release to the end of the section. The rhythmic riff-like lilting B section was taken in the twenties for the chorus of a jazz classic, *Heebie Jeebies.* It has eccentric 32nd-note triplets and a break of descending diminished triads. The ending here is also unusual, and features the "Scotch snap" rhythmic pattern, encountered infrequently in the Classic rags. The C and D sections are more predictable. Rudi Blesh recalls that Sam Patterson played the entire piece as a tango.

SCOTT HAYDEN
Born: Sedalia, Missouri, March 31,
1882
Died: Chicago, Illinois, September 16,
1915

Raised in the very place where Joplin formally created his concept of ragtime, Hayden was a schoolmate of Arthur Marshall's and attended and graduated from Lincoln High School. Under Joplin's tutelage, their collaborations are among the finest rags ever written. Hayden had a light, airy, delicate style with single notes and flowing melodic lines indicating his personal pianistic approach, much admired by Joplin. He married Nora Wright and lived with the Joplins in St. Louis in 1901. Nora died after the birth of their daughter. Hayden moved to Chicago where he married Jeanette Wilkins, who lived on in Chicago after his death. The last twelve years of his life were spent as an elevator operator in the Cook County Hospital where he died of pulmonary tuberculosis.

Pear Blossoms. November 1, 1960. Published in *They All Played Ragtime,* Oak Publications, 3rd edition, 1966. Arranged by Bob Darch, edited by Donald Ashwander.
Recording: Bob Darch, "Ragtime Piano," United Artists UAL 3120.
Structure: INTRO AA BB CC DD INTERLUDE EE CODA
Hayden wrote this while still in high school. The manuscript contains the complete melody line but only sketchy bass parts which were completed by Bob Darch, who obtained the manuscript from Sedalia musician Tom Ireland.

Sunflower Slow Drag (with Scott Joplin). March 18, 1901. John Stark & Son, St. Louis.

Recording: Dick Zimmerman, "Scott Joplin, The Entertainer," Olympic 7116.

Roll: Aeolian 8479 (65 note).

Structure: INTRO AA BB A TRIO-INTRO CC DD

While the two worked together on this piece, the trio is by Joplin alone and the rest primarily by Hayden. This rag once rivaled the popularity of *Maple Leaf Rag,* and was one of the very first Classic rags available on piano rolls. Stark advertised it as "the twin sister of *Maple Leaf"* and told of Joplin's writing of the trio during his courtship of Belle Hayden. The A section is very ingenious and extremely pianistic (Brun Campbell recalled that Hayden was one of the best players locally). The B section breaks away with:

The trio uses a wider range of keys and is dramatically marked, beginning *pianissimo,* and achieving a fine lyricism. As is true of the *Swipesy* trio, this one is also heavily pentatonic. The D section caps the lyricism with a delicate melody that nevertheless assures the firm ending of the rag.

Something Doing (with Scott Joplin). February 24, 1903. Val A. Reis Music Co., St. Louis.

Recording: The Southland Stingers, "Magnetic Rag," Angel S-36078, 1974.

Roll: Scott Joplin, Connorized 10277 ("Scott Joplin-1916," Biograph BLP 1006Q).

Structure: INTRO AA BB A CC DD

This masterwork is totally original. Its rich inspiration is reflected in its eternal springtime freshness, so characteristic of the early Classic rags. It is largely in flowing melodic lines, with a final D section that features anticipatory syncopation (notable in the 1903 rags of Joplin).

Felicity Rag (with Scott Joplin). July 27, 1911. John Stark & Son, St. Louis.

Roll: U.S. Music 65050 ("Scott Joplin Ragtime, Vol. 2," Biograph BLP 1008Q).

Structure: INTRO AA BB CC INTRO-2 AA

This was probably written during the early years in St. Louis when they lived together and, with *Kismet Rag,* were the "Joplin" rags Stark referred to (see *Sugar Cane*). The melodic lines are fresh and very busy, with a contrasting trio, probably Joplin's contribution.

Kismet Rag (with Scott Joplin). February 21, 1913. John Stark & Son, St. Louis.

Recording: Trebor Jay Tichenor, "King of Folk Ragtime," Dirty Shame 2001, 1973.

Roll: Kimball B-6793.

Structure: INTRO AA BB A CC DD

A lyrical collaboration with an unusual modulation at B which goes to the dominant. The final rhythmic theme appears to be built from a floating folk idea found with some modification in Kelly's *Peaceful Henry,* Furry's early *Robardina Rag* and in one of the so-called "rag medleys," *Bunch of Rags,* arranged by Ben Jerome (*I Don't Like That Face You Wear* by Ernest Hogan).

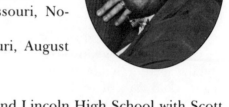

ARTHUR MARSHALL

Born: Saline County, Missouri, November 20, 1881

Died: Kansas City, Missouri, August 18, 1968

Attended grade school and Lincoln High School with Scott Hayden in Sedalia. He was a protégé of Joplin, who lived with the Marshall family when he first arrived in Sedalia. Marshall also took private classical lessons from Lillian Read and from Mrs. Teeter while in grade school. Under Joplin's influence, he played his first piano job at the Maple Leaf Club. Marshall then attended the George R. Smith College, studying music theory, and went to the Teacher's Institute, majoring in Education and obtaining a teaching license. During this time he began his professional career as a ragtime pianist and played for dances at Liberty Park and for picnics and barbecues at Forest Park. He also worked in the "parlors" where the official rate was $1.50 for the evening, but with tips take-home pay was closer to $10.00. He joined McCabe's Minstrels in 1901 as an intermission pianist and marched in their parades playing cymbals. Marshall found lots of work in St. Louis during the World's Fair. He married Maude McMannes, joining Joplin's Drama Company, along with Scott Hayden. He recalled friendly, cutting contests among the pianists—"shootin' at one another—where it caused them to write some pretty good rags." He left for Chicago in 1906 where opportunities to earn a decent living as a pianist were more plentiful. Here he married Julia Jackson, who bore him two daughters and a son. He entered a ragtime contest around 1910 at the Booker T. Washington Theatre in St. Louis, run by Charlie Turpin, and won the top prize of five dollars. He then went to work for Tom Turpin at the Eureka on Chestnut Street and 22nd Avenue. His last piano job was playing at Henry Maroche's Moonshine Gardens, when his wife died in childbirth at the end of 1916. He went to Kansas City in 1917, retired from the music business, and married for a third and last time.

Swipesy Cakewalk (with Scott Joplin). July 21, 1900. John
    Stark & Son, St. Louis.
Recording: Bob Darch, "Ragtime Piano," United Artists UAL
    3120.
Roll: QRS 3988 (65 note).
Structure: INTRO AA BB A CC DD
The title was suggested by a local Sedalia newsboy (whose photo is on the original cover) who, Stark said, "looked like he just swiped something." This has a simple folk spirit suggested by the "cakewalk" title, but is a polished Classic rag in form and

ideas, having little to do with the cakewalk tradition. An important highlight is the lyrical Joplin trio, brought in with abrupt 16th-note bass octaves, much like the embellishments on the hand-played Joplin rolls. The final section is a quintessential Folk rag style stomper—Marshall at his best.

Kinklets. December 10, 1906. Stark Music Co., New York.
Recording: Max Morath, "The World of Scott Joplin," Vanguard SRV 310.
Roll: QRS 30519.
Structure: INTRO AA BB TRIO-INTRO CC DD
Originally called *Smokeville Kinklets,* it was Marshall's own favorite, and was named after Stark first heard the rag; patting his foot, he remarked with admiration, "That tune's got plenty kinks in it." It flows beautifully throughout, and is a graceful march-like Classic rag. Section A uses a pattern that became a standard one in later years (see Joplin's *Paragon Rag*). C and D feature a Folk rag style pattern.

Lily Queen. November 8, 1907. W. W. Stuart, New York.
Recordings: Richard Zimmerman, "Scott Joplin, his Complete Works," Murray Hill 931079. The Southland Stingers, "Magnetic Rag," Angel S-36078, 1974.
Structure: INTRO AA BB A CC DD
Although the name of Scott Joplin appears as collaborator, he did not write any part of it. In a letter, Marshall explained, "Joplin told me he had a party that would publish that piece of music so I let him handle it. But for him having any part in the composing, he did not. Now he was the more popular as a composer and that is why his name was mentioned in the writing of *Lily Queen.* I got about $50 in all for it at the time. I was living in Chicago."

The D section of this march-style rag is one of the most moving climactic final strains in all of ragtime. It rolls along, sparked by repeated slurs in the treble, an explicit touch best described as "funky." It is hardly ever found in the Classic rags, but one that was popular as a performance device (see Bowman's *11th Street Rag*).

Ham And! February 24, 1908. Stark Music Co., New York.
Recording: Trebor Jay Tichenor, "Mississippi Valley Ragtime,"
    Scroll LSCR 102, 1966.
Structure: INTRO AA BB A CC DD
It is here that the Marshall style is best exemplified. A fascinating intermediary style between the less formalized Folk ragtime and the subtle restraint of the Joplin style. As the only
active performer of the Classic rag pioneers, he incorporated
many folksy, explicit performing devices into his own rags,
much as Matthews did later with his various *Pastime* rags. Once
again, this rag highlights an intense series of slurs (found in
section C), a sound usually associated with the Midwest and
Southern folk blues players. The entire rag has the feeling of
spontaneity.

The Peach. December 7, 1908. Stark Music Printing & Publish-
    ing Co., New York.
Recordings: Chris Barber, "Elite Syncopations," (E) Columbia
    33 SX 1245. Trebor Tichenor, "King of Folk Ragtime,"
    Dirty Shame 2001.
Structure: INTRO AA BB A CC DD
The trio has a strong feeling of a spiritual, and section D main-
tains his high standard with an exceptional final section. In
measure eight, he has a phrase of moving ambiguity in the
treble which is supported by a diminished chord, but also has
the feeling of a flatted "blue" third.

The Pippin Rag. December 7, 1908. Stark Music Printing &
    Publishing Co., New York.
Recording: Max Morath, "The World of Scott Joplin," Van-
    guard SRV 310.
Structure: INTRO A BB TRIO-INTRO CC A
In printing both *The Peach* and *Pippin*, a mix-up occurred in the
sub-titles: on the cover of *Peach* the subtitle is "Ragtime Two
Step," and on the *Pippin* cover we read "A Sentimental Rag."
On the inside, however, the subtitles are reversed. This is
Marshall's most unusual conception with a 24-measure A sec-
tion largely in F minor which ends, however, on the relative

major. The c section has effective call-and-response patterns and one of the most soulful endings in ragtime writing. The rag returns to the ambivalent minor-major A section to finish, trimmed to a regular 16-measure version.

Century Prize. 1966. Published in *They All Played Ragtime,* Oak Publications, 3rd edition, 1966.
Structure: INTRO AA BB A CC D INTERLUDE D
A lightly syncopated march done with great melodic flair and attention to detail characteristic of the composer.

Missouri Romp. 1966. Published in *They All Played Ragtime,* Oak Publications, 3rd edition, 1966.
Recording: Max Morath, "They All Play Ragtime," Jazzology JCE 52.
Structure: INTRO AA BB INTERLUDE VAMP CC
The soulful, spiritual overtones of Marshall's work were never stronger and reach a truly masterful height in the B section. The trio modulates to the key of C from E flat by way of an 8-measure interlude and a 4-measure vamp, marked "clap hands."

Silver Rocket. 1966. Published in *They All Played Ragtime,* Oak Publications, 3rd edition, 1966.
Recording: John Arpin, "They All Play Ragtime," Jazzology JCE 52.
Structure: INTRO AA BB A CC DD
Excellent strutting rag with extended 20-measure D section.

Little Jack's Rag. 1976. Published in *This Is Ragtime,* Hawthorne, 1976.
Structure: INTRO AA BB A TRIO-INTRO CC
One of his very finest, it was discovered posthumously as a complete manuscript by pianist-historian Terry Waldo when visiting Marshall's daughter, Mildred Steward. The title is the affectionate nickname for Mildred. Marshall performed the c section in 1959 at an early Joplin Festival in Sedalia. It must have been one of his favorite themes; it is certainly one of his most inspired.

JAMES SYLVESTER SCOTT
Born: Neosho, Missouri, 1886
Died: Kansas City, Kansas, August 30, 1938

T he second child in a family of six, Jimmy was gifted with perfect pitch. He was given piano lessons by local pianist John Coleman, who was able to give him a thorough grounding in both playing and theory. His parents, James, Sr. and Molly Thomas Scott, were former slaves who tried to find work to support their large family. They moved to Carthage in 1901 where James, Jr. completed his schooling at the segregated Lincoln School and took further lessons from Emma Johns, a Carthage piano teacher. He started playing at the famed Lakeside Park—both piano and steam calliope—and obtained a job in 1902 with the Dumars Music Store, owned by Charlie Dumars, the director of the Carthage Light Guard Band. He started out as window-washer and store sweeper, but it wasn't long before he was demonstrating music, plugging songs and playing his own tunes. Demand for Scott's music induced Dumars to publish his work. He took a trip to St. Louis in 1906 where he met Joplin, who took his work to Stark. Fortunately, the first rag Stark bought, *Frog Legs Rag,* was a hit. Thus encouraged, Stark kept on publishing whatever Scott sent until 1922 when Stark stopped publishing new works. Scott left Carthage and the Dumars firm in 1914 when he went to Kansas City, Kansas. He married Nora Johnson, who predeceased him; they had no children. One of his cousins was the famed vaudeville blues singer Ada Brown, who also lived in Kansas City. He taught piano and organ and played at moving picture theaters. At first he played at the keyboard for the Panama Theatre; then he formed an eight-piece band for which he acted as arranger. Scott played at the Lincoln and finally the Eblon. During the last years of his life, he was in poor health, but kept on composing, although nothing further was published.

The only Missourian of the "Big Three," Scott's rags reflect his activity as a professional pianist and theater organist. As with most ragtime composers, Scott wrote in one sustained mood. Joplin was the only one to use moods of varying intensity in one composition. Whereas Joplin synthesized nineteenth-century European classicism with Mississippi Valley Afro-American folk roots, Scott synthesized the folk tradition with his professional career in popular and jazz music. This resulted in a developmental feeling in his rags, a spirit more characteristic of twentieth-century music to come, and one step further away from the oldest concept of ragtime, that of a patchwork of various different musical ideas. He was undoubtedly the best keyboard man of the Classic ragtimers, and loved to punctuate his lyrical melodies with short, abrupt phrases. Toward the end of his published writing career, his rags became more thickly textured with much varied bass work. Scott, much more than Joplin, was concerned with exploring the form pianistically more than emotionally.

A Summer Breeze. March 14, 1903. Dumars Music Co., Carthage, Mo.
Structure: INTRO AA BB A TRIO-INTRO CC DD
This first Scott work is greatly influenced by Scott Joplin's work. While the format is identical, the first three sections indicate a general appreciation of Joplin's ideas, but the D section is an outright steal from the B section of *Elite Syncopations.* Nevertheless, there is an indication of originality, especially in the trio, which has a brassy but artistic use of parallelism.

The Fascinator. September 23, 1903. Dumars Music Co., Carthage, Mo.
Structure: INTRO AA BB A CC DD
Scott's cleverness is clearly illustrated in this rag. His long,

elegantly flowing melody is amply demonstrated in the B section, heralding beautiful melodies to come. The C section takes a Joplinesque turn: in tune with the heavy influence of the 1901–2 Joplin rags, he modulates at the trio from A flat to C, copying the same idea in Joplin's *Breeze From Alabama.* The D section has ideas incorporated from the *Peacherine Rag* trio by Joplin.

On the Pike. April 13, 1904. Dumars Music Co., Carthage, Mo.
Structure: INTRO AA BB A CC
A section starts out like the B section of *At a Georgia Camp Meeting,* but includes a vigorous left hand which is extended in an unusual C section of 32 measures. Of these first three rags published by Dumars, this one makes a more complete break with Joplin and is the most original of the three, foretelling later Scott rags. This one was dedicated to visitors at the 1904 St. Louis World's Fair and named after the amusement section of the fair where most of the ragtime pianists were playing.

Frog Legs Rag. December 10, 1906. John Stark & Son, New York.
Recording: Ralph Sutton, Down Home 9, November, 1949.
Roll: U.S. Music 1255 (65 note) ("James Scott Volume 1," Biograph BLP 1016Q).
Structure: AA BB A TRIO-INTRO CC DD
His first real masterpiece, it contains many of what were to become typical Scott devices. The crisp freshness of the A section gives way to a sophisticated use in the B section of the *Maple Leaf Rag* B section. The lyrical C is an interesting development in feeling of the A section, with similar harmonics. The D section introduces us to one of Scott's favorite devices, the echo, or call-and-response phrasing in which an idea (usually of one measure) is stated and then repeated an octave higher. This theme develops the feel of B, once again, with the use of similar chords. The modulation at the trio is unusual in that it goes to the dominant (A flat) instead of the subdominant, which would have put sections C and D in the key of G flat. Perhaps Stark objected to a score with six flats—he did later with Lamb's *Excelsior,* but then gave in.

Kansas City Rag. January 2, 1907. Stark Music Co., St. Louis.
Roll: QRS 30566 ("James Scott Volume 1," Biograph BLP 1016Q).
Structure: INTRO AA BB CC BB
A beautiful A section flows directly into an imaginative B section which teases with its insistent melody trying to escape from its confines. The C section is brilliantly original in phrasing which creates 1-measure breaks, such as jazz bands were to do on recordings ten years later.

Great Scott Rag. August 18, 1909. Allen Music Co., Columbia, Mo.
Recording: John Arpin, "Concert in Ragtime," Scroll 101, September, 1965.
Roll: QRS 31138 ("James Scott Volume 1," Biograph BLP 1016Q).
Structure: INTRO AA BB CC BB
A lovely rag filled with Scott's reworkings of favorite ragtime devices. The first two measures of A are identical with the opener of Chas. L. Johnson's *Scandalous Thompson* of 1899. Though the two Kansas City composers never met, it is highly probable that Scott was familiar with this fine early work. The B section contains another variation of Joplin's B section to *Maple Leaf Rag,* with the Scott echo effect interwoven. The C section has the interesting device of alternating the syncopation between the left and right hands, the bass in syncopated octaves similarly done in *Kansas City Rag.*

The Ragtime Betty. October 5, 1909. Stark Music Co., St. Louis.
Roll: Electra D-76018–3.
Structure: AA BB A CC DD
His most complex essay of 1909, it contains all his hallmarks in a more demanding and involved format than in the preceeding rags. Section C has short 1-measure runs of single-note lines which Scott was to make greater use of later on.

Grace and Beauty. November 12, 1909. Stark Music Co., St. Louis.

Recording: Ralph Sutton, Down Home 10, November, 1949, ("Backroom Piano," Verve MGV 1004).

Rolls: U.S. Music 63294 ("James Scott Volume 1." Biograph BLP 1016Q). W. Arlington. Connorized 20460 ("Scott Joplin 1916," Biograph BLP 1006Q).

Structure: INTRO AA BB A TRIO-INTRO CC DD

Undoubtedly Scott's most brilliant ragtime work. In the finest Classic rag tradition, this scintillating composition flows smoothly from one section to the next, progressively developing fresh ideas. Section C starts with the echo device which is imaginatively used again in the D section.

Sunburst Rag. Not copyrighted but published 1909. Stark Music Co., St. Louis.

Recording: John Arpin, "The Other Side of Ragtime," Scroll 103, April, 1966.

Roll: U.S. Music 62261 ("James Scott Volume 1," Biograph BLP 1016Q).

Structure: INTRO AA BB A TRIO-INTRO CC B

One of the great joys of Classic ragtime. The intensely pianistic C section has an ascending break of triads that foretells Novelty ragtime. Scott uncannily predicted specific tunes in much later popular music. This trio, for instance, is identical with a Herb Albert tune called *Spanish Flea.*

Ophelia Rag. June 6, 1910. Stark Music Co. St. Louis.

Recording: Dave Jasen, "Rip-Roarin' Ragtime," Folkways FG-3561, June 1977.

Roll: U.S. Music 64138 ("James Scott Volume 1." Biograph BLP 1016Q).

Structure: INTRO AA BB TRIO-INTRO CC B

Scott made direct use of folk elements of pianistic ragtime. The chromatic ascent in the A section is identical with Turpin's dramatic use of it in his *Ragtime Nightmare.* B section is outstanding here both for its melody and for its variation of the B section of *Maple Leaf Rag.* The C section has a most unusual left hand which isn't merely used as an arresting device as in *Great Scott Rag,* but as an integral part of the melody.

Hilarity Rag. September 15, 1910. Stark Music Co., St. Louis.
Recording: John Jensen, "Piano Rags by James Scott," Genesis
  GS 1044. 1974.
Roll: U.S. Music 64542 ("James Scott Volume 1," Biograph
  BLP 1016Q).
Structure: AA BB CC DD
A highlight in the development of the Classic rag. Sections A
and D are in the Folk rag style and enclose two richly harmonic
and heavily syncopated sections. The C section is an ingenious
extension of the B section. The D section is Joplinesque in its
strong finish but distinctively original in concept.

Quality. July 27, 1911. Stark Music Co., St. Louis.
Rolls: U.S. Music 65270 ("James Scott Volume 1," Biograph
  BLP 1016Q). W. Arlington, Connorized 20461 ("Scott
  Joplin 1916," Biograph BLP 1006Q).
Structure: INTRO AA BB A CC INTRO B
A graceful and characteristic rag with an unusual adaptation of
Joplin's C section of *Maple Leaf Rag,* in this C section (it is
usually the B section which is borrowed).

Ragtime Oriole. December 10, 1911. Stark Music Co., St.
  Louis.
Recording: Fred Van Eps & Frank Banta, Pathe 021088, September, 1923 ("Kings of the Ragtime Banjo." Yazoo 1044).
Rolls: U.S. Music 65311 ("James Scott Volume 1." Biograph
  BLP 1016Q). W. Arlington. Connorized 10311 ("Scott
  Joplin 1916," Biograph BLP 1006Q).
Structure: INTRO AA BB A CC DD A
An outstanding rag which pioneered the use of bird calls in
ragtime. Among the greatest syncopated masterpieces, the
unity of feeling is superb. The A section looks ahead to what
was going to happen in the Novelty rags. The C section is, of
course, another way of stating the C and bits of B from the
Maple Leaf Rag. The D section illustrates the high degree of
musicianship which Scott possessed; he took a Midwestern
blues device and reshaped it on an ascending circle-of-fifths
connected with chromatic runs.

Princess Rag. Not copyrighted but published 1911. Stark Music Co., St. Louis.
Structure: INTRO AA BB CC B
This is a light work in a lyrical cakewalk style (see *Evergreen Rag*).

Climax Rag. March 5, 1914, Stark Music Co., St. Louis.
Recordings: Jelly Roll Morton's New Orelans Jazzmen, Bluebird 10442, September, 1939. Ralph Sutton, Down Home 8, November, 1949 ("Piano Ragtime of the Forties," Herwin 403). Turk Murphy Jazz Band, "The Many Faces of Ragtime," Atlantic SD 1613. 1972.
Rolls: 88 Note Aeolian 301037 ("James Scott Volume 1," Biograph BLP 1016Q). Max Kortlander, QRS 100395.
Structure: INTRO AA BB A CC B
A section begins with the echo which usually comes at the end section. It has been suggested that this piece was inspired by the silent movie accompaniments. The C section is extraordinarily clever in the descending approach of the left hand which swells from being part of the right hand to a full traditional left hand. The effect is orchestral and a welcome break from the usual approach.

Evergreen Rag. Not copyrighted but published 1915. Stark Music Co., St. Louis.
Roll: U.S. Music 7278 ("James Scott Volume 1," Biograph BLP 1016Q).
Structure: INTRO AA BB CC INTRO-2 BB
A charming departure from Scott's excursions into the heavier textured rags. Lightly syncopated, it is dance music. The B section evokes pleasant memories of such pieces as Joplin's *Elite Syncopations* and *Weeping Willow*.

Prosperity Rag. March 10, 1916. Stark Music Co., St. Louis.
Roll: U.S. Music 7905.
Structure: INTRO AA BB A TRIO-INTRO CC B_1B_1
This rag is to *Grace and Beauty* as *Gladiolus Rag* is to the *Maple Leaf Rag*. Each section reflects its companion, but with ad-

vanced conception and writing. An interesting touch is the restatement of B at the end with a change of bass. The original line is much like that described in C of *Ophelia,* but for the finish Scott adopts the traditional Octave-Chord pattern, giving the rag a stronger finish.

Honey Moon Rag. August 15, 1916. Stark Music Co., St. Louis.

Roll: Steve Williams (pseudonym of Ernest L. Stevens), Artempo 9935 ("James Scott Volume 1," Biograph BLP 1016Q).

Structure: AA BB A TRIO-INTRO CC BB

The Steve Williams piano roll is one of the finest Classic rag performances on roll. The A section of *Honey Moon* is a variation to the A section of *Maple Leaf Rag.*

Efficiency Rag. January 10, 1917. Stark Music Co., St. Louis.

Recording: William Bolcom, "Pastimes & Piano Rags," Nonesuch H-71299.

Roll: U.S. Music 8397 ("James Scott Volume 1," Biograph BLP 1016Q).

Structure: INTRO AA BB A TRIO-INTRO CC BB

A great rag reflecting the joyousness and sunny spirits inherent in the ragtime tradition. Contains all of Scott's hallmarks and could be used to sum up the best of Scott.

Paramount Rag. November 24, 1917. Stark Music Co., St. Louis.

Recording: John Jensen, "Piano Rags by James Scott," Genesis GS 1044, 1974.

Roll: Music Note 1074.

Structure: INTRO AA BB CC DD

A very ambitious rag that combines most features of the composer. Section A has a brassy, almost funky quality, making use of a pianistic device considered under *Paragon Rag* and *Kitten on the Keys.* B takes Scott's echo one step further, with two repeats of the one measure idea, ranging high up the keyboard. These dramatic register shifts seem difficult for piano, but are much easier for a multiple-keyboard theater organ such as one used by Scott. Instead of having to move quickly in a horizontal movement up and down the piano, one moves vertically, minimizing actual physical movement. The c section is a surprise in its almost uninterrupted lyrical flow.

Rag Sentimental. Not copyrighted but published 1918. Stark Music Co., St. Louis.
Roll: Music Note 1075 ("James Scott Volume 1," Biograph BLP 1016Q).
Structure: INTRO AA BB A CC DD
The fascinating A section uses the minor mode, but a major key feeling dominates the rag. This is the more usual use of the minor tonality in ragtime, as a change in color, unlike Joplin's use to effect a melancholy mood.

Dixie Dimples. Not copyrighted but published 1918. Will L. Livernash Music Co., Kansas City, Mo.
Structure: INTRO AA BB A CC A
Unlike the other Scott rags, this one is written in dotted-rhythm—in the style of the late teens' foxtrots. The A section cleverly uses the final section of *Climax Rag.* In the B section, which is linked and can be considered a development of A, we can hear what would become in 1950 part of *The Old Piano Roll Blues.* A most charming addition to the Scott catalogue.

Troubadour Rag. February 7, 1919. Stark Music Co., St. Louis.
Recording: John Arpin, "The Other Side of Ragtime," Scroll 103, April, 1966.
Roll: Music Note
Structure: AA BB A TRIO-INTRO CC DD
A typical late-Scott rag, heavily textured. Unusual feature is the dotted-note writing for part of the A section. The rag includes variations of his familiar devices but beautifully articulated.

New Era Rag. June 1, 1919. Stark Music Co., St. Louis.
Recording: William Bolcom, "Pastimes & Piano Rags," Nonesuch H-71299, 1974.
Structure: INTRO AA BB A CC INTRO B

The B section is a reworking of the B section of Joplin's *Cascades*. C section is a tour de force and is a fine contrast to B—an answer, in effect, to Joplin's pianistics. Stark adapted an earlier cover for this tune, Ed Hallway's *Tango Tea*, which accounts for the potted-palm dance salon of the title page.

Peace and Plenty Rag. December 1, 1919. Stark Music Co., St. Louis.
Recording: John Jensen, "Piano Rags by James Scott," Genesis GS 1044, 1974.
Structure: INTRO AA BB A TRIO-INTRO CC INTERLUDE C
A peculiar mixture of march-like features and typical late-Scott ragtime complexities. He even makes use of the old march-styled interlude or "dogfight" before the repeat of C.

Modesty Rag. September 15, 1920. Stark Music Co., St. Louis.
Structure: INTRO AA BB A CC B
Section A uses varied bass patterns to excellent effect. Starting with the sixth and eighth measures in the B section and continuing with the second, fourth and tenth measures of the trio, Scott employs phrasing in the right hand which became popular in piano roll performances of popular songs.

Pegasus. September 15, 1920. Stark Music Co., St. Louis.
Recording: William Bolcom, "Pastimes & Piano Rags," Nonesuch H-71299.
Structure: INTRO AA BB CC INTRO BB
The trio uses the same harmonic progression found in such later popular songs as *Birth of the Blues* and *Tip Toe Through the Tulips*.

Don't Jazz Me—Rag ("I'm Music"). September 18, 1921. Stark Music Co., St. Louis.
Structure: INTRO AA BB A TRIO-INTRO CC BB
Undoubtedly a Stark title (he was known to have disliked jazz). Ironically, the rag uses many devices which would become common in the twenties' jazz band performances.

Victory Rag. Not copyrighted but published 1921. Stark Music
   Co., St. Louis.
Structure: INTRO AA BB A TRIO-INTRO CC BB
Has the most involved and varied bass work of any of his rags.
Section B contains a left hand alternating between a regular
ragtime bass and single-note runs.

Broadway Rag. January 3, 1922. Stark Music Co., St. Louis.
Structure: INTRO AA BB A TRIO-INTRO CC BB
A bravura finish to the Scott rags, thickly textured in his late
style. The melodic flair of the trio suggests Jelly Roll Morton.

Calliope Rag. 1966. Published in *They All Played Ragtime,* Oak
   Publications, New York, 3rd edition, 1966. Arranged and
   edited by Donald Ashwander.
Recording: Donald Ashwander, "They All Play Ragtime," Jazzology JCE 52.
Structure: INTRO AA BB A CC A
An enchanting work discovered by Robert Darch, who obtained the manuscript from one of Scott's sisters, with the
information that Scott played it on the steam calliope at Lakeside Park, located between Carthage and Joplin, Missouri.
Probably written prior to 1910.

JOSEPH FRANCIS LAMB

Born: Montclair, New Jersey, December 6, 1887

Died: Brooklyn, New York, September 3, 1960

The youngest son in a family of four children, Lamb grew up in an Irish Catholic neighborhood. His father James was born in Drogheda, Ireland, married Julia Henneberry of Kilkenny and settled in Montclair in a home which he built. A successful building contractor, he taught Joe carpentry and mechanics. Joe attended the Catholic grammar school attached to the Church of the Immaculate Conception. At about eight years of age he asked his older sisters to teach him the piano lessons they were taking. Katherine became a church organist and professional piano teacher. Anastasia was awarded a piano scholarship at St. Elizabeth's Convent. Aside from these infrequent lessons and studying a beginner's book, he was self-taught. Upon his father's death in 1900, he was sent to St. Jerome's College in Berlin, Ontario, where he enrolled as a pre-engineering student. His interest in music flourished, and he composed waltzes, songs and other popular dance music which the Harry H. Sparks Music Publishing Company of Toronto issued. He got a job as office boy in a wholesale drygoods company in the summer of 1904 and never returned to school. He spent some time with his brother in San Francisco, returning home shortly before the earthquake, and then worked first for a clothing company and then a publishing house. He was attracted to Joplin's ragtime, and in 1907 he went to the Stark office in Manhattan where he purchased most of their rags. There he met Joplin, his ragtime idol, who liked his rags and got Stark to publish them. After the first published rag, which listed Joplin as "arranger," Stark took everything Lamb sent to him. Lamb formed the Clover Imperial Orchestra which performed at church and lodge dances. In 1911 Joe married Henrietta Schultz and moved from Montclair to Brooklyn, where he also briefly entered the Tin Pan Alley world as an arranger for the J. Fred Helf Music Publishing Company. In April, 1914 he went to work for L. F. Dommerich & Company, Inc., which financed accounts of manufacturers and guaranteed their sales. Joe retired in December, 1957. Henrietta died during the flu epidemic in early 1920, leaving Joe with a five-year-old son. In November, 1922 Joe married Amelia Collins and moved into a large house on East 21st Street in the Sheepshead Bay section of Brooklyn. Four more children were born to the couple who became solidly entrenched in their neighborhood, so solidly, in fact, that when the local grammar school celebrated its fiftieth anniversary in May, 1976, its name was changed from P. S. 206 to the Joseph F. Lamb School. Fame for the ragtimer came with the publication of *They All Played Ragtime,* when it was learned that he was still alive and living in Brooklyn. The ragtime revival of the forties and fifties brought him fan mail and visits from dedicated ragtimers. It also stimulated him to compose new rags and dust off older ones to complete or revise. Bob Darch arranged to have Lamb play at the Club 76 in Toronto in October, 1959, his first and only professional engagement. Earlier that summer, Sam Charters recorded Joe for an album of reminiscences and playing (Folkways FG-3562). He died of a heart attack at home.

The strength of Joplin's ideas in ragtime is best exemplified by the rags of Joe Lamb. Rags written before 1907 (which is to say before he became aware of the Joplin rags), recently found in manuscript form, show a rather mediocre attempt at composing rags, using all of the overworked devices of the cakewalk, Popular rag and song. From the twelve works published between 1908 and 1919, we find that his rags are more predictable, as he synthesized the Joplinesque legato melody style with Scott's expansive keyboard work. Then, Lamb replaced Joplin's phrase structure, making the first half of a section contrasting rather than parallel. He also avoided the short, motivic phrasing of James Scott, but used Scott's echo effect and rhythmic exuberance. Among Lamb's greatest original stylistic features are his use of sequences for developmental purposes and his diversity of texture, not only from light to heavy rags, but from section to section and even phrase to phrase, with the total eclipse of the 4-measure phrase in three of his best rags (A sections of *American Beauty Rag, Top Liner Rag* and *Cottontail Rag*). Whereas Joplin preferred 4-measure phrases and Scott 2-measure ones, Lamb developed 8-measure phrases. These rags published by Stark can be placed in two groups: easy and hard. The easy-to-play ones are light-hearted and reflect Scott's expansive keyboard approach. The hard-to-play ones illustrate Lamb's deep understanding of Joplin's ideas. They have rich and unusual harmonies and varied yet exciting rhythms. In both types, however, his intuitive feeling for the Missouri folk sounds is not imitative, but imaginatively original. Lamb was the consummate ragtime composer, the genius who possessed the ability to synthesize the best from all of the Folk, Classic and Popular ragtime music worlds into stirring works of his own great originality.

There are a great number of rags, some of which were published posthumously, some still in manuscript form, which are part of Lamb's oeuvre. For the sake of simplicity, we shall discuss the rags Stark published first, then group the rest in alphabetical sequence. Many of these other works were written much earlier but were revised and rewritten during the 1950s. Some bear no date at all. We are sure that *Alaskan Rag* was a new one written to celebrate that territory's entrance into the United States in 1959.

Sensation Rag. October 8, 1908. Stark Music Co., New York.
Recordings: Hank Jones, "This Is Ragtime Now!" ABC-Paramount 496, April, 1964. Joe Lamb, "Joseph Lamb: A Study in Classic Ragtime," Folkways FG 3562, August, 1959.
Roll: QRS 30845.
Structure: AA BB A CC D
The most interesting feature of the rag is the way popular harmonic devices were used to construct a Classic rag.

Ethiopia Rag. Not copyrighted but published 1909. Stark Music Co., New York.

Recording: John Jensen, "Piano Rags by Joseph Lamb," Genesis GS 1045.

Structure: INTRO AA BB A CC DD

A startling change of style from *Sensation Rag.* The trio is one of the most imaginative found in ragtime featuring varied bass patterns with single notes as well as octaves. The riff pattern here (measures 5, 6 and 7) is unique.

Excelsior Rag. Not copyrighted but published 1909. Stark Music Co., New York.

Recordings: John Arpin, "The Other Side of Ragtime," Scroll 103. Patrick Gogerty, "American Beauty Rag," Sound Current, February, 1976.

Roll: U.S. Music 62255.

Structure: AA BB A CC DD

This reveals Lamb's genius for intricate rhythmic forms and full, rich harmonies. A beautifully complex structure of syncopation, built on sequences (measures 6, 7 and 8), it is in reality an homage to Joplin, as the A, B and C sections are inspired improvisations on the respective sections of *Maple Leaf Rag.* It is also the only Classic rag published in the keys of D flat and G flat. When Stark saw it, he asked Lamb to transpose it to the keys of C and F. After he heard it, he agreed with Lamb that it sounded better in the more difficult keys.

Champagne Rag. September 15, 1910. Stark Music Co. St. Louis.

Recording: Dave Jasen, "Rip-Roarin' Ragtime," Folkways FG-3561, June 1977.

Roll: U.S. Music 64523.

Structure: INTRO AA BB A CC INTERLUDE A INTERLUDE A

An eloquent rag in a light vein which reveals ragtime's link with the march and cakewalk forms. The A section has a lovely melody with a march-like quality. In the B section that quality is more insistent, with a descending chromatic flow of the melody. C section has the stately but sprightly quality of the cakewalk. When repeated, it has an added burst of optimism which is more richly scored, with the melody in octaves. A march interlude with dramatic stop-time effects follows. With old world charm, it glides into the repeat of the A section, but this time in the subdominant, as in the structure of the cakewalk.

American Beauty Rag. December 27, 1913. Stark Music Co. St. Louis.
Recording: Wally Rose, "Whippin' the Keys," Blackbird C-12010. June 28, 1971.
Rolls: Max Kortlander, QRS 100299.
Structure: AA BB A TRIO-INTRO CC DD
One of the greatest rags of all and a splendid example of the best of the Classic rags, it simply must be heard to be appreciated. It reveals the depth of Lamb's conceptions, his bold originality, and his use of unusual harmonies. The melodic lines alternate between long, sweeping phrases and short, skipping melodies. While section B compliments the A section, the tour de force comes with the short introduction into the C section and throughout C leading to section D with its powerful development into the finale. These sections are more rhythmic than melodic. Austere yet elegant in its sweeping beauty, it is an astonishing yet fitting rag in the development following *Excelsior Rag.*

Contentment Rag. January 10, 1915. Stark Music Co., St. Louis.
Recording: Dave Jasen, "Rompin' Stompin' Ragtime," Blue Goose 3002.
Roll: Steve Williams, Artempo 2815.
Structure: AA BB A C DD
Written as a present for the Starks' wedding anniversary in 1909, it wasn't published then because of Mrs. Stark's illness which lead to her death the following year. Illustrating a more subdued side of Lamb, it makes a perfect counterpart to *Ethiopia Rag.* The B section quotes two measures of *Maple Leaf's* B section but quickly returns to the body of the development. In an unusual design, the C section is used as an introduction to the D section (as *Maple Leaf Rag's* A section introduces the B).

This is a most delightful section which is striking in its strength and grandeur.

Ragtime Nightingale. June 10, 1915. Stark Music Co., St. Louis.
Recordings: Hank Jones, "This Is Ragtime Now!" ABC-Paramount 496. Hitch's Happy Harmonists, Gennett 5633, January, 1925.
Roll: Steve Williams, Artempo 3855.
Structure: INTRO AA BB A CC INTRO-2 B
One of the all too rare descriptions of how a great rag was inspired and set about is Joe's story of how he was inspired by Scott's *Ragtime Oriole* and the concept of a bird-call rag. He didn't know what a nightingale sounded like, but took a bit from Chopin's *Revolutionary Etude* and another bit from Ethelbert Nevin's *Nightingale Song*. Highlight comes in section A which sets a majestic mood, largely in C minor.

Cleopatra Rag. June 16, 1915. Stark Music Co., St. Louis.
Recording: Joe "Fingers" Carr and Tiny Little, "Mr. Ragtime Meets Mr. Honkytonk," Coral CRL 57444.
Structure: INTRO AA BB A TRIO-INTRO CC B
A light, high-stepping prance-like A section indicates an extensive use of dotted notes to form a single note melody line—a device rarely found in a Classic rag, as this group preferred a legato melody line. An excellent example of the variety of Lamb's syncopations.

Reindeer. Not copyrighted but published 1915. Stark Music Co., St. Louis.
Recording: John Jensen, "Piano Rags by Joseph Lamb," Genesis GS 1045.
Roll: U.S. Music 7272.
Structure: INTRO AA BB A CC BB
One of Lamb's light cakewalk-march inspired rags. In contrast to his more serious legato rags, part of A is marked to be played staccato. The tempo marking is a quarter note equals 100. The B section has a most beautifully flowing melody.

Top Liner Rag. January 4, 1916. Stark Music Co., St. Louis.
Recordings: Wally Rose, "Ragtime Classics," Good Time Jazz
    M-12034. December, 1958. Dave Jasen, "Rompin' Stom-
    pin' Ragtime," Blue Goose 3002, April, 1974.
Rolls: Felix Arndt. Metro Art. 202626. Howard Lutter. Ar-
    tempo 8834.
Structure: AA BB A TRIO-INTRO CC DD
Undoubtedly Lamb's greatest rag and among the three greatest rags of all time. In its construction and development, it is
a perfect rag. Lamb consistently returned to this rag as his own
favorite, and the Wally Rose recording was Lamb's favorite
recording of any of his rags.

Patricia Rag. November 19, 1916. Stark Music Co., St. Louis.
Recording: Tony Parenti, "Ragtime Jubilee," Jazzology J-21.
Structure: AA BB A TRIO-INTRO CC DD
The A section is a clever working of its counterpart in the *Maple
Leaf Rag.* It also contains two of Lamb's creative devices: a use
of sequences to develop the mood and a characteristic dimin-
ished seventh chord which appears in many of his best rags.
The trio is especially original in measures 1, 2 and 3, which
contains one descending melody line but before completion,
an ascending melody line overlaps in a broad sweep.

Bohemia. February 17, 1919. Stark Music Co., St. Louis.
Recordings: Dave Jasen, "Rompin' Stompin' Ragtime." Blue
    Goose 3002, April, 1974. Chris Barber, "Elite Syncopa-
    tions," (E) Columbia 33SX-1245. January, 1960.
Structure: INTRO AA BB A C INTERLUDE-C INTERLUDE-C
Most advanced use of tonality in Lamb, with the key in section
A not sure until the twelfth measure. A most unusual beginning, starting in the minor mode and ending up in the major.
The grace and charm of the B section is achieved by the subtle
use of passing tones and syncopation crossing the bar lines
which enhances the delicate quality. This section also has an
alternate "ad lib" bass in octaves at its start. The high spirits
of the C section gives way to an interesting but unusual device
for a Classic rag, the 12-measure interlude leading to a repeat

of the C section—a throwback to an old cakewalk pattern, much as Joplin did in *Eugenia.* The repeat marks indicate that the interlude is to be included in the last repeat. A thoroughly delightful rag.

Alabama Rag. *Ragtime Treasures,* Mills Music, Inc. New York, 1964.
Recording: John Jensen, "Piano Rags by Joseph Lamb," Genesis GS 1045.
Structure: AA BB A CC B
A delightful composition in the Folk rag style.

Alaskan Rag. *They All Played Ragtime,* Oak Publications, New York, 1966, 3rd edition.
Recordings: Joseph Lamb, "They All Play Ragtime," Jazzology JCE-52. John Arpin, "The Other Side of Ragtime," Scroll 103.
Structure: INTRO AA BB A CC DD
An extension of his great complex rags of the teens and a beautiful addition to the Classic rag repertoire. It is certainly Lamb's most intricate and detailed conception. His final breakthrough in Classic rag composition, he begins the A section with rests in both hands.

Arctic Sunset. *Ragtime Treasures,* Mills Music, Inc., New York, 1964.
Structure: AA BB A CC DD
A section begins with a Novelty rag influence and proceeds to an ambitiously syncopated B section crossing the bar lines. C, however, brings an almost Joplinesque change of mood with a brief "serenade" marked to be played "slow." The final section again designates a tempo change, marked *allegretto.* Such a format is rare with Lamb.

Bee Hive. March 27, 1959. Not published.
Structure: AA BB A CC DD
Of all the unavailable Lamb rags, this is most like his hard-to-play Classics. The trio is one of his most monumental creations,

with frequent chord changes occurring in rapid succession in a heavy texture of diminished chords that seems to be Lamb's answer to the trio of his favorite Joplin rag, *Gladiolus.*

Bird-Brain Rag. *Ragtime Treasures,* Mills Music, Inc., New York, 1964.
Recording: John Arpin, "Concert in Ragtime," Scroll 101, 1965.
Structure: INTRO AA BB A CC DD
Expansive later style with thinner texture to allow for a wider ranging melodic line. In sections C and D, tenths are used in the bass instead of the conventional octaves.

Blue Grass Rag. *Ragtime Treasures.* Mills Music, Inc., New York, 1964.
Recording: John Jensen, "Piano Rags by Joseph Lamb," Genesis GS 1045.
Structure: INTRO AA BB A TRIO-INTRO CC DD
One of Lamb's very best. It remained unfinished until during the 1950s when he finally wrote its trio. The bass is varied in section B and the rousing D section is capped by a Novelty rag break.

Chasin' the Chippies. Not published but written in 1914 and copyrighted in 1961.
Structure: INTRO AA BB CC A DD EE INTRO-2 B
Simple Folk-style rag, much like his earliest efforts, but a bit more organized.

Cottontail Rag. *Ragtime Treasures,* Mills Music, Inc., New York, 1964.
Recording: Max Morath, "The Best of Scott Joplin," Vanguard VSD 39/40, 1972.
Structure: AA BB A CC DD
A marvelous rag in the Classic rag tradition, even the D section being a variation of the same section in his *Top Liner Rag.* Elegant, sparkling with rich harmonies and beautiful flowing melodies.

Firefly Rag. *Ragtime Treasures,* Mills Music, Inc., New York, 1964.

Structure: AA BB A TRIO-INTRO CC DD

Contains his most unusual harmonic touch: a break midway into the A section is spiced with chromatic augmented chords, revealing Lamb's knowledge of the later twenties writing style.

Good and Plenty Rag. *Ragtime Treasures,* Mills Music, Inc., New York, 1964.

Structure: AA BB A CC DD

An exciting and thrilling work. Mixing the Joplin and Folk rag styles with his own originality, this unusual rag creates a happy-go-lucky atmosphere. One in his experimental group of rags from the 1907–1914 period.

Greased Lightning. March 27, 1959. Not published.

Structure: AA BB CC D

Section A recalls *Excelsior Rag.* B and C are folksy, but D is an astounding finale—a bold through-composed theme with ascending and descending runs capped by a blaze of Novelty devices.

Hot Cinders. *Ragtime Treasures,* Mills Music, Inc., New York, 1964.

Structure: AA BB A C A

This was one from his Novelty rag days when Mills, publishers of Zez Confrey's super Novelties, asked for the same from Lamb. He obliged with this clever, un-Classic rag.

Jersey Rag. March 17, 1959. Not published.

Structure: AA BB A CC D

One of the Folk-style rags written during the same time as *Sensation Rag.* A pure joy, the C section contains a startling key change from G flat to G natural, effected cleverly by way of a D_7 chord at the beginning of the section. D section extends the motive of the *Maple Leaf Rag* B section for a whirlwind finish.

Joe Lamb's Old Rag. Written in 1908, originally titled *Dynamite Rag,* copyrighted in 1962 but not yet published.

Structure: A B CC A DD E

One of the best of the unpublished experimental rags and certainly one of the most adventurous. It is in a romping Folk rag style throughout. The through-composed D section is a major achievement.

The Old Home Rag. *Ragtime Treasures,* Mills Music, Inc., New York, 1964.

Structure: AA B A CC D

Another adventurous ragtime experiment pre-dating the more orthodox Joplin influence. Lamb draws on another Tin Pan Alley device as he climaxes the rag with a syncopated transformation of *Home Sweet Home.*

Ragged Rapids Rag. Written in 1905, copyrighted in 1962, but not yet published.

Structure: INTRO AA BB A CC (ms. unfinished.)

Ragtime Bobolink. *Ragtime Treasures,* Mills Music, Inc., New York, 1964.

Recording: Patrick Gogerty, "American Beauty Rag," Sound Current, Feb. 1976.

Structure: AA BB A CC DD

Intricate, challenging Lamb rag in his most advanced Classic rag style.

Ragtime Special. March 27, 1959. Not published.

Structure: INTRO AA BB C DD E

"Respectfully dedicated to my friend, Scott Joplin." A curious Lamb reflection on the earliest Folk rag style compilations, this seems almost a medley of various ideas, although it is finely put together. Sections C and E contain only 8 measures each and the tonal plan of the entire rag keeps moving as in the early rags (it begins in the key of G, goes to C and finally to F).

Rapid Transit Rag. March 17, 1959. Not published.

Structure: INTRO A BB ½A CC D

A rag of motion, beginning with a minor strain, but one which could be used for chase scenes in the silent movies. The rest of the rag rolls along merrily in the major tonality.

Thoroughbred Rag. *Ragtime Treasures,* Mills Music, Inc., New York, 1964.
Structure: AA BB A TRIO-INTRO CC DD
Section A recalls *Excelsior Rag* but, in typical Lamb fashion, the texture changes with the B section to a thinner, more intricate one. D is a dramatic ending.

Toad Stool Rag. *Ragtime Treasures,* Mills Music, Inc., New York, 1964.
Structure: INTRO AA BB A CC D
The trio is a beautiful reflection on Joplin's *Cascades* trio. Section D is an 8-measure conception repeated.

Walper House Rag. Written in 1903, copyrighted in 1962, but not yet published.
Structure: INTRO AA BB A CC INTERLUDE CC
Lamb's first rag. Folksy and rambunctious, using a simple cakewalk pattern. Not an immortal work.

Popular Ragtime 1906-1912

Popular ragtime came into its own with the huge success of Charles L. Johnson's *Dill Pickles Rag.* It was published by the Carl Hoffman Music Company of Kansas City, Missouri, the same firm which published Joplin's *Original Rags.* And, the man who bought the Joplin number for the Hoffman firm was the same one who bought *Dill Pickles* for his new firm, the Jerome H. Remick Company of Detroit, Michigan. That man was famous composer-arranger-publisher Charles Neil Daniels, who made this rag the first Tin Pan Alley million-selling hit which established the form and device for most rags that followed.

Tin Pan Alley became the collective name for the popular sheet music publishers who made it their business to publicize, market and distribute their wares on a large scale, concentrating on the national marketplace. Selling popular sheet music to the masses was a new idea in the early 1890s and it worked mainly by means of song pluggers. These were men who were hired by the publishers to ensure that the firm's songs were being played and sung in saloons, vaudeville houses, restaurants and music stores. Most of the time they had to play the songs themselves.

With the creation of Tin Pan Alley came the composer—a person hired at a stated salary and paid a weekly advance against future royalties for creating songs on demand. There was no waiting for the muse or inspiration, but rather a turning out of a product either for general popular consumption or for a specific performer or client. As ragtime became part of the pop music scene, publishers had their own composers write easy-to-play rags for the amateur pianist. Ragtime was now big business, with schools like Axel Christensen's which advertised "Ragtime Taught in Ten Lessons." The large firms not only employed staff composers to turn it out, but bought rags from outsiders. The demand was so great that everyone had an opportunity to be published—amateur and professional alike.

The most significant ragtime entrepreneur besides John Stark was Charles Neil Daniels, manager of Tin Pan Alley's largest firm, Jerome H. Remick & Company. Born in Leavenworth, Kansas on April 12, 1878, Charles grew up in Kansas City, Kansas with his small family: his father, Alfred Edward from Ireland (the original surname was O'Daniels), his mother, Agnes Tholen from Hanover, Germany and his sister, Elizabeth. While not affluent, the Danielses were comfortable because the father made a good living as a watch and jewelry repairman. Charles graduated from high school in Kansas City; this was the end of his academic training. During high school he accompanied singers and played piano in a dance orchestra. He could sight read well, play by ear and improvise beautifully. It was also during this time that he learned music calligraphy. He was justly proud of his pen and ink manuscripts, which were among the most attractive ever seen. He studied harmony, composition and arranging with Carl Pryor. Upon graduation he worked at the Carl Hoffman Music Company as a song demonstrator during the day, and for the Kronberg Concert Company at night, accompanying the singers. In 1898 the Hoffman firm offered a prize of $25.00 for the best two-step by a local composer. Daniels, after much prodding by friends, finally competed for the prize, and his composition, *Margery*, won. At that time John Phillip Sousa was playing at the Coats Opera House. He heard of the contest, offered to perform the work and, much to everyone's amazement, it became an instant success. This led to a lasting friendship which was to come in handy for Daniels more than once. While *Margery* sold 275,000 copies, Daniels had to content himself with the prize money and some favorable publicity. But the tune's success led to his being promoted to manager. In December, 1898 he purchased Joplin's *Original Rags*. He still maintained two jobs and, in the next year, he was accompanying Harry Haley, featured singer with Epperson's Minstrels. He wrote *You Tell Me Your Dream, I'll Tell You Mine* for Haley. The song became a bigger hit than *Margery*. But this time he published it himself, starting the firm of Daniels, Russel and Boone. The following year he left Kansas City and moved the new firm to St. Louis where he stayed for the next two years. By coincidence, John Stark arrived in St. Louis during this same period. During his St. Louis days, Daniels managed the sheet music department of the Barr Dry Goods Company. In 1901 the firm published his new Indian tune, *Hiawatha*, which became another success when Sousa was prevailed upon to perform and record it. The firm of Daniels, Russel and Boone was purchased by the Detroit-based publishing house of Whitney-Warner so that they could have *Hiawatha*. Daniels was paid $10,000.00 for it, which created a sensation in the music world; it was the highest sum then paid for a song. With it went an offer to head up the company as manager. Daniels accepted, and moved to Detroit in 1902. The following year words were added and sales zoomed into the millions. Thus started the trend toward Indian songs which were extremely popular during the first decade of this century. For many of his songs, he used the pseudonym of Neil Moret. He also used the names of L'Albert, Lamonte C. Jones, Jules Lemare, Charlie Hill and Sidney Carter. He married Pearl Hamlin on New Year's Eve of 1904. A son, Neil Moret Daniels, was born in 1907 and a daughter, Dana Agnes Daniels was born the following year. Because Dana was in poor health, Daniels was advised to move to the West Coast, which he did in 1912, giving up his position in Detroit (Whitney-Warner became the Jerome H. Remick Company in 1905), and created his own firm once again, this time in partnership with Weston Wilson, the new firm being known as Daniels and Wilson, Inc. Most notably, they published in 1918 the Daniels song commissioned by Mack Sennett for his movie starring Mabel Normand, *Mickey*. This was the first motion picture theme song. From 1924 to 1931 Daniels was president of Villa Moret, Inc. Sensing that the movies, with their new soundtracks, and commercial radio were cutting into sheet music sales, he decided to withdraw from active management in the music business.

After a lengthy illness, he died of kidney failure in Los Angeles, California on January 23, 1943. During the years he owned his own firms, he composed many popular hit songs selling into the millions: *Moonlight and Roses, Mello Cello, Song of the Wanderer, Chloe, She's Funny That Way, In Monterey, Sweet and Lovely.* A pioneering music publisher and manager of the largest music publishing firm in the United States, he contributed greatly during the boom years of ragtime, which he helped to create and maintain. His thorough knowledge of the business and of the public's taste helped him to sustain the popularity of ragtime for many years. He encouraged the composing of rags by his staff by accepting unsolicited manuscripts and by purchasing small-town publishers' rags. Daniels, heretofore, has been remembered by ragtime scholars as the "arranger" of *Original Rags,* but that was only the beginning. He nurtured ragtime until it was a flourishing and significant part of the popular sheet music industry.

For the most part, the rags created by Tin Pan Alley were done by professional tunesmiths, not particularly dedicated to the art of ragtime. They created their rags for the seemingly insatiable market which made ragtime a fad.

Dill Pickles Rag was the next big hit after *Maple Leaf Rag,* written by composer-publisher Charles L. Johnson. It is interesting to see how Johnson adapted Joplin's framework of a rag to suit his own work style. Keeping the essence of Joplin's structure of a five-part rag, Johnson made a slight but commercially important change. Instead of the AA BB A CC DD formula, Johnson created a three-section rag and substituted a repeat of either the first or second section which saved him from having to write a fourth section. The Johnson formula, therefore, looked like this: AA BB A CC AA or AA BB A CC BB. For this particular rag, however, the structure he used was INTRO AA B A CC B.

The chief device which made *Dill Pickles Rag* such a hit was what is known as the "three-over-four" pattern (discussed under *12th Street Rag*). This configuration was then used so much that it became the first of several musical clichés in ragtime writing. The public seemed not to tire of it, since they made substantial hits of *Black and White Rag, Spaghetti Rag, Crazy*

Bone Rag, Grizzly Bear Rag, Hungarian Rag and the most widely known of them all—*12th Street Rag.*

Recordings from this period feature the military band, the five-string banjo (accompanied by either piano or military band) or some other percussive or high-pitched instrument like the piccolo, accordian and xylophone. The first ragtime piano recording we know of occurred on December 2, 1912 when the champion "Rag Time King of the World,"* Mike Bernard recorded Wallie Herzer's popular rag, *Everybody Two Step,* for Columbia ("Ragtime Piano Interpretations," Folkways RBF-24). Mike was the orchestra leader and chief accompanist at Tony Pastor's Music Hall, the leading variety and vaudeville showplace in New York. Perhaps the greatest display of his talents on record appears in his own composition, *Blaze Away,* which Columbia also issued ("Ragtime Piano Originals," Folkways RBF-23).

Player piano rolls were still not true recordings, but conceived by arrangers away from any recording piano. The catalogs from the major roll companies detail ragtime's popularity as it kept pace with the ballads and comic songs of the day.

With the concentration of publishing houses in the large cities, most of the working composers lived there. New York was the leading center, offering employment not only to composers of popular songs, but work for people in the musical theater as well. Such composers as Albert Gumble, Jean Schwartz, Harry Tierney, Ford Dabney and Ted Snyder—who also functioned as a publisher (first as Seminary Music which issued several Joplin rags, then as Ted Snyder Company and then as Waterson, Berlin & Snyder)—all wrote popular rags. In Chicago, always right behind New York, rags from the gifted pens of Egbert Van Alstyne, Bernie Adler and Percy Wenrich were being published. With the prolific composer and publisher Charlie Johnson headquartered in Missouri, Kansas City became a ragtime center where Johnson's success, particularly as a ragtime composer, served as an on-the-spot example for

---

*Title and diamond-studded medal so stated in the giant ragtime contest run by the *Police Gazette* at Tammany Hall in New York City on January 23, 1900.

others like Ed Kuhn, Maude Gilmore and Charles A. Gish. Although hardly a Tin Pan Alley area, Indianapolis became a center of ragtime publishing through the efforts of John H. Aufderheide, a pawnbroker turned publisher issuing rags by his daughter, May, and her similarly-minded ragtime composing friends—Julia Lee Niebergall, Cecil Duane Crabb, Will Morrison and Paul Pratt.

The best of the ragtime composers of Popular ragtime were not the hacks found in the back rooms in Tin Pan Alley, but dedicated craftsmen who took pains to produce quality work, yet managed to please the public time and again, as their output demonstrates, with easily playable works which convey the happy sprightliness inherent in ragtime's charm.

GEORGE BOTSFORD

Born: Sioux Falls, South Dakota, February 24, 1874
Died: New York, New York, February 11, 1949

Although born in South Dakota and raised in Iowa, Botsford spent his professional life as a composer-conductor in New York City. His second rag was a smash hit and established him as a professional. His *Grizzly Bear Rag* was also a tremendous hit and became an even greater seller when Irving Berlin wrote words for it. *Sailing Down the Chesapeake Bay* was another enormous success, and with the proceeds he started his own publishing firm, experimenting with miniature opera to be sung by only three or four people. The idea didn't catch on and he went to work for Remick Music Corporation as arranger and chief of their harmony and quartet department. He arranged music for amateur minstrel shows and became the director of the New York Police Department's Glee Club.

Though, overall, the Botsford rags are a fine group, he was more dependent on the "three-over-four" formula than other writers for major companies. Half of his rags have the following pattern: A BB A CC B. In general, he preferred not to repeat A before stating the B section and moved directly to the trio after the second A.

Klondike Rag. January 23, 1908. William R. Haskins Co., New York.
Structure: INTRO AA BB A CC INTRO-2 B
More ambitious than later, more formulated rags, this has effective syncopation crossing the bar line, a good chromatic melody, and an orchestral concept in section C where the bass echoes the treble melody.

Black and White Rag. Not copyrighted but published 1908. Jerome H. Remick & Co., New York.
Recordings: El Cota, Columbia A-1118, December, 1911. ("Ragtime Entertainment," Folkways RBF-22). Winifred Atwell, (E) Decca F-9790, June, 1951, ("Piano Ragtime of the Fifties." Herwin 404).
Roll: Universal 75569.
Structure: INTRO AA BB A CC B
One of the most popular rags, it is incredible that it was not originally copyrighted. It wasn't until November 13, 1924 that Botsford had it copyrighted in a revised arrangement. This popular rag featured the "three-over-four" device in its A section. The C section is from Max Hoffman's rag of 1904, *Yankee Land.* Later that same year Seymour used it for his trio in *The Black Laugh.*

Old Crow Rag. April 13, 1909. Jerome H. Remick & Co., New York.
Roll: Standard Electra 76014.
Structure: INTRO A BB A CC B

Pianophiends Rag. May 17, 1909. William R. Haskins Co., New York.
Roll: Universal 78475.
Structure: INTRO AA BB A CC

Texas Steer. October 15, 1909. Jerome H. Remick & Co., New York.
Roll: Connorized 5415.
Structure: INTRO A BB A CC A

Wiggle Rag. October 15, 1909. Jerome H. Remick & Co., New York.
Roll: QRS 30847.
Structure: INTRO AA BB A CC B

Grizzly Bear Rag. April 18, 1910. Ted Snyder Co., New York.
Recordings: Wally Rose, "Cakewalk to Lindy Hop," Columbia CL-782. Max Morath, "In a Scintillating Program of Waltzes, Shouts, Novelties, Rags, Blues, Ballads and Stomps," Epic LN-24066, 1963.
Roll: Universal 77815 (65 note).
Structure: INTRO AA BB AA CC BB
The San Francisco Barbary Coast version of the teen dance fad, the turkey trot. A joyous number and a fine rag.

Lovey-Dovey Rag. May 19, 1910. Ted Snyder Co., New York.
Structure: INTRO A BB A CC B

Chatterbox Rag. October 4, 1910. Jerome H. Remick & Co., Detroit.
Recording: Fred Van Eps, Zonophone 5828, 1911.
Roll: U.S. Music 64618.
Structure: INTRO A BB A C B
An imaginative rag with a trio which combines features from sections A and B effectively.

Royal Flush. March 27, 1911. Jerome H. Remick & Co., Detroit.

Roll: QRS 30992.
Structure: INTRO AA BB A CC B

Hyacinth. December 11, 1911. Jerome H. Remick & Co., New
    York.
Rolls: U.S. Music 65189. George Botsford & Albert Gumble,
    Solo Style A-3022.
Structure: INTRO A BB A CC B
A graceful rag with long flowing melodic lines at the end of the
extended sixteen-measured introduction, and again in section
B. The trio is one of the finest in all Popular ragtime.

Honeysuckle Rag. December 19, 1911. Jerome H. Remick &
    Co., New York.
Recording: John W. "Knocky" Parker, "Golden Treasury of
    Ragtime," Audiophile AP-92.
Roll: QRS 31172.
Structure: INTRO A BB A CC B
One of the composer's best. A section is in minor using the
"three-over-four" syncopation. B breaks away beautifully on
the dominant of the relative major, and has longer phrases of
syncopation using another pattern, the delayed entrance of the
melody in the right hand. The trio is another fascinating excursion utilizing several ragtime devices in a fresh manner.

Universal Rag. February 14, 1913. George Botsford, New
    York.
Rolls: Universal 100019. Metrostyle Themodist 300282.
Structure: INTRO A B A CC B
A rouser apparently written exclusively for issue on Universal
piano rolls (see Joplin's *Silver Swan*).

Rag, Baby Mine. March 28, 1913. Jerome H. Remick & Co.,
    New York.
Structure: INTRO A BB A CC B

The Buck-Eye Rag. June 11, 1913. George Botsford, New York.
Roll: Uni-Record 300559.
Structure: INTRO A BB A CC B

The Incandescent Rag. October 21, 1913. Jerome H. Remick
& Co., New York.
Roll: QRS 31390.
Structure: INTRO A BB A CC B
An excellent rag featuring the "three-over-four" device in section A spiced with anticipatory syncopation, and an intricate B
section climaxed by a great ascending break (measures 7 and
8). This is an ambitious syncopated figure, apparently first used
in *Mandy's Broadway Stroll,* later more dramatically by Lamb in
his B section of *Ethiopia,* and, finally, received its most advanced use in Janza's *Lion Tamer.*

Boomerang Rag. June 21, 1916. Jerome H. Remick & Co.,
New York.
Recording: Charlie Rasch, "Ragtime Down the Line," Ragtime
Society RSR-4, January 8, 1966.
Roll: U.S. Music 68047.
Structure: INTRO A BB A CC B

THOMAS HENRY LODGE
Born: Providence, Rhode Island, February 9, 1884
Died: West Palm Beach, Florida, February 16, 1933

Lodge was the eldest of four brothers and one sister. His father
had come from Manchester, England and worked in a
textile mill. His mother came from Maryland. There was no
musical background in the family but, with an acquired piano,
Lodge took lessons when he was twelve. After school he ob-

tained a job demonstrating and selling pianos at Meiklejohn's Music Store. In 1906 he married Sarah Agnes Mackie. Their only child, Mary, was born in 1907. In 1912 they moved to New York City, where he played piano in cabarets. He worked as pianist for Irene and Vernon Castle at Castle House, where they gave private dance instructions for very high fees. Lodge hung around the publishers' offices where he was hailed as a fine composer of Popular rags. His *Temptation Rag* of 1909 was an outstanding success, and was played most often in vaudeville. He led bands in vaudeville and in dance halls. He moved to Atlantic City, New Jersey, where his orchestra played on the Million Dollar Pier. In 1918 his wife died. In the early twenties he wintered in West Palm Beach, Florida, where his orchestra played for the wealthy. It was there he met and eventually married his second wife, Irene. They had three children— Sally, Arthur and Theodore. He started writing background music for films and, in 1930, lived in Los Angeles while working for Universal and MGM. At the end of the year his family moved back to the New York area, but continued to winter in West Palm Beach where he unexpectedly died in 1933.

The late rags from 1917 and 1918 are written in a more advanced style, using more complex tonal plans, odd harmonies and surprising textures. Those called "blues" are rags with some emphasis on minor chords to effect a slightly melancholy aura, and are far from the down-home blues style. They are a complete departure from his earlier rags which are very danceable, and in the Popular ragtime format. In all his work Lodge was fascinated with the minor tonality and made more creative use of it than any other composer. His predeliction was for a pattern of three minors: Dm/Am/Gm. This became a staple of much later writing in pop music, especially during the Rock era.

Temptation Rag. September 9, 1909. M. Witmark & Sons, New York.
Recordings: Arthur Pryor's Band, Victor 16511, June, 1910. Dave Van Ronk, "Ragtime Jug Stompers," Mercury MG-20864.

Rolls: U.S. Music 3047. QRS 30750.

Structure: INTRO AA BB A C D ½C B

A unique rag. The overall tonal plan rejects the classic splitting-in-half in favor of one major key and its relative minor. This, combined with Lodge's flair for long lyrical lines, results in an unusually cohesive and forward-moving rag. But the internal element that makes it a success is a masterful use of varied syncopated patterns for each section. The B section introduces a different idea from A. Section C begins with still another, yet also recalls that of B. D functions as an interlude of largely unsyncopated staccato sixteenths; however, its one syncopation is derived from the opening C pattern. This all lends a developmental air to the rag and contributes to its unity. His greatest success and one of the biggest rag hits of its day, it was appropriately most always performed by a band. Although he composed at the piano, he was, from all accounts, a good performer, but his rags did not become pianistic until 1917.

Sure Fire Rag. March 15, 1910. Victor Kremer Co., Chicago.

Roll: Master Record 7.

Structure: INTRO AA BB A CC B

Sneaky Shuffles. October 4, 1910. Jerome H. Remick & Co., New York.

Roll: U.S. Music 64040.

Structure: INTRO AA BB A CC B

An odd rag with unexpected harmonies in section B, followed by a clever trio involving syncopation in both hands, but in a lyrical and original format.

Red Pepper, A Spicy Rag. December 19, 1910. M. Witmark & Sons, New York.

Recording: Fred Van Eps, Victor 17033, December, 1911, ("Kings of the Ragtime Banjo," Yazoo L-1044).

Roll: Universal 8507.

Structure: INTRO AA BB A TRIO-INTRO C INTERLUDE C

No less ingenious and more of a rouser than *Temptation.* The idea of A is an unusually long series of sixteenths:

B has the following pattern combined with the "three-over-four" and chromatic descents in the form of one measure breaks:

C is one of the most joyous strains in ragtime, and combines syncopations from A and B. The interlude is in minor and cleverly written to lead back into C, which also begins on minor but ends in the relative major. Another popular Lodge hit.

Black Diamond, A Rag Sparkler. February 5, 1912. M. Witmark & Sons, New York.
Recording: Fred Van Eps, Victor 17168, May, 1912. ("Kings of the Ragtime Banjo," Yazoo L-1044).
Roll: Kimball C-6441.
Structure: INTRO AA BB A C INTERLUDE ½ C B

Tokio Rag. May 27, 1912. M. Witmark & Sons, New York.
Roll: U.S. Music 65405.
Structure: INTRO AA B A TRIO-INTRO C

Pastime Rag. April 28, 1913. M. Witmark & Sons. New York.
Recording: National Promenade Band, Edison 50158. ("Ragtime Entertainment," Folkways RBF-22).
Roll: Arr. B.G. Howard, Pianostyle 85487.
Structure: INTRO AA BB A CC

Moonlight Rag. May 5, 1913. M. Witmark & Sons, New York.
Recording: New York Military Band, Edison 50135.
Structure: INTRO A BB A CC A

Oh You Turkey. January 20, 1914. Waterson, Berlin & Snyder Co., New York.

Roll: Frederick Arno & F. A. S., Rhythmodik A-9212.
Structure: INTRO AA B A CC B

Gum Drops. July 1, 1915. Popular Music Distributing Co., San Francisco.

The Baltimore Blues. June 20, 1917. Jerome H. Remick & Co., New York.
Structure: A ½A TRIO-INTRO BB A
Weird tonal plan for a blues concept. It begins in the key of D major, modulates to C and then onto F, finishing with a repeat of the first section. A touch of true blues feeling occurs at the start of the C section, where a very pianistic bass run in triplets ends on a minor seventh.

Remorse Blues. July 30, 1917. Jerome H. Remick & Co., New York.
Structure: AA BB A CC A

The Bounding Buck. March 1, 1918. M. Witmark & Sons, New York.
Structure: AA BB A C B CODA
One of his most lyrical, yet certainly his most advanced rag. The A section is masterful: after establishing the tonality of E flat, he introduces a sequence which suggests the key of E natural. The eighth measure ends on a B_7 which has the feeling of the lowered sixth chord, since it is followed by a return to the first 4 measures, which re-establishes E flat. The B strain is one of the composer's most beautiful, enhanced by his clever use of minors. C extends the mood of B and is the most melodic of the three.

Hifalutin Rag. March 28, 1918. M. Witmark & Sons. New York.
Structure: INTRO AA BB A C INTERLUDE C

Misery Blues. May 1, 1918. M. Witmark & Sons. New York.
Structure: AA BB CC B CODA

MAY FRANCES AUFDERHEIDE

Born: Indianapolis, Indiana, May 21,
　1888
Died: Pasadena, California, Septem-
　ber 1, 1972

A popular pianist whose first rag was a hit. The large sale of *Dusty Rag* impressed her father, John H. Aufderheide, enough to start his own music publishing company. Located in the Lemcke Building, the firm was managed by Paul Pratt who, along with May's friends, Julia Niebergall and Gladys Yelvington, also contributed three rags to the catalog. May married Thomas M. Kaufman, who worked for her father in his Commonwealth Loan Company and permanently left the music business. They had one son.

Dusty Rag. February 6, 1908. Duane Crabb Pub. Co., Indianapolis.
Recording: Turk Murphy's Jazz Band, "The Many Faces of Ragtime," Atlantic SD-1613, 1972.
Roll: Connorized 315.
Structure: INTRO AA BB CC
An unadorned rag in a folk style, but with the emphasis on non-chord tones and melodic chromaticism which brings about a softer lyricism than those older Folk rags. This was the first hit rag of the Indianapolis-Ohio Valley ragtime group which surfaced at this time.

Buzzer Rag. September 4, 1909. J. H. Aufderheide, Indianapolis.
Roll: QRS 30910.
Structure: INTRO AA BB CC A

The Thriller. September 4, 1909. J. H. Aufderheide, Indianapolis.
Recording: Neville Dickie, "Ragtime Piano," (E) Saydisc SDL-
118, 1966.
Roll: Angelus 90172.
Structure: AA BB A CC
This has a very chromatic melody and a Classic rag style change
in section A with the introduction of the minor of the dominant.
Sections B and C are more orchestral with the B section a
remarkable blend of chromaticism and the use of blue thirds
and sevenths, with a call and response phrasing in C. It is a
companion to *Dusty Rag* and a fine example of blending both
black and white folk music materials in a ragtime composition.

A Totally Different Rag. July 16, 1910. J. H. Aufderheide,
Indianapolis.
Roll: QRS 03380.
Structure: AA BB CC B
The title is descriptive of unusual melodic construction of sec-
tion B, achieved partially by a suspended fourth, another fea-
ture of Ohio Valley rags after 1908.

Blue Ribbon Rag. October 3, 1910. J. H. Aufderheide, In-
dianapolis.
Roll: QRS 30930.
Structure: AA BB CC AA

Novelty Rag. April 11, 1911. J. H. Aufderheide, Indianapolis.
Roll: Kimball B 5904
Structure: INTRO AA BB CC A

J. RUSSEL ROBINSON

Born: Indianapolis, Indiana, July 8,
1892
Died: Palmdale, California, September 30, 1963

He attended Shortridge High School. Always fooling around the piano as a youngster, he finally took lessons and concentrated on reading. During high school he and his brother John, a drummer, played for lodge dances and other social functions. From 1905–9 the family accompanied the "Famous Robinson Brothers" as they toured the South, settling in Macon, Georgia, where they accompanied the silent movies. His first composition was *Sapho Rag*, which was published by Stark. During his stay in Macon he became acquainted with Ferd Guttenberger, a fine pianist and co-owner of the local music store. Robinson arranged and wrote down two of Ferd's rags, *Kalamity Kid* and *Log Cabin Rag*. He wrote rags first, he remembered, because there was no demand for songs. In 1910 the family went to New Orleans to play at the Alamo Theatre and the Penny Wonderland. He wasn't impressed with the pianists there and called them fakers (they couldn't read music). The following year the brothers played in Montgomery, Alabama, where two more rags were written. He heard W. C. Handy's band at Memphis and said that they, too, were fakers. By 1912 the family had returned to Indianapolis, where *That Eccentric Rag* was written during a short walk with the publisher to his music store. At the store Robinson played it for him, wrote it down and sold it for twenty-five dollars. "I don't know which made me most excited, the money or the prospect of getting another song in print . . . probably the latter." From 1917–25 he worked for the Imperial Company and QRS (he was introduced by QRS in their catalog as "the White Boy with the colored fingers"), making two rolls a month and getting fifty dollars apiece. During the day he worked as a demonstrator for Leo Feist, Inc. in Chicago. In 1918 he played at the Starr Theatre and began recording for Gennett. He wrote the words and music to *Singin' the Blues,* which became a hit song in 1921. Finally, in late 1918 he went to New York, where he became W. C. Handy's personal manager. He met Al Bernard, lyric writer and blackface singer, and formed the famous vaudeville team called the Dixie Stars. They recorded for Columbia, Brunswick, Cameo and Okeh. Robinson joined the famous Original Dixieland Jass Band in 1919 and went to London with them. He returned home at the end of the year, but rejoined the group in mid-1920 and persuaded them to add the alto saxophone virtuoso, Bennie Krueger. He also accompanied Lou Holtz, Kate Smith and Marian Harris in vaudeville. Robinson wrote such great pop song hits during the twenties as *Margie* (earlier song in different tempo called *Lullaby Blues*), *Aggravatin' Papa*, *Rhythm King* (as Joe Hoover), *Mary Lou, Palesteena,* and *Beale Street Mama.* He went to the West Coast to freelance as composer.

Sapho Rag. October 5, 1909. Stark Music Co., St. Louis. *Roll:* QRS 30781.
Structure: INTRO AA BB C TRIO-INTRO D E C
Named after a popular New Orleans dancer, this is an impressive first rag of five sections. It is a folksy composition with a bucolic flavor effected by the use of a dotted rhythm and phrasing that suggests a country Schottische. c has a pattern that folk rag performer Brun Campbell used:

Dynamite Rag. October 1, 1910. Southern California Music
   Co., Los Angeles.
Structure: INTRO AA BB A CC DD

The Minstrel Man. July 27, 1911. Stark Music Co., St. Louis.
Recording: Tony Parenti's Ragtime Band, "Ragtime Jubilee,"
   Jazzology J-21.
Roll: U.S. Music 65156.
Structure: INTRO AA BB A C DD
Section A is reminiscent of *Maple Leaf*'s A section, but is a
creative reworking of the phrasing. C and D are folk strains,
with D's stomping finish especially reminiscent of Brun Camp-
bell's playing.

Whirl Wind. December 11, 1911. Stark Music Co., St. Louis.
Roll: U.S. Music 65194.
Structure: INTRO AA BB A CC DD

That Erratic Rag. Not copyrighted at this time but published
   1911. Stark Music Co., St. Louis.

Erratic. October 17, 1923. Jack Mills Inc., New York.
Recording: Tony Parenti's Ragtime Band, "Ragtime Jubilee,"
   Jazzology J-21.
Structure: INTRO AA BB A CC A
Section A features unusual harmonies in a downward chromatic
run which suggests the title. B has a touch rarely encountered:
the bass in the fifth and sixth measures join the syncopated
treble pattern, abandoning briefly the traditional ragtime bass.

That Eccentric Rag. January 22, 1912. I. Seidel Music Pub.
   Co., Indianapolis.

Eccentric. October 17, 1923. Jack Mills Inc., New York.
Recording: New Orleans Rhythm Kings, Gennett 5009, August
   29, 1922.
Roll: QRS 31211.
Structure: INTRO AA BB A CC DD
Because this rag has an orchestral feeling, it is a favorite with

jazz bands. Noteworthy is the dotted-note writing in the melody of the D strain which is done to effect a swinging feeling, as used on many late ragtime and dance tunes. Robinson's idea to swing, and so indicate it in the music, is unusual and compares favorably to Jelly Roll Morton's musical ideas.

Rita (with Bernie Cummins). May 20, 1929. Vincent Youmans Music Pub., New York.
Fine Novelty rag.

HARRY AUSTIN TIERNEY
Born: Perth Amboy, New Jersey, May 21, 1890
Died: New York, New York, March 22, 1965

H is musical education began with his mother, continued with Nicholas Morrissey and he subsequently attended the Virgil Conservatory of Music in New York City. Tierney toured the country as a concert pianist. He went to London in 1916, where he wrote music for a show and revue and returned the following year to embark on a career in popular music. He joined the publishing firm of Jerome H. Remick & Co. and, in 1919, wrote the complete score to *Irene,* which had the longest run for a musical comedy up to that time on Broadway (the most famous tune from the show was the lovely waltz, *Alice Blue Gown*). He wrote for several Ziegfeld Follies and, in 1927, again composed the entire score for a smash musical comedy, *Rio Rita,* which, in addition to the title song, also contained a clever syncopated number, *The Kinkajou.* He went to Hollywood in 1931 under contract to RKO.

The Bumble Bee. November 24, 1909. Ted Snyder Co., New York.
Roll: Connorized 1347.
Structure: INTRO A B A TRIO-INTRO C INTERLUDE C

The Fanatic Rag. February 15, 1911. Ted Snyder Co., New York.
Roll: Universal 78679.
Structure: INTRO AA BB A C INTERLUDE C

Uncle Tom's Cabin. March 14, 1911. Jos. W. Stern & Co., New York.
Roll: U.S. Music 64871.
Structure: INTRO AA BB A C INTRO-2 C_1 C_2
A good rag with a truly exceptional trio. The initial C states a great lyrical melody. C_1 thickens the texture with octaves in the treble. C_2 is the ragged transformation using the pattern:

Dingle Pop Hop. April 12, 1911. Ted Snyder Co., New York.
Roll: U.S. Music 64938.
Structure: INTRO AA BB A C INTERLUDE C

Black Canary. May 5, 1911. Ted Snyder Co., New York.
Structure: INTRO AA BB AA C INTERLUDE C

Checkerboard. May 13, 1911. Ted Snyder Co., New York.
Structure: INTRO A B A C INTERLUDE C

Crimson Rambler. May 19, 1911. Ted Snyder Co., New York.
Roll: U.S. Music 64973.
Structure: INTRO AA BB A C INTERLUDE C

William's Wedding. June 23, 1911. Ted Snyder Co., New York.
Roll: QRS 31114.
Structure: INTRO AA BB A C INTERLUDE C INTERLUDE C

Rubies and Pearls. June 24, 1911. Ted Snyder Co., New York.
Roll: U.S. Music 65336.
Structure: INTRO AA BB A C INTERLUDE C INTERLUDE C

Fleur De Lis. August 16, 1911. Jos. W. Stern & Co., New York.
Roll: U.S. Music 65011.
Structure: INTRO AA BB A CC INTRO-2 C

Cabaret Rag. Not copyrighted or published.
Recording: Prince's Band, Columbia A-1164, March 1912.

Variety Rag. July 1, 1912. George W. Meyer Music Co., New
   York.
Roll: U.S. Music 65625.
Structure: INTRO AA BB A C INTERLUDE C INTERLUDE C
The introduction is scored as 7 measures with an introductory
measure to A. This same measure is used again to bring back
A after B.

Louisiana Rag. May 3, 1913. Jos. Krolage Music Co., Cincin-
   nati.
Structure: INTRO A B A INTERLUDE C A
The trio is a blues (12 measures with a reprise of the last four).
This is a rare, idiomatic score with indications of ragtime per-
forming conventions usually found only on rolls.

Chicago Tickle (also known as "The Tierney Rag"). August 8,
   1913. Chas. T. French, New York.
Recording: Prince's Band, (E) Regal G-6845, July, 1913. ("A
   Programme of Ragtime," E, VJM-1).
Structure: INTRO A B A CC INTERLUDE C A B A
C section is very fine but familiar.

1915 Rag. August 8, 1913. Chas. T. French, New York.
Recording: Mike Bernard, Columbia A-1427, June, 1913.
   ("Early Ragtime Piano," Folkways RBF-33).
Roll: Aeolian Themodist T-300618.
Structure: INTRO AA BB A CC INTRO-2 B

H. CLARENCE WOODS
Born: Blue Earth, Ohio, June 19, 1888
Died: Davenport, Iowa, September
    30, 1956

Woods grew up in Carthage, Missouri, where he and James Scott took piano lessons from the same teacher, Emma Johns. He spent many early years as a pianist with a traveling drama troupe, a silent film pianist, an accompanist and soloist in vaudeville throughout Texas and Oklahoma; he became a theater manager, an organist in movie houses, an orchestra leader, a radio entertainer and, finally, ended his career as a professional musician as chief organist, composer and arranger for the Ringling Brothers-Barnum & Bailey Circus.

Slippery Elm Rag. December 2, 1912. Bush & Gerts Piano Co., Dallas.
Recording: Max Morath, "Plays the Best of Scott Joplin & Other Rag Classics," Vanguard VSD 39/40.
Roll: U.S. Music 66075.
Structure: INTRO AA BB CC B
Section A combines three features: the "three-over-four," an even flow of sixteenth notes and the syncopation:

A and B are chromatic melodically, and C has a fine and unusual break which, with the indicated slurs, achieves a blues quality. The whole composition balances chromaticism and blues writing to become one of the most original rags ever written.

Sleepy Hollow Rag. Not copyrighted but published 1918. Will L. Livernash Music Co., Kansas City, Mo.
Recording: John Arpin, "Concert in Ragtime," Scroll LSCR-101, September 21, 1965.
Structure: AA BB A C C$_1$ B
The title refers to a black community just outside Carthage. A most unusual and expressive rag. Section A is built around a tremolo effect. B has written fill-ins in small notes to be executed lightly above the sustained chord. C has a lyrical, otherwordly aura, intensified in C$_1$ with a return to the delicate tremolo.

Black Satin Fox Trot. Not copyrighted or published.
Roll: U.S. Music 9235.
Structure: INTRO AA BB CC DD
A great advanced foxtrot rag done exclusively for U.S. Music piano roll company.

OTHER IMPORTANT RAGS

Angel Food. Al F. Marzian. December 16, 1911. Forster Music Pub., Chicago.
Recording: Joe "Fingers" Carr, "Bar Room Piano," Capitol T-280.
Roll: U.S. Music 66238.
Structure: INTRO AA BB CC INTERLUDE C
A string bass player from Louisville, Kentucky, who published several rags of others, this is his only rag and is an absolute joy. The interlude in minor recalls the *Dance of the Seven Veils* and provides a wonderful contrast to the rest of the piece.

Bachelor's Button. William C. Powell (Polla). May 3, 1909. J. W. Jenkins' Sons Music Co., Kansas City, Mo.
Structure: INTRO AA BB A CC DD A B A

Black Beauty. Jean Schwartz. November 9, 1910. Jerome H.
  Remick & Co., New York.
Rolls: Metrostyle 94711. QRS 30952.
Structure: INTRO A BB A TRIO-INTRO C INTERLUDE C

Black Wasp Rag. H. A. Fischler. February 21, 1911. Vandersloot, Williamsport, Pa.
Roll: QRS 30978.
Structure: INTRO AA BB CC BB
One of a half-dozen or so rags published by Vandersloot, who
specialized in easy-to-play rags, mostly scored in single-note
melody lines and phrased with rather busy, relentless syncopations that vary greatly in inventiveness.

Bolo Rag. Albert Gumble. November 11, 1908. Jerome H.
  Remick & Co., New York.
Recording: Bill Mitchell, "Ragtime Recycled," Ethelyn ER-
  1750, 1972.
Roll: QRS 30659.
Structure: INTRO AA BB A CC A CODA
A fine rag climaxed by a sweeping descent of sixteenth notes
in the trio. Instructions read to be played "slowly but surely."

Bombshell Rag. Thomas R. Confare and Morris Silver. Not
  copyrighted, but published 1909. Charles I. Davis Music
  Pub., Cleveland.
Structure: INTRO AA BB CC DD INTRO A CODA
An important recent discovery that would indicate that Con-
fare, who arranged the famous *Cannon Ball,* might have had a
heavier hand in the rag than the "composer," Jos. Northup.
This is in the same style, but is a more complex work.

A Certain Party. Tom Kelly. October 3, 1910. Maurice
  Shapiro, New York.
Roll: Kimball B-5318.
Structure: INTRO AA BB A C INTERLUDE C

Chimes. Homer Denney. July 20, 1910. Jos. Krolage, Cincinnati.
Roll: Universal 27133.
Structure: INTRO A BB A TRIO-INTRO C DD C
The composer was a popular calliope performer in Cincinnati who introduced most of his rags on the excursion steamboat, Island Queen.

Chow-Chow Rag. Phil Schwartz. August 12, 1909. Jerome H. Remick & Co., Detroit.
Structure: INTRO AA BB A TRIO-INTRO C INTERLUDE A CODA

Clover Leaf Rag. Cy Seymour. March 1, 1909. Albright Music Co., Chicago.
Structure: INTRO AA BB CC BB

Crab Apples. Percy Wenrich. January 27, 1908. Brehm Bros., Erie, Pa.
Roll: QRS 30684.
Structure: INTRO AA BB TRIO-INTRO CC DD
One of his more inspired rags and with his characteristic folk touch. Section B has imaginative harmonic changes.

Dat Lovin' Rag. Bernard Adler. October 25, 1906. F. B. Haviland Pub. Co., New York.
Recording: Lou Busch, "Honky Tonk Piano," Capitol T-188, (recorded as *That Ever-Lovin' Rag*).
Roll: Melographic (65 note).
Structure: INTRO A B CC

The Entertainer's Rag. Jay Roberts. September 30, 1910. Pacific Coast Music Co., Oakland.
Recording: Joe "Fingers" Carr, "Mister Ragtime," Capitol T-760.
Roll: W. Arlington. Connorized 20350.
Structure: INTRO AA INTRO-2 B C D C E INTERLUDE FF
One of the most popular rags of its day, written by a virtuoso vaudeville pianist. Actually, it is a collection of rather hack-

neyed, though dazzling, ragtime licks. It was used by pianists to win contests, as the counterpoint of *Yankee Doodle* and *Dixie* assured the contestant a hand from both sides of the Mason-Dixon line.

Evolution Rag. Thomas S. Allen. December 16, 1912. Walter
    Jacobs. Boston.
Rolls: U.S. Music 66097. Perfection 80459.
Structure: INTRO AA BB A CC INTERLUDE C
The best in a fairly impressive series of rags by Allen, a prolific writer of instrumentals, who had a flair for syncopated melodic lines in long phrases.

Father Knickerbocker. Edwin E. Wilson. August 19, 1907.
    Jos. W. Stern & Co., New York.
Structure: INTRO AA BB A TRIO-INTRO CC INTERLUDE BB

'Frisco Frazzle. Nat Johnson. June 27, 1912. M. Witmark &
    Sons, New York.
Structure: INTRO AA BB A CC B

Frisco Rag. Harry Armstrong. November 6, 1909. M. Witmark
    & Sons, New York.
Roll: QRS 30769.
Structure: INTRO AA BB A TRIO-INTRO CC

Gasoline Rag. Louis Mentel. July 23, 1906. Mentel Bros. Pub.
    Co., Cincinnati.
Recording: Dave Jasen, "Rip-Roarin' Ragtime," Folkways FG-
    3561. June, 1977.
Structure: INTRO AA B CC DD

The Georgia Rag. Albert Gumble. December 15, 1910.
    Jerome H. Remick & Co., New York.
Recording: Dave Jasen, "Rompin' Stompin' Ragtime," Blue
    Goose 3002, 1974.
Roll: Connorized 4525.
Structure: INTRO A BB A CC B

Glad Rag. Ribe Danmark (pseud. for J. B. Lampe). May 18, 1910. Jerome H. Remick & Co, Detroit.
Roll: U.S. Music.
Structure: INTRO AA BB A CC B
One of only two known rags by an early and very prominent arranger of Tin Pan Alley, he was also a leading cakewalk composer at the turn of this century. The pseudonym is a slight change from his birthplace—Ribe, Denmark.

Gold Dust Twins Rag. Nat Johnson. June 20, 1913. Forster Music Publisher, Chicago.
Roll: Supertone 860344.
Structure: INTRO AA BB A CC DD
An ebullient rag, one of several named after a popular product —in this case, a cleanser.

Harmony Rag. Hal G. Nichols. September 25, 1911. Sam Fox Pub. Co., Cleveland.
Recording: Pete Daily's Dixieland Band, Capitol 1588, May, 1951, ("Dixie By Daily," Capitol T-385).
Roll: Artistone 41717.
Structure: INTRO AA BB A C BB

Haunting Rag. Julius Lenzberg. December 4, 1911. M. Witmark & Sons, New York.
Recording: Victor Military Band, Victor 17319, March, 1913. ("Ragtime Entertainment," Folkways RBF-22).
Rolls: Felix Arndt. QRS 100044. U.S. Music 65179.
Structure: INTRO AA BB A C INTERLUDE C

Heavy on the Catsup. Lewis F. Muir. December 26, 1913. F. A. Mills. New York.
Structure: INTRO AA BB A TRIO-INTRO CC
Muir was a self-taught pianist who played exclusively in the key of F sharp. He played on the pike at the St. Louis World's Fair in 1904 and later became one of the great Tin Pan Alley songwriters.

Honey Rag. Egbert Van Alstyne. July 7, 1909. Jerome H. Remick & Co., New York.

Recording: Neville Dickie, "Rags and Tatters," (E) Contour 2870–190, 1972.

Roll: QRS 03190 (65 note).

Structure: INTRO AA BB A CC

Extraordinary harmonic color is achieved in section A with the use of the major seventh and sixth. He attended the Chicago Musical College.

Hoosier Rag. Julia Lee Niebergall. November 1, 1907. Jerome H. Remick & Co., New York.

Recording: Max Morath, "The Ragtime Women," Vanguard VSD-79402, 1977.

Roll: QRS 30598.

Structure: INTRO AA B A CC B_1

An apt title for an Indiana rag, and one of the best. A characteristic lyricism is achieved here and in other rags of this Ohio Valley group by emphasis on major sevenths, sixths and ninths.

Horseshoe Rag. Julia Lee Niebergall. April 1, 1911. J. H. Aufderheide & Co., Indianapolis.

Recording: John W. "Knocky" Parker, "Golden Treasury of Ragtime," Audiophile AB-92.

Roll: Melographic 02187.

Structure: INTRO AA BB CC A

Section A is perhaps her finest melody. It alternates four even eighth notes in the treble with the pattern:

and has a Classic rag style ending à la Joplin. C has parts of the bass in chromatic sixths, a characteristic of Midwestern rags that Jelly Roll Morton picked up:

Hot Chocolate Rag. Malvin Franklin & Arthur Lange, April 6, 1909. Jos. W. Stern & Co., New York.
Recording: Dave Jasen, "Rompin' Stompin' Ragtime," Blue Goose 3002, April, 1974.
Roll: Connorized 4429.
Structure: INTRO AA BB CC A
Melodic phrasing in the A section teases one's perception of the actual tonic key.

Jamaica Jinjer, A Hot Rag. Egbert Van Alstyne. March 19, 1912. Jerome H. Remick & Co., New York.
Rolls: Egbert Van Alstyne, QRS 100036. U.S. Music 65315.
Structure: INTRO AA BB TRIO-INTRO C INTERLUDE C
The composer's version on piano roll is interesting because he slows down for the final repeat of C. Vintage recordings of ragtime reveal that this device, as well as its reverse, was a common practice in performance.

Ketchup Rag. Irene M. Giblin. March 5, 1910. Jerome H. Remick & Co., New York.
Roll: QRS 30854.
Structure: INTRO AA B A TRIO-INTRO C B

The Lion Tamer Rag. Mark Janza, January 2, 1913. A. F. Marzian. Louisville.
Roll: U.S. Music.
Structure: INTRO AA BB VAMP CC DD ½B CODA
The most adventurous of the Ohio Valley rags, is accurately subtitled, "Syncopated Fantasia." It combines a circus pomposo air with surprises at every turn. Measures 15 and 16 in the trio are the most ambitious, creative use of an idea that dates from 1898 (see *Incandescent Rag*). Here the pattern is executed in the bass, combined with a "three-over-four" treble.

Louisiana Rag. Leon Block. February 6, 1911. Will Rossiter, Chicago.
Recording: Paul Lingle, Good Time Jazz 88, February, 1952. ("Piano Ragtime of the Fifties," Herwin 404).

Roll: Artistone 31593.
Structure: INTRO AA BB A TRIO-INTRO CC

Nat Johnson's Rag. Nat Johnson, December 16, 1911. Forster
   Music Publisher, Chicago.
Roll: Herbert.
Structure: INTRO AA BB A CC B

Nonsense Rag. R. G. Grady. January 14, 1911. Jos. W. Stern
   & Co., New York.
Recording: Wally Rose, "Ragtime Piano Masterpieces," Co-
   lumbia CL-6260 (10"), May, 1953.
Roll: U.S. Music 64823.
Structure: INTRO AA BB A TRIO-INTRO CC B

Oh You Angel. Ford T. Dabney. January 4, 1911. Maurice
   Shapiro, New York.
Roll: U.S. Music 64769.
Structure: INTRO AA BB A CC INTRO-2 A

Oh You Devil. Ford T. Dabney. July 2, 1909. Maurice Shapiro,
   New York.
Roll: Universal 77837 (65 note).
Structure: INTRO AA BB A CC INTRO-2 AA CODA
A sophisticated rag with extensive use of non-chord tones. The
trio harmony creates an unusual effect with a continued emphasis (in the key of C) on A in the melody—first as the sixth
of tonic, then as fifth combined with the ninth (E) over a D_7,
then as ninth over a G_7, then again as the sixth of C. The home
key of C is not stressed at all until the fifteenth measure.

Peaches and Cream. Percy Wenrich. November 27, 1905.
   Jerome H. Remick & Co., New York.
Roll: Angelus 25590 (65 note).
Structure: INTRO AA BB TRIO-INTRO CC DD
An important yet overlooked early rag which anticipated *Dill
Pickles* with the "three-over-four" device.

Perpetual Rag. Harry Thomas. May 29, 1911. Harry Thomas, Montreal.
Roll: Harry Thomas, Uni-Record.
An explosive performance with triplets, breaks, dramatic tremolos and walking bass. The "perpetual" effect comes from not resolving the melody in the final measure of the A section.

Persian Lamb Rag. Percy Wenrich. June 15, 1908. Walter Jacobs, Boston.
Recording: Vess L. Ossman, Victor 16127, October, 1908.
Roll: QRS 30647.
Structure: INTRO AA BB CC D INTRO-2 A
He had a truly great flair for writing lyrical popular song melodies with a genuine folk flavor. Although he had heard the legendary ragtime pioneers in his youth play at the House of Lords, one of the most plush sporting emporiums, his total output of first-rate rags is less than one might expect. Only a few are in that category, but his forte was the pop song (*Put On Your Old Grey Bonnet, When You Wore a Tulip*). The A section of *Persian Lamb* is reminiscent of an old fiddle tune known as *Whiskers,* played in his hometown of Joplin, Missouri.

The Phantom Rag. Sol Violinsky and Al W. Brown. June 9, 1911. J. Fred Helf Co., New York.
Structure: INTRO AA BB A TRIO-INTRO CC

Pitter-Patter Rag. Jos. Michael Daly. April 1, 1910. Jos. M. Daly, Boston.
Structure: INTRO AA BB A TRIO-INTRO CC BB

Poison Ivy Rag. Herbert Ingraham. March 9, 1908. Maurice Shapiro, New York.
Recording: Dave Jasen, "Fingerbustin' Ragtime," Blue Goose 3001.
Roll: Connorized 4403 (65 note).
Structure: INTRO AA BB CC B
One of several imaginative rags by a writer who died of tuberculosis at the age of twenty-seven.

The Pop Corn Man. Jean Schwartz. December 15, 1910. Jerome H. Remick & Co., Detroit.
Structure: INTRO AA BB A CC A CODA
The most lyrical of the Schwartz rags, with interpolated "steamboat whistle" in the A section and "pop" written above several afterbeats in the trio, commemorating the ubiquitous popcorn man of earlier years.

Popularity. George Michael Cohan. August 27, 1906. F. A. Mills, New York.
Recording: Vess L. Ossman, Columbia 3529, October, 1906, ("Kings of the Ragtime Banjo," Yazoo L-1044).
Roll: Universal 74209 (65 note).
Structure: INTRO AA BB A TRIO-INTRO C INTERLUDE C
An instrumental composed for his show of the same name, it was an extremely popular rag. It has a cakewalk flavor, but with much more syncopation and imaginative use of harmonies.

The Queen Rag. Floyd Willis. June 16, 1911. Joseph Krolage Music Co., Cincinnati.
Roll: Connorized 4562 (65 note).
Structure: AA BB A CC B
This rag celebrates the most famous excursion boat from Cincinnati in the ragtime era: the Island Queen. Rags, like Denney's *Chimes* were written for her steam calliope.

Ragtime Chimes. Percy Wenrich. July 26, 1911. Jerome H. Remick & Co., New York.
Recording: Trebor Jay Tichnor, "King of Folk Ragtime," Dirty Shame 2001, 1973.
Roll: U.S. Music 65017.
Structure: INTRO AA BB A CC A
A clever chimes effect on a very pianistic figure in section A.

Ramshackle Rag. Ted Snyder. March 10, 1911. Ted Snyder Co., New York.
Recording: Dawn of the Century Ragtime Orchestra, "Silks and Rags," Arcane 602, April, 1972.
Roll: Universal 11333 (65 note).

Structure: INTRO AA BB A CC INTERLUDE C
A good rag with clever phrasing in the introduction and ambitious harmonies in the interlude.

Red Onion Rag. Abe Olman. January 17, 1912. George W. Meyer Music Co., New York.
Recording: Roy Spangler, Rex 5342, March, 1911, ("Piano Ragtime of the Teens, Twenties & Thirties," Herwin 402).
Roll: QRS 31216.
Structure: INTRO AA BB A CC

Red Rambler Rag. Julia Lee Niebergall. July 16, 1912. J. H. Aufderheide, Indianapolis.
Recording: Max Morath, "The Ragtime Women," Vanguard VSD-79402, 1977.
Roll: U.S. Music 65411.
Structure: INTRO AA BB CC A

Rigamarole Rag. Edwin Kendall. Not copyrighted, but published 1910. Jerome H. Remick & Co., New York.
Recording: Joe "Fingers" Carr, "Bar Room Piano," Capitol T-280.
Roll: U.S. Music 4628 (65 note).
Structure: INTRO AA B A CC INTERLUDE C

Riverside Rag. Charles Cohen. August 8, 1910. Cohen Music Co., Binghamton, New York.
Recording: Neville Dickie. "Creative Ragtime," Euphonic 1206.
Roll: QRS 31030.
Structure: INTRO AA BB A C A

Sleepy Sidney. Archie W. Scheu. August 22, 1907. Archie W. Scheu, Cincinnati.
Recordings: Sousa's Band, Victor 16278, October, 1908. Johnny Maddox, Dot 45–15028, "Authentic Ragtime," Dot 102 (10″).
Roll: Universal 75565 (65 note).
Structure: INTRO AA BB A CC B

The Smiler Rag. Percy Wenrich. January 2, 1907. Arnett-Delonais Co., Chicago.

Recording: Vess L. Ossman, Columbia A-972, December, 1910. ("Kings of the Ragtime Banjo," Yazoo L-1044).

Rolls: Universal 3361 (65 note). Felix Arndt, Duo Art 5551.

Structure: INTRO AA BB TRIO-INTRO CC DD

His best rag with four strong sections of varying character. A has a fine folk flavor, B features a break, C has a Joplin lyricism since it is stolen from his *Peacherine Rag* trio, and D is high-lighted by treble runs.

Sour Grapes. Will B. Morrison. November 11, 1912. Will B. Morrison, Indianapolis.

Roll: Connorized 2539.

Structure: INTRO AA BB A CC B

A rather athletic A strain melody precedes an imaginative B section of involved syncopation.

Spaghetti Rag. George Lyons and Bob Yosco, April 11, 1910. Maurice Shapiro, New York.

Recording: Robert Maxwell, Tempo 634, ("String Ragtime," Yazoo L-1045).

Rolls: J. Lawrence Cook, QRS 8641. U.S. Music 64042.

Structure: INTRO AA BB CC A

This was composed by an unlikely vaudeville duo which featured mandolin and harp. Only a modest success in its day, it became a favorite during the fifties revival of ragtime interest.

Swanee Ripples. Walter E. Blaufuss. December 27, 1912. Frank Clark Music Co., Chicago.

Recording: Victor Dance Orch., Victor 17585, February, 1914.

Roll: Pierre LaFontaine, QRS 100048.

Structure: INTRO AA BB CC DD

Arranged by another rag composer, Harry Thompson, this is a most imaginative rag with an ambitious syncopated B strain and dotted-note phrasing much like an Advanced rag. Blaufuss was a Milwaukee-born musician whose first rag appeared in 1899 (*Chicago Rag,* named after the Chicago Musical College, the training ground for many of the ragtime composers). He went on to become music director for the popular radio program, "Don McNeil's Breakfast Club" (also, see Bill Krenz).

That Demon Rag. Russell Smith. January 27, 1911. I. Seidel, Indianapolis.
Roll: QRS 31145.
Structure: INTRO AA BB TRIO-INTRO CC DD
An original conception by a black Indianapolis composer who also worked in vaudeville and minstrelsy. C is especially beautiful as the syncopated patterns alternate between the bass and treble, rejecting the traditional ragtime bass. Section D breaks away with a burst of sixteenths—a fine touch.

That Madrid Rag. Julius Lenzberg. May 31, 1911. Ted Snyder Co., New York.
Structure: INTRO AA BB A CC B

Vivacity Rag. Frank C. Keithley. February 5, 1910. New York & Chicago Music Pub. House, Chicago.
Structure: INTRO AA BB A CC
Nice variation on *Maple Leaf Rag* and *The Naked Dance.*

The Watermelon Trust. Harry C. Thompson. May 25, 1906. Barron & Thompson Co., New York.
Structure: INTRO AA BB CC DD
One of the most lyrical works which makes inspired use of non-chord tones in the melody to produce a sensitive rag.

Whitewash Man. Jean Schwartz. September 8, 1908. Cohan & Harris Pub. Co., New York.
Recordings: Ralph Sutton, Circle 1052, January, 1949, ("Piano Ragtime of the Forties," Herwin 403). Turk Murphy's Jazz Band, "The Many Faces of Ragtime," Atlantic SD-1613, 1972.
Roll: U.S. Music 61151.
Structure: INTRO A BB A TRIO-INTRO C INTERLUDE C
A prolific song-writer and composer of show tunes, Schwartz had a flair for smooth harmonic changes, frequently with the bass moving downward adding interesting color in an orthodox tonal format.

Wild Cherries. Ted Snyder. September 23, 1908. Ted Snyder
 Co., New York.
Recording: Frank Banta, Gennett 4735, May, 1921. ("Piano
 Ragtime of the Teens, Twenties & Thirties," Herwin 402).
Roll: U.S. Music 61137.
Structure: INTRO AA BB A C INTERLUDE-C INTERLUDE-C
A major ragtime hit. The A section has a descending progression which is a floating folk strain (as used in Morton's *Perfect Rag*). B cleverly utilizes bass octaves effecting harmonic changes. C is climaxed by a sustained lowered sixth (or raised fifth) chord.

~~5~~
Advanced Ragtime
1913-1917

After ragtime's popularity peaked around 1912, there wasn't the sudden dismissal that occurs with musical fads of today. Ragtime in 1913 still had a powerful draw, not only in this country, but in England and Europe as well. Tin Pan Alley was continuing to grind out large quantities of songs with the magic word *rag* in their titles. But other things were also happening to ragtime.

Composers were starting to experiment with the Popular rag, not in form, but in content—creating new musical ideas within the same structure. Now that the pressure to create popular hits was removed, other composer-performers were attracted to ragtime as a composed music. Unusual harmonies were initially used by Georgia-born Malvin Franklin when he came to New York City and his *Hot Chocolate Rag* was published. As New York-born Harry Jentes entered the field with his *California Sunshine,* and later his *Bantam Step,* people noticed a decided difference in the rags. There were colorations and new dissonances to be used later in jazz; blues elements and the blues form integrated with traditional ragtime writing to tantalize the by-now jaded listener. But it wasn't all confined to New York City. Sydney K. Russell in Berkeley, California was turning out imaginative rags like *Too Much Raspberry;* Irwin P. Leclere in New Orleans, Louisiana, with his inventive *Triangle Jazz Blues;* Fred Heltman in Cleveland, Ohio, with his *Fred Heltman's Rag;* and the cradle of ragtime, St. Louis, Missouri, was maintaining its creativity with the widest variety of musical ideas incorporated into the ragtime form as demonstrated by Artie

Matthews and his five diverse *Pastime Rags*, Rob Hampton's *Cataract Rag* and *Agitation Rag*, Lucien P. Gibson's *Jinx Rag* and *Cactus Rag* and, finally, Charles Thompson's unassuming but highly exciting ragtime compositions, *The Lily Rag* and *Delmar Rag*.

The black ragtime pianist-composers from the East Coast began being heard from. Luckey Roberts from Philadelphia was the first of this crowd to be published and to record. Unfortunately, his earliest recordings (on Columbia) were not issued at the time and have since disappeared, presumably destroyed. At the time they were recorded, in 1916, only Mike Bernard and the Englishman-turned-Canadian, Harry Thomas, had made ragtime piano discs of major consequence; but they were soon to be joined by the touring vaudeville favorite, Roy Spangler, who can be heard on "Piano Ragtime of the Teens, Twenties and Thirties," (Herwin 402), performing songwriter-publisher Abe Olman's *Red Onion Rag*. The "Pride of Baltimore," Eubie Blake, followed Luckey in publishing rags, but his numbers fell between the pop song and the rag tradition. Finally, New Jersey-born James P. Johnson composed several rags which, like Luckey's and Eubie's, had a pronounced lyrical quality seldom found in the rags of the time. It is not surprising, then, that a few years later all three would make significant contributions to the world of popular music by writing beautiful ballads, memorable dances and sparkling, foot-tapping music. Their creativity easily matched their counterparts in St. Louis, but their originality took on a completely different character.

One of the oldest show business devices is to take a classical composition and syncopate it. The ragging of the classics suddenly blossomed forth in this era with great skill and cleverness. Julius Lenzberg led the pack with *Operatic Rag* and *Hungarian Rag*, while Edward Claypoole from Baltimore published the widely copied and wildly successful *Ragging the Scale*. Paul Pratt contributed *Springtime Rag*, which was given twenties dance-band treatment in an unusual recording by Vic Meyers and his Orchestra. George L. Cobb created the masterpiece *Russian Rag*, from Rachmaninoff's *Prelude*, Op. 3, No. 2, which was so successful that a few years later he was forced to write

The second cover but the first one published in St. Louis with composer's picture of 1899

Ragtime's first best-seller as played by the composer

A rare recording of the ragtime masterpiece

TO PLAY RAGTIME IN EUROPE

SCOTT JOPLIN.

Director Alfred Ernst of the St. Louis Choral Symphony Society believes that he has discovered, in Scott Joplin of Sedalia, a negro, an extraordinary genius as a composer of ragtime music.

So deeply is Mr. Ernst impressed with the ability of the Sedalian that he intends to take with him to Germany next summer copies of Joplin's work, with a view to educating the dignified disciples of Wagner, Liszt, Mendelssohn and other European masters of music into an appreciation of the real American ragtime melodies. It is possible that the colored man may accompany the distinguished conductor.

When he returns from the storied Rhine Mr. Ernst will take Joplin under his care and instruct him in the theory and harmony of music.

Joplin has published two ragtime pieces, "Maple Leaf Rag" and "Swipesey Cake Walk," which will be introduced in Germany by the St. Louis musician.

"I am deeply interested in this man," said Mr. Ernst to the Post-Dispatch. "He is young and undoubtedly has a fine future. With proper cultivation, I believe, his talent will develop into positive genius. Being of African blood himself, Joplin has a keener insight into that peculiar branch of melody than white composers. His ear is particularly acute.

"Recently I played for him portions of 'Tannhauser.' He was enraptured. I could see that he comprehended and appreciated this class of music. It was the opening of a new world to him, and I believe he felt as Keats felt when he first read Chapman's Homer.

"The work Joplin has done in ragtime is so original, so distinctly individual, and so melodious withal, that I am led to believe he can do something fine in compositions of a higher class when he shall have been instructed in theory and harmony.

"Joplin's work, as yet, has a certain crudeness, due to his lack of musical education, but it shows that the soul of the composer is there and needs but to be set free by knowledge of technique. He is an unusually intelligent young man and fairly well educated."

Joplin is known in Sedalia as "The Ragtime King." A trip to Europe in company with Prof. Ernst is the dream of his life. It may be realized.

The *St. Louis Post-Dispatch* of February 28, 1901

Joplin was "King of Ragtime Writers" but Chauvin was "King of Ragtime Players."

Celebrating the St. Louis Exposition

Scott's first hit

Among the most
creative rags written

Och Himmel! the carpets wave up und wave down
Und der light she go 'round mit a schwing
Dot hot razzle dazzle—I can't find der notes
Und der time he gone crazy by Jing
'Raus mit der new fangled stuff of to day
I blays der same biece dot my grand vatter blays

RAGTIME THAT IS DIFFERENT

A BREEZE FROM ALABAMA—A story in transitions. Scott Joplin

AFRICAN PAS—Easy and brilliant. Good to catch the ragtime swing. Maurice Kirwin

BLUE JAY RAG. Frank Wooster

BRAIN STORM—A Rag Wake-out. Bud Manchester

CALLA LILY RAG. Logan Thane

CARNATION—From the fountain of the Simon pure. A good one. Douglas

CASCADES—Inimitable. The melody glides through a labyrinth of harmony with a surprise at every turn. A classic Scott Joplin

CHAMPAGNE RAG—The greatest brilliency with the lest difficulty. Lamb

CHRYSANTHEMUM—The product of a dearm. An inspiration. Scott Joplin

CLOVER BLOSSOMS RAG. Manchester

COLLARS AND CUFFS—A Rousing Rag. C. H. St. John

COLE SMOAK—Intellectual and sentimental. A top liner Clarence St. John

COMUS—Brilliant, showy and not difficult. Bruggeman

CORRUGATED RAG—A new style of rag. Get it. Mellinger

DARKTOWN CAPERS—A white man's rag. Starck

EASY WINNERS—Joplin's favorite. Joplin

ELITE SYNCOPATIONS—Syncopation in last part are actually frenzied. Scott Joplin

ENTERTAINER Scott Joplin

ETHIOPIA—Different from all rags. Great. Lamb

EXCELSIOR—A heavy weight. Lamb

FIG LEAF—A high-class rag. Scott Joplin

FELICITY RAG—It is Joplinese throughout. Joplin

FROG LEGS—Now we need adjectives in fifteen degrees with a rising inflection. We need letters a foot high and a few exclamation points about the size of Cleopatra's needle—but we won't tell you of this piece, we want to surprise you. James Scott

FUSS AND FEATHERS—Dramatic. You can read the title page a country block away. Exceedingly showy inside and out. Morehead

GRACE AND BEAUTY—A classy rag. James Scott

HAM AND—A sentimental rag. Arthur Marshall

HAVANA RAG—Corrugated to a finish. Exhilarating. Maurice Kirwin

HELIOTROPE BOUQUET—The audible Poetry of Motion. Scott Joplin

HILARITY RAG—Positively the best rag since Maple Leaf. Scott

HONOLULU PRANKS—Thoroughly warranted—warp and woof. Sykes

KANSAS CITY RAG—This is a chip off the same block as Frog Legs, and written by the same man. Any comments would weaken it. James Scott

KENTUCKY WALK-AWAY—Easy and quite catchy. Very popular. Cummins

KINKLETS—Very ingenious and strictly up-to-date. Very popular. Cummins

KYRENE—All to the good. High class without a struggle. E. J. Stark

MANHATTAN RAG—Fluted and frilled, good and proper. Hear it. Brownold

MAPLE LEAF—The king o fall rags. Description impossible. Scott Joplin

MEDDLESOME—Prepare for a surprise. St. John

MINSTREL MAN RAG—Rare and catchy. If you don't rave over it we are insulted. Robinson

MY SOUTH SEA ISLAND QUEEN. Woster

NONPAREIL—The latest by Joplin—That's all. You will want it. Scott Joplin

ONE MORE RAG—Easy and catchy. Berger

OPHELIA RAG—Will certainly add a chapter to the gaiety of Nations. Fine three color title page. Scott

ORIOLE RAG. Scott

PEACHERINE—Somewhat easier, but all on the spot. Scott Joplin

PEACH—Nothing finer. Marshall

PIPPIN—A fine sentimental rag. Marshall

PRINCESS RAG—Exquisitely beautiful. Scott

QUALITY RAG—One of Scott's best. Scott

RAGTIME BETTY—The best since Maple Leaf. Scott

RAGTIME DANCE—Thrilling, stop-time, two-step or buck and wing. Scott Joplin

SAND PAPER RAG. Ellman & Schwab

SAPHO. J. Russel Robinson

SCHOOL OF RAGTIME—It teaches you thoroughly. Joplin

SENSATION. Lamb

STRENUOUS LIFE—Joplinese and eccentric; away up. Scott Joplin

SUNBURST—Equal to Frog Legs. Scott

SUNFLOWER SLOW DRAG—Twin sister of Maple Leaf. Equally good. Scott Joplin

SWIPESY—Fine but don't take our word for it; get it. Scott Joplin

SYMPATHETIC JASPER—The name pipes its quality to a hair's breadth. Catlin

TEN PENNY RAG. Brandon

THE CLIMBERS RAG—Title page has a halftone picture of each player on the St. Louis Cardinal team. Sizemore

TOPSY'S DREAM—A vision bliss. Williams

TROMBONE JOHNSEN—Tells the artistic story with a smile. E. J. Stark

UNIVERSAL RAG—Reminds us of the Akound of Swat, or something. Wooster

WHIRLWIND RAG. Robinson

In this collection you have the storm-center of high-class ragtime. The fountain from which composers draw their inspiration.

The gauge by which publishers test their manuscript.

Ingenious, unique and original. Trenchant, terse and scholarly. They are the philosophy of Bacon clothed in the keen wit of Falstaff. They are the rag classics. There are no others.

You don't have to take our word for it; get the entire list and see for yourself.

EXTRA SELECTED WALTZES.

ACHING HEARTS—Best of Kirwin's Waltzes. Beautiful melody. Kirwin

AUGUSTAN CLUB—Joplin's best waltz. Suberb arrangement. Scott Joplin

BERTRAM WALTZES. York

CASTLE SQUARE—These glittering arpeggios awaken the fairies. Brownold

CAVALIER—Good waltz and fine three-color title-page. Brownold

CLARICE. Ilgenfritz

CYNTHIA. Ilgenfritz

A typical Stark ad—at its hyperbolic best

Charles N. Daniels, when he purchased
Joplin's *Original Rags* in 1898

Jerome H. Remick, largest publisher
of rags in the United States

Ted Snyder,
composer-publisher
of ragtime hits

Even Jimmy Durante played this one at Coney Island.

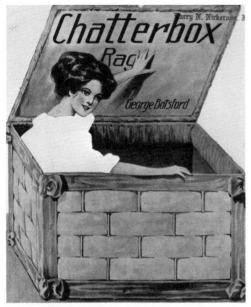

Another successful rag by Botsford

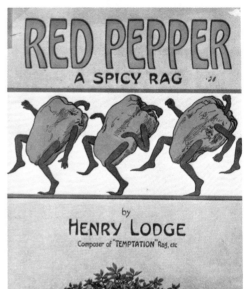

Continuing the vogue for "vegetable" rags

Dedicated to "The Minstrel Boys of America"

Muir's only rag

Julia Lee Niebergall in the mid-1930s

Chicagoan Egbert Van Alstyne

Jean Schwartz, composer of the popular *Whitewash Man*, in 1908

An early Cobb rag

The artwork creates
a double pun.

Nat Johnson in 1911

The figures were the trademark for the famous Gold Dust detergent

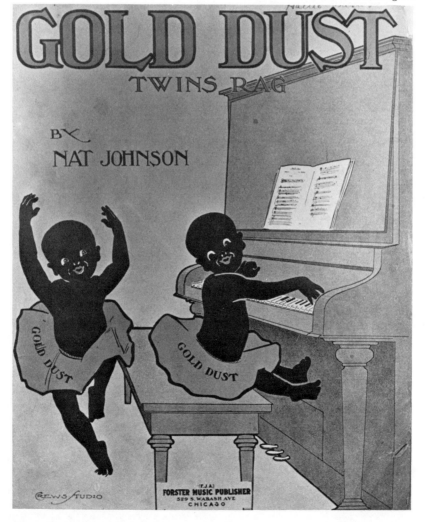

The Baltimore composer
Julius Lenzberg in 1911

Sid Le Protti, legendary Barbary Coast performer and composer of
Canadian Capers, in Berkeley, California at his shoeshine parlor, 1920

another one which was called *The New Russian Rag.*

Throughout these imaginative years, the Folk rags were still being written and published in the small towns, and the Joplin school was well represented by James Scott and Joseph Lamb. The Advanced rag writers were no longer writing for the at-home amateur pianist, as were the Popular rag composers, but were writing for themselves and for other professional performers. Consequently, the Advanced rag was not only harmonically advanced, but was more difficult to play than the preceding Popular rag.

It was around 1913 that a revolution in producing player piano rolls took place. This was the advent of hand-played rolls. Before then all rolls were created by technicians who read music scores and punched out the notes they wanted on a continuous sheet of paper placed on a table with the piano keyboard marked. In many cases the rolls exactly reproduced the sheet music score. One firm, however, hired a brilliant arranger to enrich the plain, unadorned sound. When pumping alone in a living room or parlor, a full, rich series of sounds would make the pumping seem worthwhile. U. S. Music Rolls employed Mary (Mae) Brown, the most gifted arranger of mechanical cut popular rolls.

Two outstanding player-artists in these years created certain rags which are found only on rolls. These rags were never published or recorded on disc, and many were never even copyrighted. The men were Imperial Industries manager, Charley Straight, and QRS's eventual owner, Max Kortlander.

GEORGE L. COBB

Born: Mexico, New York, August 31, 1886

Died: Brookline, Massachusetts, December 25, 1942

C obb attended the School of Harmony and Composition at Syracuse University in 1905. He won a contest for the best composition in Buffalo. He was a distinguished arranger and composer for the Boston publisher, Walter Jacobs. His rags covered three phases—Popular, Advanced and Novelty. During the teens, he wrote several very popular songs, among them *Are You From Dixie, All Aboard For Dixie Land, Listen to That Dixie Band,* and *Alabama Jubilee.*

Rubber Plant Rag. June 14, 1909. Walter Jacobs, Boston.
Structure: INTRO AA BB A CC
The B section has rapid harmonic rhythm, where the chord changes come quickly, creating a silent-movies aura, foretelling his later extensive music writing for the motion pictures.

Aggravation Rag. March 1, 1910. Walter Jacobs, Boston.
Roll: U.S. Music 63869.
Structure: INTRO AA BB A TRIO-INTRO CC

Canned Corn Rag. March 1, 1910. Bell Music Co., Buffalo, New York.

That Hindu Rag. October 15, 1910. Walter Jacobs, Boston.

Bunny Hug Rag. August 4, 1913. Chas. E. Roat Music Co., Battle Creek, Mich.
Structure: INTRO AA BB A TRIO-INTRO C INTERLUDE C
An interesting rag pointing to the next one which fulfills the promise inherent in this one.

The Midnight Trot. April 5, 1916. Will Rossiter, Chicago.
Recording: Dave Jasen. "Rip-Roarin' Ragtime," Folkways FG-3561, June 17, 1977.
Structure: INTRO AA BB A TRIO-INTRO C A
Perhaps Cobb's best rag, with an inspired trio consisting of extremely adventurous key changes. For example, the second 8 measures in section C, which is in the key of B flat, looks harmonically like this: B flat/B flat/D/D-B_7/E_7/A_7/D-E flat$_7$^{0}/C_7-F_7

Nautical Nonsense. Not copyrighted, but published 1917. Walter Jacobs, Boston.
Structure: INTRO AA BB A CC

Cracked Ice. Not copyrighted, but published 1918. Walter Jacobs, Boston.
Structure: INTRO AA BB A CC

Irish Confetti. Not copyrighted, but published 1918. Walter Jacobs, Boston.
Structure: INTRO AA B A C A

Russian Rag. April 27, 1918. Will Rossiter, Chicago.
Recording: Joe Fingers Carr, Capitol 1311, August, 1950.
Roll: Max Kortlander, QRS 100870.
Structure: INTRO AA BB A TRIO-INTRO C INTERLUDE C
This is the famous adaptation of Rachmaninoff's *Prelude in C Sharp Minor;* it was a hit for many years and the vaudeville virtuoso's favorite.

Feedin' The Kitty. Not copyrighted, but published 1919. Walter Jacobs, Boston.
Structure: INTRO AA BB A CC

Say When. Not copyrighted, but published 1919. Walter Jacobs, Boston.

Stop It. Not copyrighted, but published 1919. Walter Jacobs, Boston.

Water Wagon Blues. Not copyrighted, but published 1919. Walter Jacobs, Boston.

Structure: INTRO AA BB A TRIO-INTRO CC

It is a fine example of humor and prohibition affecting ragtime as the C section quotes *How Dry I Am* in a very effective blues-tinged ragtime style.

Dust 'em Off. Not copyrighted, but published 1920. Walter Jacobs, Boston.

Structure: INTRO AA BB A CC INTERLUDE C

Hop Scotch. Not copyrighted, but published 1921. Walter Jacobs, Boston.

Structure: INTRO AA BB A CC

An ingenious and moving composition. Section A begins as an updated movement through a circle-of-fifths with a chromatic melody line, stressing flatted ninths and fifths with ninth and thirteenth chords. The phrasing and bass movement in B suggests the title. The C section is an inspiration with a wistful blues flavor.

Piano Salad. January 18, 1923. Walter Jacobs, Boston.

Structure: INTRO AA BB A TRIO-INTRO CC

Fine Novelty rag with an especially clever C section.

The New Russian Rag. May 16, 1923. Will Rossiter, Chicago.

Roll: Buck Johnson, Vocalstyle 50409.

Structure: INTRO AA BB A TRIO-INTRO C INTERLUDE C

A more pyrotechnical conception of *Russian Rag,* reflecting musical changes that occurred from the Advanced rag to the Novelty rag:

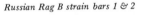

Russian Rag B strain bars 1 & 2

New Russian Rag B strain bars 1 & 2

Chromatic Capers. June 12, 1925. Walter Jacobs, Boston.
Structure: INTRO AA BB A TRIO-INTRO CC INTRO A
Another fine Novelty rag.

Procrastination Rag. June 29, 1927. Walter Jacobs. Boston.
Structure: INTRO AA BB A CC

Piano Sauce. August 13, 1927. Hub Music Co., Boston.

Cubistic Rag. October 14, 1927. Walter Jacobs, Boston.
Structure: INTRO AA BB A TRIO-INTRO CC INTRO-2 A

Snuggle Pup. March 4, 1929. Walter Jacobs, Boston.
Structure: INTRO AA BB AA
Clever Novelty rag taken from *Doll Dance.*

HARRY JENTES

Born: New York, New York, August
28, 1887
Died: New York, New York, January
19, 1958

J entes was a pianist in vaudeville who made a few piano rolls
and gramophone records. He composed such early teen favorites as *Put Me To Sleep With An Old Fashioned Melody, I Don't
Want To Get Well,* and *All By Myself.*

Rhapsody Rag. January 17, 1911. Maurice Shapiro, New York.
Roll: U.S. Music 64765.
Structure: INTRO A BB A TRIO-INTRO CC A

California Sunshine. November 29, 1913. Theron C. Bennett
Co., New York.
Rolls: Harry Jentes, Rhythmodik A7362. Max Kortlander, QRS
100277.
Structure: INTRO A BB INTRO A CC CODA
Only last section is in ragtime.

Soup and Fish Rag (with Pete Wendling). December 11, 1913.
George W. Meyer Music Co., New York.
Structure: INTRO AA B A CC
A wandering labyrinth of strange harmonies. The B strain is an
experiment in chromatic writing. It has a 4-measure sequence
on a previous four, with the same melodic intervals, only one-
half step higher; but in character with the rest of the tune, there
is a clever modulation back to the home key as soon as the
feeling of a new key becomes established.

Bantam Step. February 21, 1916. Shapiro, Bernstein & Co., New York.

Recordings: Conway's Band, Victor 18141, October, 1916, ("Ragtime Entertainment," Folkways RBF-22). Dave Jasen, "Rip-Roarin' Ragtime," Folkways FG-3561, June, 1977.

Roll: Harry Jentes, QRS 100340.

Structure: INTRO AA BB A CC A

One of the most singular Advanced rags. Section A's unusual harmonies achieve a haunting quality, unlike most late rags. His piano roll performance is important because it illustrates how he altered some of the harmonies of the score in performance, and is especially enjoyable because of his great broken bass octave figures which are at variance from the printed score.

Rag-Man-I-Noff. December 19, 1919. Irving Berlin, Inc., New York.

The Cat's Pajamas. January 10, 1923. Jack Mills, Inc., New York.

Recordings: Harry Jentes, Okeh 4850, February, 1923. Harry Jentes, Arto 9221, April, 1923.

Rolls: Harry Jentes, QRS 101023. Harry Jentes, Melodee 204139.

Structure: INTRO AA BB CC INTERLUDE A

The QRS piano roll is one of the most exciting Novelty rag performances of the era.

Tricky Trix. June 13, 1923. Jack Mills, Inc., New York.

Recording: Cecil Norman, (E) Homochord DO-929, 1926.

Structure: INTRO AA BB CC A

Rag-O-Rhythm. May 17, 1924. Harry Jentes Company, New York.

Structure: INTRO AA BB A INTRO CC CODA

PAUL CHARLES PRATT

Born: New Salem, Indiana, November
1, 1890
Died: Indianapolis, Indiana, July 7,
1948

Pratt was a vaudeville pianist who made a few piano rolls under the name Paul Parnell—a name he also used as conductor of musical shows on the road. In December, 1908 he became general manager of J. H. Aufderheide Publishing Co. The firm did well under his direction, and in 1911 he went to Chicago to open a branch office. There he married Beatrice Harcourt. He collaborated briefly with Will Callahan on popular songs. His second wife was Edythe Lee, and they had a daughter, Sharon Gaye. From 1934 until his death he owned and operated the Pratt Photo Studio in Indianapolis. Among his other compositions are *Everybody Tango, 'Mid the Purple Tinted Hills of Tennessee,* and *Dreamy Days of Long Ago.*

Vanity Rag. April 17, 1909. J. H. Aufderheide, Indianapolis.
Recording: Knocky Parker, "Golden Treasury of Ragtime,"
    Audiophile AP-91.
Roll: QRS 30708.
Structure: INTRO AA BB CC A

Colonial Glide. January 13, 1910. J. H. Aufderheide, In-
    dianapolis.
Structure: INTRO AA BB CC INTRO A B
The title reflects the popular dance craze of the teens with its plethora of "glide" tunes. The joke here is a very brief suggestion of the minuet in the introduction which yields to a rag of imagination and skill. The changes come up one measure at a time and are rapid harmonic rhythm for a rag written in 1910. Section A begins on a diminished chord and arrives at the home key thus: A flat⁰/A flat/F₇/B flat minor/B flat₇/E flat₇/A flat.

But the real tour de force occurs in section c: Fm/C/
A flat₇/D₇/D flat₇/Fm/C₇/Fm (it repeats for the last 8 measures).

Walhalla. January 13, 1910. J. H. Aufderheide, Indianapolis.
Structure: INTRO AA BB A CC INTRO-2 B

Hot House Rag. July 27, 1914. Stark Music Co., St. Louis.
Recording: Wally Rose, "Ragtime Piano Masterpieces," Columbia CL-6260 (10″), May 15, 1953.
Roll: Steve Williams (Ernest Stevens), Artempo 1884.
Structure: INTRO A BB TRIO-INTRO CC INTERLUDE A
A truly brilliantly inspired conception by the crack pit-band pianist of Indianapolis. The first two measures of section A anticipate the Novelty rag with its descending octaves broken into a three-eight figure, executed with both hands.

Spring-Time Rag. January 4, 1916. Stark Music Co., St. Louis.
Recordings: Vic Meyers Orch., Brunswick 2630, March, 1924, ("Toe Tappin' Ragtime," Folkways RBF-25). Wally Rose, "Ragtime Classics," Good Time Jazz M-12034, December, 1958.
Roll: Metrostyle 302454.
Structure: INTRO AA BB A C INTERLUDE C
Pratt's most lilting rag, and the finest creative use in ragtime of Mendelssohn's *Spring Song,* a favorite of Tin Pan Alley writers.

On the Rural Route. May 10, 1917. Stark Music Co., St. Louis.
Structure: INTRO AA B INTERLUDE B INTERLUDE TRIO-INTRO CC
INTRO A CODA

Little Bit of Rag. Not copyrighted or published.
Roll: U.S. Music 8005.
This is another rag written solely for piano roll issue. The tremolo effect, which became standard during the twenties, was usually arranged in the middle range of the piano carrying the melody while in the upper treble there were syncopated embellishments. Such rolls were marketed as "saxo-rags," "cello rags" and even "jug band rags." Interestingly, these

arrangements were very much in the style of recorded ragtime group arrangements of the teens. The complex nickelodeon pianos, with xylophone, flute pipes, drums, etc. went one step further in imitating the sound of these early ragtime groups.

Prattles. Not copyrighted or published.
Roll: U.S. Music 7916.

Wailana Rag. Not copyrighted or published.
Roll: U.S. Music 7917.

ARTIE MATTHEWS
Born: Braidwood, Illinois, November
15, 1888
Died: Cincinnati, Ohio, October 25,
1958

Matthews moved to Springfield, where his father's job of sinking shafts for coal mines necessitated travel. Here he took piano lessons from his mother and then from a teacher. He did not learn to read music, but was taught pieces. He first played ragtime around 1905 after he heard Banty Morgan, a dope addict. He played in wine rooms at the back of saloons where women could be found (women were not allowed to stand at bars). He settled in St. Louis around 1908, but traveled frequently to Chicago. There he heard and met Tony Jackson and Jelly Roll Morton. He thought Morton was better than Jackson, and he was, in turn, recalled by Jelly Roll as "the best musician in town" when Jelly visited St. Louis in the teens. He also considered Clarence Jones and Ed Hardin to be outstanding players. He arranged for Stark and wrote much of the music with Tom Turpin for the Booker T. Washington Theatre shows. By now he had not only learned to read music, but was considered the best sight reader of all the pianists in the district. Early in 1913 one of the Starks heard Matthews and offered him fifty dollars for each rag he turned in. Five eventually saw publication, but there had been more. He also arranged and wrote down music for other composers like Thompson *(The Lily Rag)* and Hampton *(Cataract Rag)*. He finally moved to Chicago in 1915, where he played at the Berea Presbyterian Church. At the end of the First World War he was offered the job of organist at the church in Cincinnati. He moved there permanently and in 1921 founded the Cosmopolitan School of Music, a conservatory where blacks could study classical music. He taught there until his death. The five *Pastimes* reveal his milieu in theater work; they are bold and dramatic, extraordinarily pianistic, reflecting the vaudeville side of ragtime, but within the polished Classic rag format. From the perspective of early Classic ragtime, these works are innovations in the idiom. However, some of the devices used in them were probably not new to the more articulate ragtime performers.

Pastime Rag No. 1. August 15, 1913. Stark Music Co., St. Louis.
Recording: Terry Waldo, "Snookums Rag," Dirty Shame 1237, 1974.
Roll: U.S. Music 66071.
Structure: INTRO A BB A TRIO-INTRO C C_1
An exposition of breaks, featured in all three sections. The unusual and delightful A section was bodily stolen by Muriel Pollock for her A section of *Rooster Rag*. Section B is basically a Folk rag-style circle-of-fifths, but here arranged with the finesse characteristic of the composer. C is the climax, with a slurred effect in the right hand which is traded for a walking broken-octave bass pattern in the variation. Those broken octaves hint of the boogie-woogie bass which would be prominently featured throughout the twenties.

Pastime Rag No. 2. Not copyrighted, but published 1913. Stark Music Co., St. Louis.

Recording: Terry Waldo, "Snookums Rag," Dirty Shame 1237, 1974.

Structure: INTRO AA BB CC DD

This was probably used in one of the musical dance routines at the Booker T. Washington Theatre or Princess roadhouse, for which Matthews composed the scores along with Tom Turpin. The A section features a break of chromatic descending triads as does the same section of *No. 1.* The bass line is largely in sixteenths, a variation on the regular ragtime bass pattern of octaves alternating with chords. The rest of the rag is lightly syncopated and suggests dancing. C has a stop-time pattern in which the pianist is instructed to clap hands—a popular performing trick with ragtime pianists.

Pastime Rag No. 3. Not copyrighted, but published 1916. Stark Music Co., St. Louis.

Recording: Paul Lingle, "They Tore My Playhouse Down," Good Time Jazz L-12025, February, 1952.

Roll: George Gershwin, Perfection 86738.

Structure: INTRO AA B A TRIO-INTRO CC DD

A beautiful reflective tango in section A climaxed with syncopated bass octaves. B section is an interlude which complements the mood in the relative minor. C has thickly textured treble chords, rich harmonies and a fine stop-time effect. Section D has a repeated rhythmic figure largely on tonic-dominant harmonies.

Pastime Rag No. 5. Not copyrighted, but published 1918. Stark Music Co., St. Louis.

Recording: Wally Rose, "Live From the Dawn Club," Fairmont 102, August, 1946.

Structure: INTRO AA B A CC DD

A section is a bright tango in the minor mode. Section B employs a mixture of standard Popular ragtime with the bird calls so loved by Scott and Lamb. C section is a development from B using a different minor at the sixth measure. Section D starts off as a variation of *Maple Leaf*'s A section but continues the developmental feeling, beginning with tonic-dominant harmonies, as in sections B and C, but substituting a different idea in measures 6 through 9. It is the most heavily textured of the *Pastimes* and, in the fashion of many late rags, alternates the dotted rhythm with a straight one (here in D), simulating a looser swing (see note on J. Russel Robinson's *Eccentric Rag* for a varied use of this rhythm).

Pastime Rag No. 4. September 15, 1920. Stark Music Co., St. Louis.
Recording: Terry Waldo, "Snookums Rag," Dirty Shame 1237, 1974.
Structure: INTRO AA BB CC
The most advanced of the five, Stark held back on this until the last. Section A is the most arresting by the use of tone clusters —the major and minor seconds adding much dissonance to a basic dominant-tonic harmony. B is dramatically pianistic with a descending series of sixteenths in triplet formation, complemented by the same phrasing in a long chromatic ascending bass run to cap the section. The chromaticism is climaxed in C as the melody rises in half steps from the bass register over a repeated low F pedal tone. Truly an innovative rag.

CHARLES HUBBARD THOMPSON
Born: St. Louis, Missouri, June 19, 1891
Died: St. Louis, Missouri, June 13, 1964

A professional pianist at age twenty in 1911, Thompson teamed with a white player, Rudy Gibson, touring Ohio and Indiana, playing duets and solos. By 1916 he was back in

St. Louis where he entered a mammoth ragtime piano competition lasting eight weeks in which sixty-eight contestants were eliminated before he was declared winner. Shortly thereafter, in a special contest with the Missouri State Champion, Thompson defeated none other than Tom Turpin. Thompson was a solo pianist aboard riverboats and played in such local bands as Charles Creath's Jazz-O-Maniacs and with the Dewey Jackson organization. In 1919, in Toledo, Ohio, he met James P. Johnson, whose unique style influenced his own. A quiet, unassuming musical illiterate, he nonetheless created original and unique rags. His rags are an original blend of late Missouri ragtime and Harlem Stride influences. In true Midwestern style he also had a great flair for the blues, which he preferred up-tempo and mixed with his ragtime licks. He was a "black key player," preferring A flat, D flat and G flat. He abandoned early in his career playing in the easier keys such as C because, as he commented, "you run all over yourself." His playing had a bounce and sprightliness which is to be found nowhere else. After the St. Louis district shut down, he became a chef at the famous Greenbriar resort where his specialty was preparing pheasants and guinea hens. During the Depression he worked as a chef on the Pennsylvania railroad. In October, 1945 he opened his own cafe and ran it until he retired. In the late '50s, Thompson regularly played at the St. Louis Jazz Club. In 1960 he joined oldtimers Eubie Blake and Joe Jordan in Bob Darch's "Reunion in Ragtime" project for Stereoddities.

The Lily Rag. Not copyrighted, but published 1914. Syndicate Music Co., St. Louis.

Recordings: Charles Thompson, American Music 527, August, 1949, ("Piano Ragtime of the Forties," Herwin 403). Tony Parenti's Ragtimers, Circle 1056, January 1949, ("Ragtime," Jazzology J-15).

Roll: U.S. Music 6797.

Structure: INTRO A BB CC CODA

A masterpiece with which he won cutting contests and became the ragtime champion of Missouri. The A section features contrasting syncopations skillfully juxtaposed. Section B is delicate and lyrical. C builds tension with sustained arpeggios on a circle-of-fifths, climaxed by a syncopated bass break in octaves. This break is not in the original score, but was always included by Thompson, at least in his later years.

Delmar Rag. Not copyrighted or published.
Recording: Charles Thompson, American Music 528, August 1949, ("Piano Ragtime of the Forties," Herwin 403).
This is named after a St. Louis street formerly called Morgan Street. The A section is similar to Joe Jordan's *J. J. J. Rag* in its A section. Both Jordan and Thompson credited the idea to Conroy Casey, a St. Louis pianist whom Joplin also admired. This rag also shows the influence of Robert Hampton.

CHARLES LUCKEYTH ROBERTS
Born: Philadelphia, Pennsylvania, August 7, 1887
Died: New York, New York, February 5, 1968

R oberts began his show business career at five years old in Gus Seekes' Pickaninnies, which toured the country in vaudeville. He became an expert tumbler, in addition to being a singer and dancer, and traveled to Europe as part of Mayne Remington's Ethiopian Prodigies. He started learning piano at age five and quickly became New York's premier performer, playing at the Little Savoy Club in 1910. Luckey was unusually short, four feet, ten inches, but had long arms and massive hands that could stretch fourteen keys. He taught James P. Johnson and George Gershwin. Eubie Blake, with the same finger span, quickly became his friend. He studied counterpoint, fugue and composition in private lessons. Roberts wrote musical revues and Broadway shows. He made his first recordings, which were never released, in 1916. He was the first of the Harlem Stride ticklers to be published. He found his niche as an orchestra leader playing for the socialites in Palm Beach, Newport and New York. When the Second World War put an end to the big parties, Luckey purchased a restaurant, the Rendezvous, in Harlem and ran it with singing waiters from 1942 till 1954, when he retired. He recorded solo piano sets in 1946 for Circle Sound and once more in 1958 for Good Time Jazz. He composed special material for radio, stage and screen. His most popular songs include *Rosetime and You, Railroad Blues* and *Moonlight Cocktail,* taken from one section of his rag, *Ripples of the Nile.* His piano roll of *Mo'Lasses* (QRS 2306) is one of the greatest of all hand-played rolls and can be heard on "Parlor Piano," Biograph BLP-1001Q.

The Junk Man Rag. May 26, 1913. Jos. W. Stern & Co., New York.
Recordings: Luckey Roberts, Circle 1026, May, 1946. Fred Van Eps, Columbia A-1417, September, 1913, ("Kings of the Ragtime Banjo," Yazoo L-1044).
Roll: Felix Arndt, Uni-Record 200985.
Structure: INTRO AA B A C INTERLUDE C
One of the most joyous romps in ragtime literature.

Pork and Beans. June 24, 1913. Jos. W. Stern & Co., New York.
Recordings: Luckey Roberts, Circle 1027, May, 1946, ("Piano Ragtime of the Forties," Herwin 403). Earl Fuller's Orch., Columbia A-2370, July 1917, ("Toe Tappin' Ragtime," Folkways RBF-25). Wally Rose, "Blues Over Bodega," Fantasy 5016, 1964.
Roll: U.S. Music 66186.
Structure: INTRO AA B A C D C
Named after a favorite sandwich combination, it is unique and stands out in ragtime literature for its originality. It was the first rag to go back and forth from the minor to the parallel major modes. Between Wally Rose's performance and Luckey's own,

we can hear the difference between printed score (which Wally follows) of a rag and a performance by its creator. That ragtime is mainly a performer's tradition, the Joplin School notwithstanding, is proved, thanks to the recordings of these pioneers.

The Music Box Rag. October 23, 1914. Jos. W. Stern & Co., New York.
Recording: Luckey Roberts, Circle 1027, May 1946.
Roll: Connorized 2890.
Structure: INTRO AA BB A CC CODA
While supposedly an imitation of its name, it clearly illustrates Luckey's melodic flair and skill at writing for musical shows.

Shy and Sly. May 7, 1915. G. Ricordi & Co., New York.
Recording: Luckey Roberts, Circle 1028, May 1946, ("Piano Ragtime of the Forties," Herwin 403).
Structure: INTRO AA BB A CC
Except that the A section closely resembles Charles L. Johnson's *Southern Beauties* B section, this is a great example of taking one idea and fitting perfectly with developing ideas. A well-constructed rag.

Bon Ton. May 7, 1915. G. Ricordi & Co., New York.
Recording: Conway's Band, Victor 17851, August 1915.
Roll: Universal 302037.
Structure: INTRO AA B C INTERLUDE C
An inverted version of *Junk Man Rag.*

Ripples of the Nile. Not copyrighted or published.
Recording: Luckey Roberts, Circle 1028, May 1946.
Only syncopated section is C. A (from which was taken *Moonlight Cocktail*) and B (which develops from A) are ballad-type material.

Nothin'. Not copyrighted or published.
Recording: Luckey Roberts, "Harlem Piano Solos," Good Time Jazz M-12035, March 1958.
A great rag and the last word in cutting contest pieces from around 1908, Roberts dug it out of his archives just for this

recording session. C section is outstanding. The first time through he plays it lyrically punctuated with his famous quick and furious treble runs. The repeat is a whirling stride finish.

JAMES HUBERT (EUBIE) BLAKE
Born: Baltimore, Maryland, February
    7, 1883

From early lessons on the organ (at age six) and piano (at age seven) to the sporting houses where he learned the latest rags as an adolescent, Eubie Blake began to compose rags (*Charleston Rag* in 1899), ballads and waltzes with equal facility and invention. He studied with Margaret Marshall and later with Llewellyn Wilson, and became star attraction in cafes, first in Baltimore, then in Atlantic City. He began his professional career on July 4, 1901 as a dancer and accompanist in a medicine show. Blake met singer and lyricist Noble Sissle on May 15, 1915 at the River View Park in Baltimore. This was the start of a lasting partnership (Sissle died December 17, 1975), as both songwriters and as "The Dixie Duo," headliners in vaudeville. On May 23, 1921 the team had their first Broadway musical produced at the 63rd Street Theatre— *Shuffle Along*. The success of this show gave other black songwriters a chance to write for Broadway. Throughout the twenties and early thirties he wrote for many such shows, both in New York and in London. During World War II he toured with the U.S.O. With the ragtime revival, Eubie has come out of retirement to record (1951, 1958, 1968 and from 1971 on) and perform at ragtime and jazz festivals around the world. He regularly attends the annual Ragtime Society Bash, frequently appears on radio and television, composes new rags, and has formed a record company, Eubie Blake Music, which has produced ten albums so far, and one sheet music folio—"Sincerely, Eubie Blake." An excellent pictorial book on his life was published by Viking Press in 1973 (*Reminiscing with Sissle and Blake,* by Robert Kimball and William Bolcom). Standard popular songs include *I'm Just Wild About Harry, Memories of You,* and *You're Lucky to Me.*

The Chevy Chase. October 28, 1914. Jos. W. Stern & Co., New
    York.
Recording: Eubie Blake, "The Eighty Six Years Of," Columbia
    C2S 847, December 1968–February 1969.
Roll: Pete Wendling & W.E.D., Rhythmodik B 10652.
Structure: INTRO AA B A TRIO-INTRO CC
The B section breaks away from A with great syncopation:

The high point in this rag is the trio.

Fizz Water. October 28, 1914. Jos. W. Stern & Co., New York.
Recording: Eubie Blake, "Featuring Ivan Harold Browning,"
    Eubie Blake Music EBM-1, 1971.
Roll: U.S. Music 67230.
Structure: INTRO AA B TRIO-INTRO C INTERLUDE C
Both of these early tunes of Eubie's are in the mold of the popular one-step and foxtrot dance tunes of the teens. This rag has the favorite syncopation of these:

Bugle Call Rag (with Carey Morgan). January 27, 1916. Jos. W. Stern & Co., New York.
Recording: Victor Military Band, Victor 35533, January, 1916.
Roll: Supertone 78323.
Structure: INTRO AA BB A TRIO-INTRO CC AA BB A CODA

Charleston Rag. August 8, 1917. Unpublished until "Sincerely, Eubie Blake," Eubie Blake Music, 1975.
Recordings: Eubie Blake, Emerson 10434, July 1921, ("Black and White Piano Ragtime," Biograph BLP-12047). Eubie Blake, "Rags to Classics," Eubie Blake Music EBM-2, July, 1971.
Roll: Eubie Blake, Ampico 54174, ("Eubie Blake Volume 1, Biograph BLP-1011Q).
Structure: INTRO A B A TRIO-INTRO C INTERLUDE C
One of the uniquely original rags and one of the most important in the entire repertoire. No part of it was ever used by anyone, including Eubie, who has reused others of his work much as Mozart did. This major work is brilliantly inspired. An interesting feature is that all of the lettered sections are 32 measures long, instead of the traditional 16. The walking bass in combination with the ambitious syncopation in the A section was truly innovative in 1899, when he composed it.

Baltimore Todolo. October 29, 1962. "Sincerely, Eubie Blake," Eubie Blake Music, 1975.
Recording: Eubie Blake, "The Eighty-Six Years Of," Columbia C2S 847.
Structure: A B A TRIO-INTRO CC A CODA
Composed circa 1910.

Brittwood Rag. September 11, 1962. "Sincerely, Eubie Blake," Eubie Blake Music, 1975.
Recordings: Eubie Blake, "The Eighty-Six Years Of," Columbia C2S 847. Dave Jasen, "Fingerbustin' Ragtime," Blue Goose 3001.
Structure: INTRO A BB CC INTRO A
Composed circa 1911. When slowed down, it becomes a beautiful ballad.

Dicty's on Seventh Avenue. July 24, 1962. "Giants of Ragtime," Edward B. Marks Music Corp., 1971.
Recording: Eubie Blake, "Featuring Ivan Harold Browning," Eubie Blake Music EBM-1, 1971.

Kitchen Tom. October 20, 1962. "Sincerely, Eubie Blake," Eubie Blake Music, 1975.
Recording: Eubie Blake, "The Eighty-Six Years Of," Columbia C2S 847.
Composed circa 1905. The third strain is one Eubie heard played by an Atlantic City pianist. Such folk strains survive because of Eubie's adaptation of these to his own style and tunes. He also did this when he cut pop blues rolls in the twenties (see "Eubie Blake, 1921," Biograph BLP-1012Q).

Melodic Rag. January 3, 1972. Unpublished.
Recording: Eubie Blake, "Featuring Ivan Harold Browning," Eubie Blake Music EBM-1, 1971.
Composed in October, 1971 to furnish himself with new material to perform at the annual Ragtime Society Bash. This is one of his most sensitive and lyrical ragtime conceptions.

Novelty Rag. January 3, 1972. Unpublished.
Recording: Eubie Blake, "Featuring Ivan Harold Browning," Eubie Blake Music EBM-1, 1971.
A complex rag in the Novelty idiom originally conceived in the twenties.

Poor Jimmy Green. October 13, 1969. "Sincerely, Eubie Blake," Eubie Blake Music, 1975.
Recording: Eubie Blake, "The Eighty-Six Years Of," Columbia C2S 847.

Poor Katie Red (Eubie's Slow Drag). August 18, 1960. "Sincerely, Eubie Blake," Eubie Blake Music, 1975.
Recording: Eubie Blake, "The Eighty-Six Years Of," Columbia C2S 847.
Eubie remarked that the A section was a folk melody played in St. Louis around the turn of this century, and indeed it is: it is

his adaptation of the notorious *St. Louis Tickle* strain (see Theron Bennett).

Rhapsody in Ragtime. March 6, 1973. "Sincerely, Eubie Blake," Eubie Blake Music, 1975.
Recording: Eubie Blake, "Live Concert," Eubie Blake Music EBM-5, May 22, 1973.
Roll: Eubie Blake, QRS CEL-123, 1973.

Tricky Fingers. October 14, 1959. "Giants of Ragtime," Edward B. Marks Music Corp., 1971.
Recording: Eubie Blake, "The Eighty-Six Years Of," Columbia C2S 847.

Troublesome Ivories (also known as "Ragtime Rag"). May 14, 1971. "Giants of Ragtime," Edward B. Marks Music Corp., 1971.
Recording: Eubie Blake, "The Eighty-Six Years Of," Columbia C2S 847.
Roll: Eubie Blake, QRS CEL-124, 1973.
This has a favorite Blake bass pattern:

and also one of his favorite tricks done on a diminished chord to punctuate a phrase:

CHARLES T. STRAIGHT
Born: Chicago, Illinois, January 16, 1891
Died: Chicago, Illinois, September 21, 1940

He completed Wendell Philips High School and then entered Vaudeville with Gene Greene, composing such songs as *King of the Bungaloos* and *Mocking Bird Rag*. Straight made recordings accompanying Greene. He became musical director of Imperial Player Roll Company and made many rolls. At the same time, he also performed for rival QRS as arranger-composer-artist. He led his own orchestra from 1920, appearing in nightclubs and hotels, and made Paramount and Brunswick recordings with them. Outstanding pianist and arranger of pop tunes and rags.

Humpty Dumpty. January 13, 1914. M. Witmark & Sons, New York.
Recording: Victor Military Band, Victor 35419, October, 1914.
Roll: Charley Straight, QRS 100137.
Structure: INTRO AA BB A TRIO-INTRO C A

Let's Go. December 30, 1915. Jerome H. Remick & Co., New York.
Roll: Charley Straight, QRS 100204.
Structure: INTRO A B A TRIO-INTRO C A

Red Raven Rag. December 30, 1915. Jerome H. Remick & Co., New York.
Recording: Prince's Band, Columbia A-5826, July, 1916.
Roll: Charley Straight, QRS 100270.
Structure: INTRO AA BB A CC

Hot Hands. February 16, 1916. Jerome H. Remick & Co., New York.
Roll: Charley Straight, QRS 100223.
Structure: INTRO AA BB CC A
A comparison of the score with the piano roll performance reveals how many rag scores are compromises for the commercial market. The melody in the published version is voiced mainly in harmonic thirds, fifths and sixths. The bass is the usual octave-chord structure. The roll, on the other hand, has the melody voiced in octaves with their harmony notes for a richer texture. The bass features tenths and alternates with the Midwestern Folk rag device of octaves with a moving added note which gives the performance a slightly funky sound.

Sweet Pickin's Rag. April 30, 1918. Forster Music Publisher, Chicago.
Rolls: Charley Straight, Imperial 510740, August 1917, Universal 303375.
Structure: INTRO AA BB A C A

The Blue Grass Rag. November 11, 1918. Joe Morris Music Co., New York.
Structure: INTRO AA BB A CC
A fascinating rag reflecting the composer's ingenuity.

Black Jack Rag. Not copyrighted or published.
Roll: Charley Straight, QRS 100705, November 1917.

A Dippy Ditty. Not copyrighted or published.
Roll: Charley Straight, Imperial 511770, April 1918.

Fastep. Not copyrighted or published.
Roll: Charley Straight, Imperial 511560, February 1918.

Itsit. Not copyrighted or published.
Roll: Charley Straight, QRS 100600.

Knice and Knifty (with Roy Bargy). (See Roy Bargy.)

Lazy Bones. Not copyrighted or published.
Roll: Charley Straight, QRS 100500.

Mitinice. Not copyrighted or published.
Roll: Charley Straight, QRS 100475.

Mow 'em Down (with Rube Bennett). Not copyrighted or published.
Roll: Charley Straight, Imperial 511940, June 1918.

Nifty Nonsense. Not copyrighted or published.
Roll: Charley Straight, Imperial 511510, January 1918.

Out Steppin'. Not copyrighted or published.
Rolls: Charley Straight, QRS 100650. Charley Straight, Imperial 510000, May 1917.

Playmor. Not copyrighted or published.
Roll: Charley Straight, QRS 100571.

Rag-A-Bit. Not copyrighted or published.
Roll: Charley Straight, Imperial 511760, March 1918.

Rufenreddy (with Roy Bargy). (See Roy Bargy.)

S'more. Not copyrighted or published.
Roll: Charley Straight, QRS 100409.
This performance highlights one of his favorite bass patterns:

In the *Music Trade Indicator* of June 7, 1919, he was referred to as the man "who is putting pep into piano rolls."

Try Me. Not copyrighted or published.
Roll: Charley Straight, QRS 100406.

Universal Rag (with McKay). Not copyrighted or published.
Roll: Charley Straight, QRS 100801.
He had an infectious swing on his early QRS Autograph rolls
that added great style and personality to the tunes he performed on that series. The B section has a characteristic descending treble figure that he loved to use. It breaks up a chord
into the pattern of a single note followed by an harmonic
interval of a third, fourth, etc.:

MAX KORTLANDER

Born: Grand Rapids, Michigan, Sep-
    tember 1, 1890
Died: New York, New York, October
    11, 1961

Upon finishing high school, Kortlander enrolled at Oberlin
Conservatory for specialized music courses and at the
American Conservatory in Chicago for piano lessons. In 1916,
he joined QRS as roll artist and arranger. Thoroughly ab-
sorbed in making rolls, his most famous pseudonym was Ted
Baxter (although all rolls credited to "Ted Baxter" are not
necessarily by Kortlander). Kortlander became president of
QRS in 1931 and owned it until his death.

Blue Clover. June 18, 1920. Jack Mills, Inc., New York.
Roll: Max Kortlander, QRS 100879.

Deuces Wild. November 17, 1923. Jack Mills, Inc., New York.
Roll: Max Kortlander, QRS 100836.
His most innovative rag; an asymmetrical effect is achieved by repeating the motive of the introduction as the first two measures of section A. At first it sounds like an extended introduction, but as the motive reappears again and again, at the middle of the A strain and at repeats of A, the idea lends the performance a seamless effect.

Funeral Rag. Not copyrighted or published.
Roll: Max Kortlander, QRS 100306.
A spirit antithetical to ragtime is nevertheless transformed into a fairly successful rag. It is based on Chopin's *Funeral March.*

Hunting the Ball Rag. June 12, 1922. Unpublished.
Roll: Max Kortlander, QRS 100470.

Let's Try It. Not copyrighted or published.
Roll: Max Kortlander, QRS 100660.

Li'l Joe. Not copyrighted or published.
Roll: Max Kortlander, QRS 100706.

Red Clover. October 17, 1923. Jack Mills, Inc., New York.
Roll: Max Kortlander, QRS 100874.

Shimmie Shoes. October 17, 1923. Jack Mills, Inc., New York.
Roll: Max Kortlander, QRS 100847.
Many of the Kortlander rolls were created for dancing the one-step and foxtrot. They are brilliant pianistic conceptions whether they are lightly syncopated dance tunes, or the more heavily syncopated rags selected here. An interesting feature is that nearly all end with a repeat of section A.

OTHER IMPORTANT RAGS

Agitation Rag. Robert Hampton. January 10, 1915. Stark
    Music Co., St. Louis.
Recording: Bill Mitchell, "Ragtime Recycled." Ethelyn 1750, 1972.
Roll: Dave Kaplan, Artempo 3027.
Structure: INTRO AA BB A CC DD
The D section has a treble figure that became a favorite in
Stride ragtime later:

Alabama Jigger. Edward B. Claypoole. January 28, 1913. Jos.
    W. Stern & Co., New York.
Recording: Max Morath & his Original Rag Quartet, "The Best
    of Scott Joplin," Vanguard VSD 39/40. 1967.
Roll: U.S. Music 63934.
Structure: INTRO AA BB A CC CODA

The Bell Hop Rag. Frederick M. Bryan. December 30, 1914.
    Jos. W. Stern & Co., New York.
Roll: QRS 31943.
Structure: INTRO AA BB A TRIO-INTRO CC D C

Billikin Rag. E. J. Stark. February 21, 1913. Stark Music Co.,
    St. Louis.
Structure: AA BB A C INTERLUDE C
Named after the St. Louis University basketball team, which
was in turn named after a coach who bore a marked resemblance to the traditional good luck doll called "Billiken," which
Stark used on the cover. Section A features an unusual chromatic descent that lasts for three measures.

Black and Blue Rag. Hal G. Nichols. January 2, 1914. Sam Fox
    Publishing Co., Cleveland.
Roll: U.S. Music 66370.
Structure: INTRO A BB A CC INTERLUDE C

Blame It on the Blues. Charles L. Cooke, March 3, 1914, Jerome H. Remick & Co., New York.

Recordings: Victor Military Band, Victor 17764, April, 1915. Paul Lingle, "They Tore My Playhouse Down," Good Time Jazz L-12025, 1952. Dave Jasen, "Rompin' Stompin' Ragtime," Blue Goose 3002, April, 1974.

Rolls: U.S. Music 66403. Arthur Prescott. Perfection 86437.

Structure: INTRO AA BB A TRIO-INTRO CC

One of the most inspired and original of these later rags, without the composer's resorting to odd harmonies or dissonances. He became famous during the twenties when he recorded as Doc Cook & His Dreamland Orchestra. He was one of the few black musicians who obtained the degree of Doctor of Music. He graduated from the Chicago Musical College.

Blaze Away. Mike Bernard. Not copyrighted or published.

Recording: Mike Bernard, Columbia A-2577, April 1918, ("Ragtime Piano Originals," Folkways RBF-23).

Bone Head Blues. Leo Gordon. Not copyrighted, but published 1917. Walter Jacobs, Boston.

Structure: INTRO AA BB A C INTERLUDE C

Some of the silent movie music issued by Jacobs are excellent original rags with frequently daring and involved harmonies. This one begins section A with a startling dissonance of augmented chords cleverly worked out over a standard dominant seventh in the bass:

Bugs Rag. Nina B. Kohler. January 22, 1913. NBK, Sherman, Texas.

Roll: QRS 66099.

Structure: INTRO AA BB A C INTERLUDE A CODA

Cactus Rag. Lucian Porter Gibson, May 10, 1916. Stark Music
Co., St. Louis.
Structure: AA BB A TRIO-INTRO CC

Calico Rag. Nat Johnson. October 19, 1914. Forster Music
Publisher, Chicago.
Recording: Vera Guilaroff, Pathe 21178, July 1926, ("Ragtime
Piano Interpretations," Folkways RBF-24).
Roll: Nat Johnson, QRS 100193.
Structure: INTRO A B A C A

Canadian Capers. Henry Cohen, Gus Chandler & Bert White.
March 26, 1915. Roger Graham, Chicago.
Recording: Jimmy O'Keefe, Puritan 11066, ("Ragtime Piano In-
terpretations," Folkways RBF-24).
Roll: Henry Cohen, Wurlitzer 50090.
Structure: INTRO AA BB A TRIO-INTRO C INTERLUDE C
An interesting rag, it is part of a much larger work by San
Franciscan pianist Sid Le Protti. Cohen happened to hear Le
Protti doing his specialty in a saloon, requested him to play it
over many times during the next few weeks and tipped him a
couple of dollars each time it was requested. Cohen wrote out
that portion of the piece he wanted and got Chandler and
White to write the lyrics. It has become one of the ragtime
favorites of this period.

Carolina Fox Trot. Will H. Vodery. July 7, 1914. Jos. W. Stern
& Co., New York.
Recording: Victor Military Band, Victor 35415, October 1914.
Roll: QRS 31619.
Structure: INTRO AA BB A C DD
Vodery was an accomplished composer and arranger who
knew Scott Joplin in New York City. This tune is one of the first
published in the Stride style and has the same feeling as found
in the earliest of Luckey Roberts' rags. The A section is remark-
ably similar to the corresponding section of James P. Johnson's
Carolina Shout.

Castle House Rag. James Reese Europe. March 9, 1914. Jos. W. Stern & Co., New York.

Recording: Wally Rose, "Ragtime Piano Masterpieces," Columbia CL-6260 (10"), May 15, 1953.

Roll: Oscar Lifshey, Rhythmodik B-8873.

Structure: INTRO AA BB A TRIO-INTRO C INTERLUDE ½C

Named after the famous dance team of the teens and their most famous teaching place. Section A is interesting in that it begins in C minor but ends up in C major. Section C is an inventive stop-time melody.

Cataract Rag. Robert Hampton. July 27, 1914. Stark Music Co., St. Louis.

Recordings: Hitch's Happy Harmonists, Gennett 5633, January 1925. Ralph Sutton, Down Home 7, November 1949, ("Backroom Piano," Verve MGV-4).

Roll: "Steve Williams" (Ernest Stevens), Artempo 1863.

Structure: INTRO A BB CC D EE CODA

The masterpiece of the virtuosic late-St. Louis style in ragtime. It has an intricate structure characterized by quick sixteenth-note movements in octaves and dramatic ascending and descending arpeggios in thirty-second note triplets, descriptive of a waterfall. Charley Thompson, Hampton's contemporary, recalled that the composer's performance was even more complex than the score—containing more "fill-ins."

Checkerboard Rag. Elijah W. Jimerson. Not copyrighted, but published 1914. Syndicate Music Co., St. Louis.

Roll: QRS 32548.

Structure: INTRO AA BB A C D

Chromatic Rag. Will Held. March 10, 1916. Stark Music Co., St. Louis.

Recording: Ralph Sutton, Down Home 8, November, 1949, ("Backroom Piano," Verve MGV-4).

Roll: U.S. Music 67906.

Structure: INTRO AA BB A TRIO-INTRO CC DD C

The chromaticism is both harmonic and melodic. Section A features long chromatic runs. By contrast, the fine trio is extremely lyrical.

Clover Club. Felix Arndt. May 9, 1918. Sam Fox Pub Co., Cleveland.
Rolls: Felix Arndt, QRS 100814. Felix Arndt, Uni-Record 201989.
Structure: INTRO A B ½A CC A
A fine rag with Novelty-style breaks by an early piano roll artist and composer of *Nola*—the most popular of the non-rag Novelties.

Cradle Rock. Abe Frankl and Phil Kornheiser. August 11, 1916. Leo Feist, New York.
Roll: Charley Straight, QRS 100503.
Structure: INTRO VAMP A VAMP A BB VAMP A VAMP A C INTERLUDE C
Section A is a genuine down-home blues over a repeated bass pattern marked "Cradle":

Cute and Pretty. Melville Morris. September 26, 1917. Jerome H. Remick & Co., New York.
Structure: INTRO AA BB A TRIO-INTRO CC AA

The Dainty Foot Glide. G. M. Tidd. February 16, 1915. G. M. T. Lancaster, Ohio.
Structure: INTRO AA BB CC A

Delirium Tremens Rag. Frank Henri Klickman. January 20, 1913. Harold Rossiter, Chicago.
Roll: U.S. Music 65944.
Structure: INTRO AA BB A C INTERLUDE C

Doctor Brown. Fred Irvin. October 27, 1914. Jerome H. Remick & Co., New York.
Roll: Charley Straight, QRS 100214.

Structure: INTRO A B A CC A

Whimsical, unforgettable early foxtrot. The A section is ingenious as it has the feeling of two melodies being played at once in the right hand:

Section B has the characteristic atmosphere of the Stride style.

Dynamite, A Noisy Rag. Paul Biese and F. Henri Klickman. September 18, 1913. Will Rossiter, Chicago.
Roll: Supertone 863340.
Structure: INTRO AA BB A CC BB

Floating Along. Henry Fredericks. August 8, 1914. McKinley Music Co., Chicago.
Structure: INTRO A BB CC A
A strain is the same as its counterpart in William Tyers' *Maori.*

Fred Heltman's Rag. Fred Heltman. February 16, 1918. Fred Heltman Co., Cleveland.
Recording: Joe "Fingers" Carr, Capitol 2834, August 1953, (recorded as *Riviera Rag*).
Structure: INTRO AA BB A C INTRO A
A fine pianistic rag by Cleveland's leading ragtime composer-performer who was also one of the all too few rag composers who cut rolls of their own compositions (Heltman for QRS Autograph series).

Georgia Grind. Ford T. Dabney. March 12, 1915. Jos. W. Stern & Co., New York.
Recordings: Signor Grinderino, Victor 17884, October 1915, ("Ragtime Entertainment," Folkways RBF-22). Trebor Jay Tichenor, "The St. Louis Ragtimers," Paseo DF-102.

Roll: QRS 32253.
Structure: INTRO AA BB A CC INTRO-2 A CODA
The "Grind" was usually a slow blues, but as done here is a beautiful rag equally effective taken at a fast or slow tempo. The Victor recording is a street-piano or hurdy-gurdy roll recording which captures a mood of bygone urban life (see comment for Turpin's *Bowery Buck*).

Gulbransen Rag. Herb Willet. Not copyrighted or published.
Roll: U.S. Music 66036.
C section is like Aufderheide's A section of *Dusty Rag.*

Harry Fox Trot. Lew Pollack. June 12, 1918. Maurice Richmond, New York.
Roll: Archie Stephens, Perfection 87270.
Structure: INTRO AA B A TRIO-INTRO C A CODA

Hot Off the Griddle. James White. December 31, 1915. Frank K. Root & Co., Chicago.
Roll: Starr 9291.
Structure: INTRO AA BB TRIO-INTRO CC
The composer was also known as "Slap Rags" in vaudeville.

Hungarian Rag. Julius Lenzberg. June 26, 1913. Jerome H. Remick & Co., New York.
Recording: Conway's Band, Victor 17392, July 1913, ("Ragtime Entertainment," Folkways RBF-22).
Roll: W. Arlington. Connorized 10340.
Structure: INTRO AA BB TRIO-INTRO C INTERLUDE C
A superb example of ragging the classics. This one owes its inspiration to Franz Liszt (1811–86).

Hysterics Rag. Paul Biese and F. Henri Klickman. December 23, 1914. Jerome H. Remick & Co., New York.
Recordings: First Life Guards Band, (E) Edison Bell Winner 3104, June, 1916. Parenti's Ragtimers, Circle 1029, November 1947, ("Ragtime," Jazzology 15).
Structure: INTRO AA BB A TRIO-INTRO C INTERLUDE C

Jinx Rag. Lucian Porter Gibson. December 7, 1911. Lucian P.
    Gibson, St. Louis.
Roll: Connorized 4598.
Structure: INTRO AA BB A TRIO-INTRO CC A
Named after a famous cartoon, this was originally published by
the composer. However, it was later published by Stark in a
much more complex version, arranged by Artie Matthews. A
comparison between the two is fascinating and demonstrates
how Matthews' skill turned a mediocre rag into an interesting
one:

The B section is stolen from Joe Jordan's *That Teasin' Rag.*

Just Blue. F. Wheeler Wadsworth and Victor Arden. Septem-
    ber 21, 1918. McCarthy & Fisher, Inc., New York.
Roll: Victor Arden & W. E. D., Rhythmodik F-19663.
Structure: INTRO AA BB A C
Still another variation on the blues-rag pattern, this one has
12-measure strains, but does not have the blues changes as one
might expect. Section C is 24 measures. Tonal color is achieved
by the use of the lowered sixth (sometimes called the raised
fifth) chord, a popular device in many of the rags called "blues"
(here A flat in the key of C). The composer was one of the most

brilliant pop pianists and was the partner of Phil Ohman—together they were the most popular piano duo of the twenties. Arden made dozens of fine piano rolls for QRS and others.

Key Stone Rag. Willie Anderson. Not copyrighted, but published 1921. Stark Music Co., St. Louis.
Structure: INTRO AA BB A CC
Named after a popular hotel in the St. Louis sporting belt, this is a beautiful, melodic rag of the end of St. Louis ragtime and one of Stark's last publications.

Meadow Lark Rag. Tom Pitts. Not copyrighted, but published 1916. Charles N. Daniels Music Pub., San Francisco.
Recording: John Arpin, "The Other Side of Ragtime," Scroll LSCR-103, April 19, 1966.
Roll: U.S. Music 7998.
Structure: INTRO AA BB TRIO-INTRO CC A B
The most delicate, subtle and pianistic of all the bird-call rags, performed masterfully by John Arpin.

Meteor Rag. Arthur C. Morse. Not copyrighted, but published 1920. Walter Jacobs, Boston.
Recording: Dave Jasen, "Rip-Roarin' Ragtime," Folkways FG-3561. June, 1977.
Roll: Columbia 95129.
Structure: INTRO AA B A CC
An excellent rag with a most optimistic A section. However, section B is sparked by an extended descent of syncopated chromatic chords.

Muslin Rag. Mel B. Kaufman. December 16, 1918. Forster Music Publisher, Chicago.
Recording: Prince's Band, Columbia A-6084, November 1918.
Roll: Universal 303403.
A fine rag by a leading composer of dance tunes during the teens specializing in one-steps. The B section has a bizarre ending which sounds like a silent movie accompaniment to a scene of sudden mayhem. The Columbia recording uses a slide whistle to heighten the effect.

Operatic Rag. Julius Lenzberg. October 27, 1914. Jerome H.
  Remick & Co., New York.
Recording: Joseph Moskowitz, Victor 17978, February 1916.
Roll: Universal 23393.
Structure: INTRO AA BB INTERLUDE C INTERLUDE C

Oriental Blues. Jack Newlon. May 25, 1933. Jack Newlon Pub.
  Co., Glenside, Pa.
Recordings: Tony De Simone Trio, Decca 29183. Tony De Si-
  mone, Epic 9059.
Structure: INTRO AA$_1$B AA$_1$CC D AA$_1$
Television comedian Ernie Kovacs used the Decca recording as
his theme song. The A section was skillfully taken from its
counterpart of the Gershwin-Donaldson *Rialto Ripples Rag.*
The introduction is surely the happiest of all introductions.
This very late rag was arranged by pop songwriter Billy James.

Rag-A-Muffin Rag. Will T. Pierson. October 3, 1913. Sam Fox
  Pub. Co., Cleveland.
Recording: Victor Military Band, Victor 17619, April 1914.
Roll: U.S. Music 66231.
Structure: INTRO AA BB A TRIO-INTRO CC INTERLUDE C

Ragging the Scale. Edward B. Claypoole, April 2, 1915,
  Broadway Music Corp., New York.
Recording: Joe "Fingers" Carr, Capitol 15727, September 1951,
  ("The Black & White Rag," Capitol ST-11303).
Roll: Charley Straight, QRS 100263.
Structure: INTRO AA BB A C INTERLUDE C
One of the most popular rag hits of this era, it has a clever use
of syncopated scale patterns. The trio is the highlight in which
the scale ascends then descends as a whole-note melody while
the rest of the right hand executes a syncopated "fill-in" figure.

The Raggy Fox Trot. Laurence E. Goffin. October 20, 1915.
  Jerome H. Remick & Co., New York.
Structure: INTRO AA BB A TRIO-INTRO C INTERLUDE C
A good and clever rag and includes some very early tricks
which would later be used in the Novelty rags of the twenties.

Rooster Rag. Muriel Pollock. February 26, 1917. Jos. W. Stern & Co., New York.

Recordings: Wally Rose, "Ragtime Piano Masterpieces." Columbia CL-6260 (10"). Max Morath, "The Ragtime Women," Vanguard VSD-79402, 1977.

Roll: U.S. Music 68429.

Structure: INTRO A BB A C

S.O.S. (Musician's Distress). K. W. Bradshaw and Joe McGrade. Not copyrighted but published 1919. Stark Music Co., St. Louis.

Roll: Keynote.

Structure: INTRO AA BB A CC INTERLUDE C

Perhaps the title reflected the oncoming change in popular music taste. The highlight is the experimental trio harmony.

Shave 'em Dry. Sam Wishnuff. May 10, 1917. Stark Music Co., St. Louis.

Roll: Musicnote 1080.

Structure: INTRO AA BB TRIO-INTRO C DD BB

A characteristic late rag mixture (one section is straight blues), very pianistic, with the three-over-four device featuring Novelty-style breaks.

Smiles and Chuckles. Frank Henri Klickman. October 8, 1917. Frank K. Root & Co. Chicago.

Recording: Six Brown Brothers, Victor 18385, May 1917, ("Ragtime Entertainment," Folkways RBF-22).

Roll: Supertone.

Structure: INTRO AA BB A TRIO-INTRO C INTERLUDE C

Klickman's main vocation was as an arranger for several publishers, although he composed many pieces. As a side line, he was the arranger for the Zez Confrey Orchestra recordings on Victor.

Snappin' Turtle Rag. Charles L. Cooke. October 27, 1913. Jerome H. Remick & Co., New York.

Roll: QRS 31389.

Structure: INTRO AA BB A TRIO-INTRO CC INTERLUDE B

The title is descriptive of the grace note used again and again here:

Such Is Life. Charles L. Cooke. December 30, 1915. Jerome
　　H. Remick & Co., New York.
Roll: U.S. Music 7816.
Structure: INTRO AA BB A CC

Talk of the Town. Elijah W. Jimerson and Marietta Cranston.
　　Not copyrighted, but published 1919. Syndicate Music
　　Co., St. Louis.
Structure: INTRO A BB CC INTRO A
A late hybrid containing a blues strain as its B section.

That's a Plenty. Lew Pollack. February 25, 1914. Joe Morris
　　Music Co., New York.
Recording: Joe "Fingers" Carr and Ira Ironstrings, "Together
　　for the Last Time, Vol. 1," Warner Bros. W-1389, 1960.
Roll: Metrostyle Themodist 301228.
Structure: INTRO AA BB A₁ C INTERLUDE C
The title reflects the popularity of *Too Much Mustard.* Television comedian Jackie Gleason used this as his "And awaaaay we go" traveling music. Although it started out as a rag, it is now a permanent part of the Dixieland repertoire. An interesting and dramatic feature is the variation on A which changes four quarter-note octaves into triplets:

Tiddle-De-Winks. Melville Morris. September 16, 1916. Jerome H. Remick & Co., New York.
Roll: Universal.
Structure: INTRO AA B A CC INTRO A
This rag uses the parallel minor (see Robert's *Pork & Beans;* Lodge's *Temptation Rag*).

Tom and Jerry Rag. Jerry Cammack. Not copyrighted, but published 1917. Stark Music Co., St. Louis.
Structure: AA BB A CC INTERLUDE AA
He was a professional musician who began his career as a ragtime pianist but who later did most of his keyboard work on the organ for circuses. This rag was written in 1906 when he was living in Marion, Indiana, where he had heard Scott Joplin demonstrating his rags on a sidewalk piano in 1903.

Too Much Raspberry. Sydney K. Russell. September 6, 1916. Charles N. Daniels, San Francisco.
Recording: Dave Jasen, "Rip-Roarin' Ragtime." Folkways FG-3561, June 1977.
Structure: INTRO AA BB TRIO-INTRO CC A
A very fine rag with unusual left hand in the A section. This is perhaps the most successful rag using unexpected harmonies which retains a cohesiveness despite its harmonic wanderings (e.g. C-E-A flat$_7$-C-A$_7$-D$_7$-G$_7$-C).

Torpedo Rag. George Oscar Young. June 5, 1917. Daniels & Wilson, San Francisco.
Structure: INTRO AA BB A CC
A rather difficult, heavily textured rag abounding in treble octaves, triplet breaks, and chromatic harmonies. The composer later recorded with the Georgia Melodians for Edison.

Triangle Jazz Blues. Irwin P. Leclere. February 21, 1917. Triangle Music Publishing Company, New Orleans.
Recordings: Wally Rose, "Ragtime Piano Masterpieces," Columbia CL-6260 (10"), May 15, 1953. Dave Jasen, "Rompin' Stompin' Ragtime," Blue Goose 3002, April 1974.
Roll: Max Kortlander, QRS 100631.
Structure: INTRO A B C

A great and very original conception of late ragtime (all sections contain 16 measures) with much jazz coloration—flatted thirds, breaks, slurs, minor seconds. Named after a theater in New Orleans where the composer performed in vaudeville, it was also the name of his publishing company.

Trilby Rag. Carey Morgan. May 11, 1915. Jos. W. Stern & Co., New York.
Recording: Wally Rose, "Ragtime Piano Masterpieces," Columbia CL-6260 (10″), May 15, 1953.
Roll: Gertrude Baum, Perfection 86508.
Structure: INTRO A B A C INTERLUDE C
An inspired rag written with a strong one-step feeling. The trio has a blues quality which is perhaps why it attracted Charles "Cow Cow" Davenport, a blues pianist who transformed it into *Atlanta Rag* and *Texas Shout* (claiming composer credit with each retitling). This transformation idea was a later Folk rag development that involved popular published rags, or parts thereof, being turned into Folk rag performances.

Whoa! Nellie. George Gould. June 4, 1925. Sherman, Clay & Co., San Francisco.
Recording: Paul Whiteman Orch., Victor 19641, September 1924.
Roll: QRS 32214.
Structure: INTRO A BB A C D C D
This is typical of many Advanced rags which are expansive and expressive, making more demands on the performer by enlarging on, but retaining a basically older rag style and flavor. The D section is pure joy.

Wild Flower Rag. Clarence Williams. August 21, 1916. Clarence Williams Music Pub. Co., New Orleans.
Recordings: Clarence Williams, Okeh 8604, July 1928 ("Piano Ragtime of the Teens, Twenties & Thirties," Herwin 402). Clarence Williams & Orch., QRS 7033, November 1928.
Roll: Kimball 7143.
Structure: INTRO AA BB A C D
His only rag and, according to Mrs. Williams (Eva Taylor), this was James P. Johnson's favorite rag.

∼6∼
Novelty Ragtime 1918-1928

Novelty piano ragtime was the product of American pianists with classical music training who originally arranged and performed popular songs on piano rolls. The idea was developed from those hand-played piano roll artists who were ordered to make full, rich arrangements so the player roll customers felt they had gotten their money's worth. Using their piano roll tricks, they put together an extremely complex rhythmic and harmonic series of progressions which demanded the greatest technical skill to perform. Just as the Advanced ragtime composers were ignoring the at-home amateur pianists, the Novelty pianists similarly put forth their efforts for themselves as special material. The big surprise, then, was the astounding hit made by Zez Confrey's warm-up exercise, *Kitten on the Keys,* which, like Joplin's *Maple Leaf Rag,* established and maintained this latest development of ragtime. Decidedly not dance music, *Kitten on the Keys* in some strange fashion appealed to the piano-playing public which avidly bought the sheet music, piano rolls and recordings. It is among the top three rags in the number of recordings made. The pattern of the Novelty rag follows the Popular rag—each has three sections. The distinctive sound of the Novelty rag is a combination of the influence of the French Impressionists—Claude Debussey and Maurice Ravel—with contrasting rhythms as used by the roll arrangers. Chromaticism is at the heart of the Novelty tradition, and the use of the whole-tone scale may have evolved from this, as it appears within the chromatic scale: in a sequence of ascending chromatic major thirds the top note of every other interval forms the whole-tone scale. Probably the most striking hallmark of Novelty writing is the use of consecutive fourths in the melody voicing.

The two publishers who consistently published and urged this new ragtime on the public were both named Jack—Mills and Robbins. It was Jack Mills who was first given the opportunity to introduce the Novelty rag to the public when he was told about the extraordinary musician at QRS who had produced an amazing roll and who had newly recorded it for the Brunswick label. And so on July 8, 1921 Jack Mills issued Confrey's *Kitten on the Keys*. Within the year, it had sold over a million copies and became the prototype for all that was to follow throughout the 1920s. Mills didn't present *Kitten* or the five other Confrey rags as either rags or popular music. Instead, he proudly presented them printed in stately grey with black rococo borders, as classical pieces.

St. Louis was the center of ragtime at the beginning of this century, but Chicago took over with the advent of the Novelty rag. The two leading piano roll companies, QRS and Imperial, had their offices and factories there. The two leading recording companies, Victor Talking Machine Company and Columbia Graphophone, had recording studios there, as well as the fledgling Brunswick-Balke-Collander Company, the experimental Autograph, and the on-the-move Okeh Record Company.

The Novelty rag's appearance coincided with the growth of the record industry. This is why so many rags appear only on recordings, performed by their composers. The industry was now in the million-dollar category and could afford the high priced vaudeville talent, and pianists began recording substantially.

The same could now be said of the player piano rolls, for it was during the twenties that the peak was reached in the manufacture of rolls. Therefore, it is no surprise that we find many great Novelty rags appearing only on piano rolls, played mostly by their composers.

EDWARD ELZEAR
(ZEZ) CONFREY

Born: Peru, Illinois, April 3, 1895
Died: Lakewood, New Jersey, Novem-
      ber 22, 1971

Zez was the youngest of five children born to Thomas J. and
Margaret Brown Confrey. When he was four, his eldest
brother Jim (who played seven instruments) was taking piano
lessons. After one of the lessons, Zez toddled over to the
piano and picked out the same piece Jim was being taught.
Lessons for precocious Zez began soon after. While attending
LaSalle-Peru High School, he played in and conducted his own
orchestra. As a senior, he played piano on the Chicago river
steamboats. After graduation, he went to study at the famous
Chicago Musical College with Jesse Dunn and Frank Denhart.
Here Zez was exposed to the French Impressionists who had
a profound influence on him and which his compositions were
to reflect. In 1915 he obtained a job demonstrating music for
the Chicago branch of the Harry Von Tilzer Music Publishing
Company. His first pieces were songs (*On the Banks of Dear Old
Illinois*), one-steps (*Over the Top*) and a revolutionary rag (*My
Pet*) which combined the Impressionist harmonies with the
rhythmic complexities of the roll arrangements in a ragtime
format. With *My Pet,* he achieved that which established Scott
Joplin nineteen years earlier. At the start of World War I, he
enlisted in the Navy and was featured in a skit with a touring
show, *Leave It To the Sailors.* Part of the routine featured Zez and
a violinist from Waukegan who eventually became known as
Jack Benny. When the show broke up, Zez auditioned for the
QRS piano roll company. Since both he and the company were
in Chicago, he was hired as pianist and arranger. Earlier, he

had a taste of rollmaking when he cut his first roll for the rival Imperial Player Roll Company *(Over the Top,* Imperial 511340). During his stay with QRS, he played and arranged 123 rolls. His arrangements were consistently tasteful and filled with inspiration. His success in making rolls and composing hit tunes led him into recording (piano solos for Brunswick, Edison and Emerson, playing with an orchestra for Victor), and appearing in vaudeville. During 1922 he composed three popular songs which further stimulated demand for his services *(Stumbling, Tricks* and *Dumbell).* The following year Mills published his phenomenally successful book, *Modern Novelty Piano Solos,* a folio still in print as late as the 1960s. On February 12, 1924 Zez participated as soloist in the historic concert at Aeolian Hall. It was billed as "Paul Whiteman and his Palais Royal Orchestra will offer an Experiment in Modern Music, assisted by Zez Confrey and George Gershwin." Later that year, he was to make rolls exclusively for Ampico. As popular music was turning more and more to jazz bands—at first small combos and then large orchestras—he turned to composition as his chief source of enjoyment and financial security. His compositions ranged from his complex Novelty rags to concert studies, miniature operas, popular songs, mood pieces and simple children's works for beginners. He retired from active composing after the Second World War. He was a victim of Parkinson's disease.

My Pet. March 11, 1921. Jack Mills Inc., New York.
Recordings: Zez Confrey, Brunswick 2082, February 1921, ("Zez Confrey, Creator of the Novelty Rag," Folkways RBF-28). Sidney Williams, Vocalion 15691, April 1928, ("Ragtime Piano Interpretations," Folkways RBF-24).
Roll: Zez Confrey, QRS 100827, July 1918, ("Zez Confrey, Creator of the Novelty Rag," Folkways RBF-28).
Structure: INTRO AA B INTRO A B TRIO-INTRO C INTRO-2 D
This is Confrey's first essay in what was to become the Novelty ragtime idiom. As we know, ragtime's ebullient feelings are obtained compositionally in the major tonality. Consider then Confrey's innovation of starting the first section in a minor

mode, but with feelings that are happy and bright. In its final printed form, it appears as a rag in four sections (illustrated above). However, in the roll version, we find five sections. He dropped the original fourth section when printed and in all recordings on disc. A unique rag and the first in the Novelty ragtime style.

Kitten on the Keys. March 11, 1921. Jack Mills Inc., New York.
Recordings: Zez Confrey, Brunswick 2082, February 1921, ("Zez Confrey, Creator of the Novelty Rag," Folkways RBF-28). Bill Krenz, MGM 30706, June 1952, ("Oh Willie, Play That Thing," MGM E-184 [10"]).
Roll: Zez Confrey, QRS 101003.
Structure: INTRO VAMP AA BB INTRO VAMP A TRIO-INTRO CC
This is the *Maple Leaf Rag* of the Novelty rags. An instantaneous success, it spawned dozens of imitators. The basic ingredient is that ragtime cliché, the "three-over-four" pattern, but instead of single notes Confrey harmonizes and creates partial dissonance with the pattern in the right hand of an augmented fourth, a third and then a single note against the steady, even duple rhythm of the left hand. To insure the proper kitten-on-the-keys effect, Confrey said of the third section, "Be sure to scramble up the octaves in the part which is supposed to sound like a cat bouncing down the keyboard. In other words, make a fist when simulating the cat running up and down, otherwise it won't sound real." The B section is a beauty. Confrey usually managed to have a ballad-like section, one which stressed melody, in at least one section of his rags.

You Tell 'em Ivories. July 19, 1921. Jack Mills Inc., New York.
Recording: Zez Confrey, Brunswick 2112, ("Zez Confrey, Creator of the Novelty Rag," Folkways RBF-28).
Structure: INTRO AA BB A TRIO-INTRO CC
A section begins with a sweeping, cheerful melodic line largely in consecutive fourths which creates a faintly mysterious atmosphere. Section B fulfills that mysterious promise with the forthright bunch of triplets we found in *Kitten*. C section combines the rhythmic contrasts of the first two sections giving a sense of completion.

Poor Buttermilk. July 22, 1921. Jack Mills Inc., New York.
Recording: Zez Confrey, Brunswick 2112 ("Zez Confrey, Creator of the Novelty Rag," Folkways RBF-28).
Structure: INTRO VAMP AA INTRO-2 BB INTRO-1 VAMP A TRIO-INTRO C
Structurally akin to *Kitten,* it is more like *Ivories* in mood. The mysterious mood is more pronounced as the introduction and A section are both in the minor mode. Section B is probably the most rhythmically complex of anything found in Novelty rags. An exotic and very typical Confrey sound here results from a series of ninth chords built on augmented triads, descending in intervals of a minor third. Section C harks back to Joplin's flag-waving endings but in the Novelty style. The ending is a rhythmic surprise.

Greenwich Witch. August 4, 1921. Jack Mills Inc., New York.
Recording: Zez Confrey, Brunswick 2167, January 1922, ("Zez Confrey, Creator of the Novelty Rag," Folkways RBF-28).
Roll: Zez Confrey, QRS 101022.
Structure: INTRO AA BB INTRO A TRIO-INTRO CC
A charming inversion of *Kitten,* it has its own distinctiveness. Section B cements its relationship to the more famous piece, but uses the groupings in a rhythmic accent rather than melodically. C section is another flag-waver, but highlights the melody rather than the rhythm.

Stumbling Paraphrase. July 1, 1922. Leo Feist Inc., New York.
Structure: INTRO A BB BB
A brilliant Novelty rag version of his song replete with the complex breaks found in the best rags.

Coaxing the Piano. March 6, 1922. Jack Mills Inc., New York.
Recordings: Zez Confrey, Brunswick 2167, January 1922, ("Zez Confrey, Creator of the Novelty Rag," Folkways RBF-28). Willie Eckstein, Pathe 20944, March 1923, ("Ragtime Piano Interpretations," Folkways RBF-24). Bill Krenz, MGM 11264, June 1952, ("Oh Willie, Play That Thing," MGM E-184 [10"]).

Structure: INTRO AA BB A TRIO-INTRO CC

Yet another variation of *Kitten.* Rhythmically more complex than *Witch,* it is also more melodic in its way. B section is unusual in that the melody is in the left hand. Altogether a first rate rag filled with inventive figures.

Nickel in the Slot. April 6, 1923. Leo Feist Inc., New York.

Recordings: Zez Confrey & Orch., Victor 19430, July 1924, ("Zez Confrey, Creator of the Novelty Rag," Folkways RBF-28). Willie Eckstein, Okeh 40018, November 1923, ("Ragtime Piano Interpretations," Folkways RBF-24). Dave Jasen, "Rompin' Stompin' Ragtime," Blue Goose 3002, April 1974.

Structure: INTRO AA BB A CC

A brilliant Novelty rag which imitates the Nickelodeon—an automated player piano machine—which frequently breaks down. The third section is the beauty with a marvelous break.

Dizzy Fingers. November 17, 1923. Jack Mills Inc., New York.

Recording: Muriel Pollock & Vee Lawnhurst, Decca 164, ("Ragtime Piano Interpretations," Folkways RBF-24).

Roll: Zez Confrey, Ampico 65581F.

Structure: VAMP A B VAMP A CC VAMP A

Confrey's second big hit; the amateur players fell all over themselves learning it.

African Suite (Mississippi Shivers, High Hattin', Kinda Careless.) July 16, 1924. Jack Mills Inc., New York.

Recording of *Mississippi Shivers:* Zez Confrey & Orch., Victor 19430, July 1924, ("Zez Confrey, Creator of the Novelty Rag," Folkways RBF-28). Sidney Williams, Gennett 6353, June 1927.

Structure of *Mississippi Shivers:* VAMP AA BB TRIO-INTRO CC

The suite consists of three Novelty rags, only the first of which has been recorded. It is also the most versatile, as it incorporates the blues with an early Romantic period flavor, and a popular ballad into the Novelty rag framework.

Humorestless. March 12, 1925. Jack Mills Inc., New York.
Recording: Zez Confrey & Orch., Victor 19606, November 1924, ("Zez Confrey, Creator of the Novelty Rag," Folkways RBF-28).
Roll: Zez Confrey, Ampico 64381F.
Structure: INTRO A B C D INTERLUDE B
Ragging the classics but in the Novelty idiom. This time Dvorak's famous *Humoresque* gets the Novelty treatment. Section D, in fact, puts *Humoresque* in counterpoint with *Swanee River.*

Jay Walk. February 12, 1927. Jack Mills Inc., New York.
Roll: Zez Confrey, Ampico 66821F, ("Zez Confrey, Creator of the Novelty Rag," Folkways RBF-28).
Structure: INTRO A B A TRIO-INTRO C LAST-1/3-OF-B A
A rollicking Novelty rag showing further refinements in the art of composition mainly with the various ways to use triplets in syncopation.

Jack in the Box. December 30, 1927. Jack Mills Inc., New York.
Recording: Arthur Schutt, Harmony 860, January 1928.
Structure: INTRO VAMP A BB A CC A
Confrey's imitation musically of the children's Jack-in-the-box toy. Lightly syncopated, it achieved popularity with the home piano players.

Smart Alec. December 27, 1933. Mills Music Inc., New York.
Structure: INTRO AA B C B A
Written ten years after *Dizzy Fingers,* it is in that same tradition and a puzzler for the student going through several Novelty patterns.

Giddy Ditty. October 24, 1935. Exclusive Publications Inc., New York.
Structure: INTRO AA INTERLUDE INTERLUDE AA BB AA
Confrey's last Novelty rag, very melodic, yet not without pitfalls. More swingy, jazzy, but with those syncopated triplets and unusual harmonies.

ROY FREDRICK BARGY

Born: Newaygo, Michigan, July 31,
1894
Died: Vista, California, January 16,
1974

Bargy grew up in Toledo, Ohio where, at the age of five, he started piano lessons. He wanted to be a concert pianist but realized at seventeen that unless he studied in Europe there would be no opportunity for such a career in this country. He hung around the district in Toledo listening to such black pianists as Johnny Walters and Luckey Roberts, started making good money playing piano and organ for silent movies and formed his own dance orchestra. Through a friend who did artwork for Imperial Player Rolls, he auditioned for Charley Straight in 1919 and in September of that year worked at Imperial full time for more than a year. His main job at Imperial was to edit the popular song rolls. Occasionally he was asked to arrange and play some himself, as well as to compose and record one Novelty rag a month. He collaborated on two with Charley Straight, who introduced him to booking agent Edgar Benson. Benson formed a band to record for the Victor Talking Machine Company and hired Bargy as pianist, arranger and director. *Ma* (Victor 18819) and *Say It While Dancing* (Victor 18938) feature him at the piano and serve to illustrate his fine abilities as arranger. He joined Isham Jones and his Orchestra in the same capacity and toured the country with them for two years. During this time, the band recorded for Brunswick and *The Original Charleston* offers a superb piano solo by Bargy (Brunswick 2970, also available on "The Dancing Twenties," Folkways RBF-27). Bargy began a twelve-year stint with Paul Whiteman, who had the greatest dance orchestra of all, in February, 1928 as solo pianist, arranger and assistant conductor. He went into radio as conductor-arranger for the Lanny

Ross Show and in 1943 he became musical director for Jimmy Durante, an association which was to last twenty years, until both of them retired.

A distinctive Bargy device was the extensive use of the "break" —a musical interruption of the melody—incorporating it as part of his melodic line. Famous ragtime artist-composer-pianist Jelly Roll Morton (see chapter 8) specifically pointed out the advantages of using breaks as a performance device. Bargy uses it as a compositional device, integrating it as part of the melodic conception. For freshness, he always used new and rhythmically different breaks throughout his rags, never boring the listener by using the same breaks over and over.

Rufenreddy (with Charley Straight). November 14, 1921. Sam Fox Publishing Co., Cleveland.
Recordings: Roy Bargy, Victor 19320, March 1924, ("Roy Bargy Piano Syncopations," Folkways RBF-35). Henry Lange, Brunswick 2344, September 1922, ("Ragtime Piano Interpretations," Folkways RBF-24).
Rolls: Charley Straight, Imperial 511360. Roy Bargy, Melodee 204027. Roy Bargy, Ampico 68641.
Structure: INTRO A BB A CC
A great Novelty rag, this turned out to compete with QRS rival Zez Confrey's. Straight and Bargy were fine pianists and roll arrangers who created rags which were not imitative of Confrey but were distinctive in themselves.

Slipova. November 14, 1921. Sam Fox Music Publishing Co., Cleveland.
Recordings: Frank Banta-Cliff Hess, Okeh 4825, April 1923, ("Ragtime Piano Interpretations," Folkways RBF-24). Patricia Rossborough, (E) Parlophone R-1599, 1933.
Rolls: Roy Bargy, Imperial 513070, May 1920. Roy Bargy, Melodee 203999, October 1922, ("Roy Bargy Piano Syncopations," Folkways RBF-35).
Structure: INTRO AA BB TRIO-INTRO CC INTRO AA
This marvelous rag incorporates several novelty embellishments, used by the more imaginative arrangers in rolls, in the melody proper. A sheer delight.

Knice and Knifty (with Charley Straight). February 7, 1922. Sam Fox Publishing Co. Cleveland.

Recordings: Roy Bargy, Victor 18969, August 1922, ("Roy Bargy Piano Syncopations," Folkways RBF-35). Willie Eckstein, Pathe 20944, March 1923, ("Black and White Piano Ragtime," Biograph BLP-12047).

Rolls: Charley Straight, Imperial 512260. Roy Bargy, Melodee 204039, ("Roy Bargy Piano Syncopations," Folkways RBF-35).

Structure: INTRO A BB A CC

Another great rag with an outstanding C section.

Sunshine Capers. February 7, 1922. Sam Fox Publishing Co., Cleveland.

Recording: Roy Bargy, Victor 19320, March 1924, ("Roy Bargy Piano Syncopations," Folkways RBF-35).

Rolls: Roy Bargy, Imperial 513080, June 1920, ("Roy Bargy Piano Syncopations," Folkways RBF-35). Roy Bargy, Melodee 204003.

Structure: INTRO AA BB AA CC

Behave Yourself. June 27, 1922. Sam Fox Publishing Co., Cleveland.

Roll: Roy Bargy, Melodee 204043, ("Roy Bargy Piano Syncopations," Folkways RBF-35).

Structure: INTRO AA BB TRIO-INTRO CC INTRO A

Jim Jams. June 27, 1922. Sam Fox Publishing Co., Cleveland.

Recordings: Roy Bargy, Victor 19537, March 1924, ("Roy Bargy Piano Syncopations," Folkways RBF-35). Ray Turner, Capitol 15437.

Rolls: Roy Bargy, Imperial 513140, July 1920, ("Roy Bargy Piano Syncopations," Folkways RBF-35). Roy Bargy, Melodee 204025.

Structure: INTRO AA BB AA CC AA

Justin-Tyme. June 27, 1922. Sam Fox Publishing Co., Cleveland.

Recording: Roy Bargy, Victor 19537, March 1924, ("Roy Bargy Piano Syncopations," Folkways RBF-35).

Rolls: Roy Bargy, Imperial 513800. Roy Bargy, Melodee 204045, ("Roy Bargy Piano Syncopations," Folkways RBF-35).

Structure: INTRO AA BB TRIO-INTRO CC DD

Pianoflage. June 27, 1922. Sam Fox Publishing Co., Cleveland.

Recordings: Roy Bargy, Victor 18969, August 1922, ("Roy Bargy Piano Syncopations," Folkways RBF-35). Fate Marable's Orch., Okeh 40113, March 1924, ("Toe-Tappin' Ragtime," Folkways RBF-25). Ray Turner, Capitol 2094, March 1952, ("Piano Ragtime of the Fifties," Herwin 404).

Rolls: Roy Bargy, Imperial 513130, August 1920. Roy Bargy, Melodee 204047, ("Roy Bargy Piano Syncopations," Folkways RBF-35). Roy Bargy, Ampico 68751.

Structure: INTRO AA BB TRIO-INTRO CC INTRO AA
Probably the finest of the Bargy rags.

Sweet and Tender. April 17, 1923. Will Rossiter, Chicago.

Recording: Dave Jasen, "Rip-Roarin' Ragtime," Folkways FG-3561, June, 1977.

Roll: Roy Bargy, Imperial 512980, ("Roy Bargy Piano Syncopations," Folkways RBF-35).

Structure: INTRO AA BB TRIO-INTRO CC INTRO A

A Blue Streak. Not copyrighted or published.

Roll: Roy Bargy, Imperial 513600, ("Roy Bargy Piano Syncopations," Folkways RBF-35).

A highlight is the great A section which is sparked by an ascending walking bass which leads to an exciting tremolo.

Ditto. Not copyrighted or published.

Roll: Roy Bargy, Imperial 513000, ("Roy Bargy Piano Syncopations," Folkways RBF-35).

Omeomy. Not copyrighted or published.

Roll: Roy Bargy, Imperial 513980, ("Roy Bargy Piano Syncopations," Folkways RBF-35).

The A section is the reverse of *Pianoflage* and, like that great rag, is quite a remarkable achievement of composition. A pity it was never written down and published.

RUBE BLOOM

Born: New York, New York, April 24, 1902
Died: New York, New York, March 30, 1976

Bloom went to public school in Brooklyn, New York, which he left at age seventeen to become an accompanist for vaudeville stars. He was entirely self-taught, composed directly at the piano, memorized it and then got someone else to write it down for publication. An extraordinarily fine pianist, he was in great demand for recording work, as a soloist, accompanist (especially for Jane Gray on Harmony) and in dance and jazz bands. Over the years he recorded with Bix Beiderbecke, Miff Mole, Frankie Trumbauer, the Dorsey Brothers, Red Nichols, Ethel Waters and Noble Sissle. His own group was called Rube Bloom and His Bayou Boys. In 1928 he won the first prize of $5,000 in the Victor Talking Machine Company's contest for his composition, *Song of the Bayou.* His songwriting career included such hits as *Give Me the Simple Life, Penthouse Serenade, Big Man From the South, Truckin!, Stay on the Right Side, Sister* and *Fools Rush In.* Although he never studied counterpoint, harmony or composition, he wrote several piano method books and was a much sought-after arranger of hit songs for various publishers.

That Futuristic Rag. April 9, 1923. Jack Mills Inc., New York. *Recording:* Rube Bloom, Okeh 41073, February 1928, ("Ragtime Piano Originals," Folkways RBF-23).
Structure: INTRO VAMP A BB TRIO-INTRO CC

Incredibly fine and, indeed, futuristic. He predicted that a distinctive national school of music was being born in the United States.

Spring Fever. June 21, 1926. Triangle Music Publishing Co., New York.
Recordings: Rube Bloom, Harmony 164-H, March 1926. Rube Bloom, Cameo 1153, April 1927, ("Black & White Piano Ragtime," Biograph BLP-12047). Dave Jasen, "Rompin' Stompin' Ragtime," Blue Goose 3002, April 1974.
Structure: INTRO A BB A TRIO-INTRO CC CODA
A brilliant original, one of the most ebullient Novelty rags with a fine jazz flavor and lyrical flair which requires great technical skill.

Soliloquy. June 21, 1926. Triangle Music Publishing Co., New York.
Recording: Rube Bloom, Harmony 164-H, March 1926.
His most famous Novelty rag, used extensively on radio throughout the next two decades.

Silhouette. May 9, 1927. Triangle Music Publishing Co., New York.
Recording: Rube Bloom, Okeh 40901, September 1927.

Jumping Jack (with Bernie Seaman and Marvin Smolev). July 3, 1928. ABC Standard, New York.
Recording: Varsity Four, Brunswick 4075, September 1928.

Aunt Jemima's Birthday. May 15, 1931. Robbins Music Corp., New York.
Recording: Rube Bloom, Victor 25227, December 1934.

One Finger Joe. May 15, 1931. Robbins Music Corp., New York.
Recording: Rube Bloom, Victor 25227, December 1934.

Southern Charms. May 15, 1931. Robbins Music Corp., New York.

BILLY MAYERL

Born: London, England, May 31, 1902

Died: London, England, March 25, 1959

A child prodigy, Mayerl was the son of an impoverished violinist. Formal training began at age five. He won a scholarship to Trinity College of Music, gave his first concert at age twelve at the Queen's Hall and, after school, played evenings in movie houses accompanying the silent films. In 1920 he had his first work with an orchestra, where he came to the attention of American saxophonist Bert Ralton who quickly hired him, first as band pianist, then as solo pianist with the Savoy Havana Band, where Billy became famous. In 1923 he became involved with the musical theater as pianist, conductor and finally as composer. At the same time, he appeared on the BBC. In 1925 he began his recording career, which lasted almost until his death. In 1927 he started what was to become the most famous and successful undertaking of its kind—the Billy Mayerl School of Music, with branches all over the world. He published his own magazine and taught many thousands of pupils by the correspondence method. This included not only instruction booklets, but recordings as well, where he personally demonstrated the various exercises and effects to be gained. He was a prolific composer with a predilection for naming his works after flowers. His most successful number, which became his theme song, was *Marigold,* followed by *Hollyhock.* While his Novelty rags were called "Syncopated Impressions" and were patterned after Zez Confrey's enormous successes, Mayerl developed his own original phrases, harmonies and rhythmical devices, as well as rich and beautiful melodies. He was probably the finest pianist of all. During the

Second World War he worked for the Light Music Unit of the BBC, broadcasting, recording and composing. He died of a heart attack.

The Jazz Master. August 4, 1925. Keith-Prowse & Co., Ltd., London.
Recording: Billy Mayerl, (E) HMV B-2131, August 1925, ("The Syncopated Impressions of," Folkways RBF-30).
Structure: INTRO AA B A TRIO-INTRO C
A magnificent example of Novelty ragtime at its most complex.

All-of-a-Twist. August 21, 1925. Keith-Prowse & Co., Ltd., London.
Recording: Billy Mayerl, (E) HMV B-2130, August 1925, ("The Syncopated Impressions of," Folkways RBF-30).

Eskimo Shivers. August 21, 1925. Keith-Prowse & Co., Ltd., London.
Recording: Billy Mayerl, (E) HMV B-2130, August 1925, ("The Syncopated Impressions of," Folkways RBF-30).

The Jazz Mistress. September 25, 1925. Keith-Prowse & Co., Ltd., London.
Recording: Billy Mayerl, (E) HMV B-2131, August 1925, ("The Syncopated Impressions of," Folkways RBF-30).

Virginia Creeper. October 12, 1925. Keith-Prowse & Co., Ltd., London.
Recording: Billy Mayerl, (E) HMV B-2203, August 1925, ("The Syncopated Impressions of," Folkways RBF-30).

Jazzaristrix. November 4, 1925. Keith-Prowse & Co., Ltd., London.
Recording: Billy Mayerl, (E) HMV B-2203, August 1925, ("The Syncopated Impressions of," Folkways RBF-30).

Antiquary. March 9, 1926. Keith-Prowse & Co., Ltd., London.
Recording: Billy Mayerl, (E) Columbia 3926, March 1926, ("The Syncopated Impressions of," Folkways RBF-30).

Loose Elbows. March 9, 1926. Keith-Prowse & Co., Ltd., London.
Recording: Billy Mayerl, (E) Columbia 3926, March 1926, ("The Syncopated Impressions of," Folkways RBF-30).

Jack-in-the-Box. July 15, 1926. Keith-Prowse & Co., Ltd., London.
Recording: Billy Mayerl, (E) Columbia 4115, June 1926, ("The Syncopated Impressions of," Folkways RBF-30).

Sleepy Piano. July 15, 1926. Keith-Prowse & Co., Ltd., London.
Recording: Billy Mayerl, (E) Columbia 4115, June 1926, ("The Syncopated Impressions of," Folkways RBF-30).

Puppets Suite (Punch, Judy, Golliwog). June 1, 1927. Keith-Prowse & Co., Ltd., London.
Recordings: Billy Mayerl *(Punch),* (E) Columbia 4677, December 1927. Billy Mayerl *(Judy and Golliwog),* (E) Columbia 4676, December 1927, ("The Syncopated Impressions of," Folkways RBF-30).

Honky Tonk. August 10, 1928. Keith-Prowse & Co., Ltd. London.
Recording: Billy Mayerl, (E) Columbia 5154, October 1928.

Jasmine. August 23, 1929. Keith-Prowse & Co., Ltd., London.
Recording: Billy Mayerl, (E) Columbia 5671, September 1929.

PHILMORE (PHIL) OHMAN

Born: New Britain, Connecticut, Oc-
    tober 7, 1896
Died: Santa Monica, California, Au-
    gust 8, 1954

After high school, Ohman became a piano demonstrator and then assistant organist in New York City. He arranged tunes and composed for QRS piano rolls in 1919 and made tours as accompanist with concert singers. He formed a wildly successful duo piano team with Victor Arden (Lewis J. Fuiks). They were perhaps the best known duo in the business; they made rolls, recordings, were featured in early Gershwin Broadway musicals (as the entire orchestra) and appeared on their own radio show. From 1934 to 1946 Phil led his own orchestra at various restaurants and cafes in Hollywood. A superb pianist who wrote brilliant rags, he employed an interesting compositional device which harked back to the Folk ragtime days—as a help in unifying a rag, he would bring back the last half of the first strain at various points.

Dixie Kisses. Not copyrighted or published.
Roll: Phil Ohman, QRS 100884.
An astounding piano roll performance which features a pyrotechnical break executed in double time and in contrary motion.

Try and Play It. August 5, 1922. Richmond-Robbins Inc., New
    York.
Recording: Arthur Schutt, (E) Regal G-8032, July 1923, ("Ragtime Piano Interpretations," Folkways RBF-24).

Up and Down the Keys. September 30, 1922. Richmond-Robbins Inc., New York.
Recording: Mike Loscalzo, Olympic 1426, December 1921.

Piano Pan. October 10, 1922. Richmond-Robbins Inc., New York.
Structure: INTRO VAMP A B ½A CC INTRO VAMP A

Sparkles. June 12, 1935. Robbins Music Corp., New York.

ARTHUR SCHUTT

ARTHUR SCHUTT
Born: Reading, Pennsylvania, November 21, 1902
Died: San Francisco, California, January 28, 1965

S chutt started his career at age thirteen playing for silent movies. From 1918–24 he was pianist and arranger for Paul Specht's orchestra. He established himself in New York as one of the top pianist-arrangers and was in great demand for recording and radio work. He regularly appeared on disc with such bands as Mike Markel's, Vincent Lopez', The Georgians, Roger Wolfe Kahn's, Fred Rich's, Nat Shilkret's, and he played with such jazz greats as Bix Beiderbecke, Benny Goodman, Red Nichols, Frankie Trumbauer and the Dorseys. During the forties and fifties he worked in Hollywood for the major studios. For the last few years of his life, he was ill and played sporadically.

Syncopating the Scales. November 3, 1922. Jack Mills Inc., New York.

The Ghost of the Piano. March 5, 1923. Jack Mills Inc., New
   York.
Recording: Arthur Schutt, (E) Regal G-8032, July 1923.

Teasing the Ivories. January 18, 1924. Francis, Day & Hunter,
   London.
Recording: Arthur Schutt, (E) Regal G-8046, July 1923.

Bluin' the Black Keys. February 24, 1926. Robbins-Engel Inc.,
   New York.
Structure: INTRO AA BB AA TRIO-INTRO CC

Rambling in Rhythm. November 5, 1927. Jack Mills Inc., New
   York.
Recording: Arthur Schutt, Harmony 860-H, January 1928.

Piano Puzzle. Not copyrighted or published.
Recording: Arthur Schutt, Okeh 41243, March 1929, ("Ragtime
   Piano Originals," Folkways RBF-23).

OTHER IMPORTANT RAGS

The Arm Breaker. Fred Rose. April 7, 1923. Jack Mills Inc.,
   New York.
Recording: Clarence M. Jones & Orch., Okeh 8404, June 1926,
   ("Toe-Tappin' Ragtime," Folkways RBF-25).
Structure: INTRO AA B C INTRO A

Blooie-Blooie. Edythe Baker. Not copyrighted or published.
Roll: Edythe Baker, Universal 203545.
She was one of the most creative piano roll artists. This work
features a striking key change from G to D flat at the trio.

The Boston Trot. Sid Reinherz. Not copyrighted or published.
Recording: Sid Reinherz, Gennett 5330, December 1923,
("Ragtime Piano Originals," Folkways RBF-23).

Bouncing on the Keys. Ed Claypoole. December 31, 1924.
Jack Mills Inc., New York.

Breakin' the Piano. Billy James. May 20, 1922. Jack Mills Inc.,
New York.
Recording: Vee Lawnhurst, Arto 9193, ("Early Ragtime Piano,"
Folkways RBF-33).

Chasing the Fox. J. Louis Merkur. August 4, 1928. Jack Mills
Inc., New York.

Cross Word Puzzle. Charles Olson. March 23, 1925. Jack Mills
Inc., New York.

Crossed Hands. Saul Sieff. November 24, 1925. Villa Moret,
Inc., San Francisco.

Cyclone. Ferde Grofe. April 7, 1923. Jack Mills Inc., New York.

Dancing Tambourine. W. C. Polla. August 4, 1927. Harms
Inc., New York.
Recordings: Pauline Alpert, Victor 21252, November 1927.
Rube Bloom, Okeh 40901, September 1927.

Dog on the Piano. Ted Shapiro. September 5, 1924. Jack Mills
Inc., New York.
Recording: Arcadia Peacock Orch., Okeh 40272, November
1924, ("Toe Tappin' Ragtime," Folkways RBF-25).

The Doll Dance. Nacio Herb Brown. July 6, 1927. Sherman,
Clay & Co., San Francisco.
Recording: Jimmy Andrews, Banner 6116, August 1927, ("Rag-
time Piano Interpretations," Folkways RBF-24).
Roll: Adam Carroll, Ampico 67741-F.
One of the most famous Novelty rags written and the subject
of countless imitations.

Fancy Fingers. Burn Knowles. July 14, 1936. ABC Standard, New York.

Feather Fingers. Claude Lapham. May 14, 1928. Alfred & Co., New York.

Fidgety Fingers. Norman J. Elholm. February 27, 1923. Jack Mills Inc., NY.
Recording: Stanley C. Holt, (E) Homochord H-434, 1923.

Fine Feathers. Larry Briers. Not copyrighted but published in 1923, Jack Mills Inc., New York City.
Recording: Willie Eckstein, Okeh 40076, March 1924, ("Early Ragtime Piano," Folkways RBF-33).

Flapperette. Jesse Greer. February 22, 1926. Jack Mills Inc., New York.
Recording: Harry Reser, (E) Brunswick 01069, October 1930, ("Harry Reser: Banjo Crackerjax," Yazoo L-1048).
Rolls: Max Kortlander, QRS 4068. Roy Bargy, Ampico 68421-B.

Gloria. Fred Hager and Justin Ring. August 10, 1926. Robbins-Engel, Inc. New York.
Recording: Vincent Lopez & Orch., Okeh 4921, August 1923, ("Toe Tappin' Ragtime," Folkways RBF-25).

Hot Fingers. Joe Gold. October 15, 1925. Jack Mills Inc., New York.

Hot Fingers. Robert Marine. June 1, 1928. Robert Marine, Inc., New York.

Hot Ivories. Ray Sinatra. April 11, 1927. Bibo, Bloedon & Lang., New York.

Igloo Stomp. Bill Wirges. January 26, 1927. Alfred & Co., New York.

Jes' Dandy. Joe Solman. March 5, 1923. Jack Mills Inc., New York.

Juggling the Piano. Sam A. Perry. December 1, 1924. Jack Mills Inc., New York.

Keen Kut-Ups. Armand Muth. Not copyrighted or published. *Roll:* Armand Muth, Staff Note 2039.

Keyboard Klassic. Robert Marine. June 1, 1928. Robert Marine, Inc., New York.

Loose Fingers. Stanley C. Holt. May 14, 1923. Lawrence Wright Music Co., London.

Lopeziana. Louis Alter. August 9, 1926. Robbins-Engel, Inc., New York.

Lotta Trix. Robert Marine. June 1, 1928. Robert Marine, Inc., New York.

Mah Jong. Sid Reinherz. March 5, 1924. Jack Mills Inc., New York.
Recording: Sid Reinherz. Gennett 5330, December 1923.

Mel-O-Dee Rag. Harry Stover. Not copyrighted or published. *Roll:* Harry Stover, Melodee 203557.

Mr. Crump's Rag. Jesse Crump. Not copyrighted or published.
Recording: Jesse Crump, Personal Gennett, July 1923, ("Black & White Piano Ragtime," Biograph BLP-12047).

Modulations. Clarence M. Jones. April 17, 1923. Will Rossiter, Chicago.
Recording: Clarence M. Jones, Autograph, January 1923, ("Ragtime Piano Originals," Folkways RBF-23).
A tour de force by one of the few black Novelty writers. He was a thoroughly schooled musician and a popular piano roll artist. Taught famous blues pianist-accompanist James Blythe.

Over the Ice. Bill Wirges. January 26, 1927. Alfred & Co., New York.

Perils of Pauline. Pauline Alpert. June 22, 1927. Jack Mills Inc., New York.

Piano Phun. Louis Alter. November 14, 1925. Robbins-Engel, Inc., New York.

Piano Mania. William Fazioli. May 26, 1922. Jack Mills Inc., New York.

Putting on the Dog. Ted Shapiro. October 17, 1923. Jack Mills Inc., New York.
Recording: Willie Eckstein, Okeh 40121, April 1924.

Racing Down the Black and Whites. Adam Carroll. April 3, 1926. Harms Inc., New York.

Rackety-Rag. J. Milton Delcamp. Not copyrighted or published.
Roll: J. Milton Delcamp, Republic 47708, 1920.

Rag Doll. Nacio Herb Brown. March 20, 1928. Sherman, Clay & Co., San Francisco.
Recording: Edna Fischer, Victor 21384, April 1928, ("Ragtime Piano Interpretations," Folkways RBF-24).
Roll: John Hunnert, Supertone 4159.
An extremely popular follow-up to *Doll Dance*.

Raindrops. Bill Wirges. June 12, 1928. William F. Wirges, New York.

Rhythmic Fantasy. Phil Saltman. February 9, 1929. Denton & Haskins, New York.

Rio de Janeiro. Willard Robison. September 14, 1926. Robbins-Engel, Inc., New York.

Sailing Along Over the Keys. Silvio De Rienzo. March 5, 1928. Bibo, Bloedon & Lang, New York.

Shootin' the Chutes. Larry Briers. March 5, 1924. Jack Mills Inc., New York.

Skidding. Ed Claypoole. April 7, 1923. Jack Mills Inc., New York.

Skipinova. Glen Barton (pseudonym of Harley F. Brocht). May 20, 1926. Jack Mills Inc., New York.

Snow Shoes. Bill Wirges. January 26, 1927. Alfred & Co., New York.

Tek-Nik-Ality Rag. Arnold Johnson. Not copyrighted or published.
Roll: Arnold Johnson, Imperial 512220.

Tenth Interval Rag. Harry Ruby. January 2, 1924. Stark & Cowan Inc., New York.
Recording: Gene Rodemich & Orch., Brunswick 2599, February 1924, ("Toe Tappin' Ragtime," Folkways RBF-25).
Roll: Ted Eastwood, Metro Art 202992.

Town Talk. Elmer Olson. November 27, 1917. E. F. Bickhart's Song Shop, Minneapolis.
Roll: U.S. Music 9100.
Structure: INTRO A B INTRO A C DD
An expansive rag spiced with flatted fifths and major sevenths. The introduction begins with a Confrey-like voicing on an augmented triad.

Up and Down in China. Willard Robison. September 14, 1926. Robbins-Engel Inc., New York.
Recording: Willard Robison, Autograph 601, September 1924.
A sense of the exotic far-off lands pervades much Novelty writing since the idiom coincided with a rage for such pseudo-oriental tunes as *Sahara, Karavan* and *Cairo,* of which Confrey made a specialty during his brilliant series of rolls for QRS in

1919. Native Missourian Robison displays an original flair for such exotica here.

Whipping the Keys. Sam Goold. Not copyrighted but published 1923. Stark & Cowan Inc., New York.
Recording: Sam Goold, Okeh 4850, June 1923, ("Ragtime Piano Originals," Folkways RBF-23).

Wippin' the Ivories. Henry Lange. May 4, 1923. Waterson, Berlin & Snyder Co., New York.

Stride Ragtime

S tride ragtime was the name given to that style created and developed by the black New York ticklers who, when they traveled around the country, wanted to be distinctive and be recognized as the finest in the country.

The word *Stride* means the syncopation alternating between the right and left hands and the counter melodies created by a moving bass line. This was putting a new twist on the regular way to play ragtime—alternating the syncopation between both hands made it twice as difficult to perform, thereby enabling the performers to win contests. It not only sounded harder to do, it was in fact harder to do. And, unlike the rest of ragtime, Stride was conceived by and originally performed solely by black artists.

It was thought to have been created by Luckey Roberts and his pupil Richard (Abba Labba) McLean, but as James P. Johnson pointed out, "I was getting around town and hearing everybody. If they had anything I didn't have, I listened and stole it. . . . I was born with absolute pitch and could catch a key that a player was using and copy it—even Luckey's. . . . In 1914 in Atlantic City, Eubie had a couple of rags. One, *Troublesome Ivories,* was very good. I caught it." And so it was that this giant of the New York scene, James P. Johnson, developed the Stride sound and became the major influence of the great jazz pianists (Willie "The Lion" Smith, Duke Ellington, Count Basie, Fats Waller, Cliff Jackson, Hank Duncan, Joe Sullivan, Teddy Weatherford, Don Lambert, Ralph Sutton, Dick Wellstood, Art Tatum and Thelonious Monk) through his many piano rolls, recordings and live performances in cafes, dance halls and, most of all, at rent parties. And, while Luckey, Eubie and James P.

were composing rags during the teens, it wasn't until 1921 that the Stride sound became definitely established. Stride rags, as composed and performed by these men, were cast in the same mold as the Popular rag. Most of the evidence comes not only from the sheet music, but from some hand-played piano rolls of the teens. In 1921 there was a startling change in performance and, simultaneously, in conception of composition. It seems as though the new Novelty ragtime was an additional challenge to the New Yorkers and they responded.

They viewed their rags, not as polished compositions as Joplin did, but as special material for their exclusive use as performers. As a consequence, most Stride rags were not published. Stride ragtime was a framework upon which they could make changes as various ideas and tricks came to them in the immediacy of performance. As with the Novelty rag, Stride ragtime became a style of playing, as well as a type of composition. The pianists, most of whom did not compose original pieces, learned many of the idiomatic tricks in this style and placed them within pop songs, hymns, marches and even classical compositions. Eubie once said, "I don't play any better than any real pianist, but it's the tricks I know. I know tricks that the average guy don't know. Because I've been playing all this time, I had to play against this guy, that guy—the finest pianists, see?"

Because the performing aspect assumed greater importance, it is essential to listen to the performer playing the same rag at different times to fully appreciate Stride ragtime. And, it is fortunate that the major composer-performers did record their rags at different times during their careers.

Being in New York, the heart of Tin Pan Alley and the Broadway musical, meant that outlets were plentiful. And so it is not surprising to find many of the leading Stride ragtimers also creating hit pop songs and writing scores for musical comedies.

JAMES PRICE JOHNSON

Born: New Brunswick, New Jersey,
    February 1, 1891
Died: Jamaica, New York, November
    17, 1955

Johnson grew up in Jersey City where his mother gave him rudimentary instruction on the piano. Born with perfect pitch, he sampled all types of piano music, taking classical lessons from Professor Bruto Gianinni for four years. In 1908, the family moved to New York City, where he heard the latest styles of playing from performers in cabarets and sporting houses from the South and West. His first professional job was in 1912 at Coney Island. He then played the popular Atlantic City resort in summers and various New York dance halls in the San Juan Hill section and clubs in Harlem during the winters. In 1919 he played in Toledo, Chicago, and other Midwestern cities. Like all top pianists, he had to play in every key. "I would hear tunes and to make sure, go home and 'woodshed' them in every key, put them in major and minor and all the ninth chords." In 1917 he began making piano rolls. They sold so well that he produced them for the next ten years. He began making records in 1921 and stopped in 1947. He became musical director for musical revues, touring the country and making a trip to England early in 1923. Later that year he collaborated on the Broadway musical, *Runnin' Wild,* from which came his popular song hit, *Old Fashioned Love.* Also from that show was a tune which was destined to be forever associated with the "roaring twenties"—the *Charleston.* During the twenties he became the favorite accompanist of blues singers, most notably Ethel Waters and Bessie Smith. Other great tunes of his were *If I Could Be With You,* the outstanding syncopated waltz, *Eccentricity,* and his most popular blues, *Snowy Morning Blues.* During the thirties he devoted his time to composing large works—symphonies, ballet music, operas and rhapsodies. During the forties he recorded, played in bands, took part in the Eddie Condon New York Town Hall concerts, appeared on the Rudi Blesh "This Is Jazz" radio show over the Mutual network, and gave a concert of his classical works with the Brooklyn Symphony Orchestra. His most memorable club date was at the Pied Piper, where he entertained his devoted fans nightly. A second stroke in 1951 made him an invalid for the last four years of his life.

Caprice Rag. Not copyrighted or published.
Recording: James P. Johnson, Blue Note 26, December 1943, ("Piano Ragtime of the Forties," Herwin 403).
Roll: James P. Johnson, Perfection 87023, July 1917, ("1917 Ragtime Vol. 2," Biograph BLP-1009Q).
He preferred a busy single-note melody line in many of his rags, especially his first two *(Caprice* and *Daintiness).* This one is spiced with quick triplets with the traditional octave-chord ragtime bass.

Carolina Balmoral. Not copyrighted or published.
Recording: James P. Johnson, Blue Note 25, November 1943.

Carolina Shout. October 16, 1925. Clarence Williams Music Publishing Co., New York.
Recordings: James P. Johnson, Okeh 4495, October 1921, ("The Father of the Stride Piano," Columbia CL-1780). James P. Johnson, Decca 24885, August 1944. Jimmy Johnson's Jazz Boys, Arto 9096, October 1921, ("Toe Tappin' Ragtime," Folkways RBF-25).
Rolls: James P. Johnson, Artempo 12975, February 1918, ("Parlor Piano Solos 1917–1921," Biograph BLP-1003Q). James P. Johnson, QRS 100999, May 1921, ("Parlor Piano Solos 1917–1921," Biograph BLP-1003Q).
To the East Coast ticklers, this was their *Maple Leaf Rag,* the tune used in all cutting contests. The QRS roll, in fact, was learned note for note by both Fats Waller and Duke Ellington. It was originally written around 1914 for cotillion dancing,

made into a roll in 1918 and recorded on disc in 1921. The A section begins with a descending progression based on a floating folk strain which was adapted and modified by rag composers and jazz musicians alike, most particularly in the respective A strains of *Wild Cherries, Perfect Rag, Buddy's Habits* and *Little Rock Getaway*. The remainder of the rag is built on call-and-response patterns shifting back and forth from treble to bass registers with dramatic syncopations. Like *Maple Leaf Rag,* it is a folk essence finely honed into a definitive masterpiece of its kind. A comparison between the QRS roll and the earlier, stilted Artempo reveals how the characteristic stride sound bloomed only after 1920.

Daintiness Rag. Not copyrighted or published.

Recordings: James P. Johnson, "The Original James P. Johnson," Folkways FJ-2850, July 1942. James P. Johnson, (F) Blue Star 198, June 1947, ("Piano Ragtime of the Forties," Herwin 403).

Roll: James P. Johnson, Universal 203107, July 1917, ("1917 Ragtime Vol. 2," Biograph BLP-1009Q).

Gut Stomp (with Willie "The Lion" Smith). Not copyrighted or published.

Recording: James P. Johnson, Blue Note 24, November 1943.

Harlem Strut. Not copyrighted or published.

Recording: James P. Johnson, Black Swan 2026, September 1921, ("Black & White Piano Ragtime," Biograph BLP-12047).

Roll: James P. Johnson, QRS 101014.

Innovation. Not copyrighted or published.

Roll: James P. Johnson, Universal 203255, October 1917, ("1917 Ragtime Vol. 2," Biograph BLP-1009Q).

Jersey Sweet. Not copyrighted or published.

Recording: James P. Johnson, "The Original James P. Johnson," Folkways FJ-2850, May 2, 1945.

Jingles. July 1, 1926. Clarence Williams Music Publishing Co., New York.

Recordings: James P. Johnson, Brunswick 4762, January 1930. Clarence Williams Orch., Paramount 12587, October 1927.

A great Novelty rag, one of the few written by a black, showing complete mastery of this complex form.

Keep Movin'. Not copyrighted or published.

Recording: James P. Johnson, "The Original James P. Johnson," Folkways FJ-2850, October 16, 1945.

Keep Off the Grass. July 1, 1926. Clarence Williams Music Publishing Co., New York.

Recordings: James P. Johnson, Okeh 4495, October 1921. James P. Johnson, Decca 24883, August 1944.

Mule Walk. Not copyrighted or published.

Recordings: James P. Johnson, "Father of the Stride Piano," Columbia CL-1780, June 14, 1939. James P. Johnson, Blue Note 27, December 1943.

Scoutin' Around. September 18, 1925. Perry Bradford Music Publishing Co., New York.

Recording: James P. Johnson, Okeh 4937, August 1923, ("Piano Ragtime of the Teens, Twenties & Thirties," Herwin 402).

Steeplechase Rag. Not copyrighted or published. Composed around 1914 and recorded as *Over the Bars.*

Recording: James P. Johnson, Decca 24884, August 1944.

Roll: James P. Johnson, Universal 203179, May 1917, ("1917 Ragtime Vol. 2," Biograph BLP-1009Q).

Johnson played this at an extremely fast tempo in the spirit suggested by the titles. The A section in minor has a typical silent-movie air. The driving trio features a favorite climactic stride figure in the treble which is repeated for nearly the entire strain:

Stop It. August 21, 1917. F. B. Haviland Publishing Co., New York.

Roll: James P. Johnson, Universal 203205, August 1917, ("1917 Ragtime Vol. 2," Biograph BLP-1009Q).

This roll has a rhythmic feeling characteristic of much black ragtime playing where subtle syncopations are achieved by the use of suspensions and quarter-note triplets in 4/4 time. Though Johnson favored octaves in the bass, this roll featured tenths with added harmonic notes. He breaks these from the bottom as harmonic fifths, followed by the upper notes. This bass playing along with his treble phrasing created a loose, jangling quality—an intricate texture that suggests the two hands working independently of each other. This feeling of detachment is the key to the more subtle and complex striding syncopations.

Toddlin'. September 18, 1925. Perry Bradford Music Publishing Co., New York.

Recording: James P. Johnson, Okeh 4937, August 1923.

Twilight Rag. Not copyrighted or published.

Recording: James P. Johnson, "The Original James P. Johnson," Folkways FJ-2850, May 2, 1945.

Roll: James P. Johnson, Metro-Art 203274, November 1917, ("1917 Ragtime Vol. 2," Biograph BLP-1009Q).

You've Got to Be Modernistic. November 3, 1933. Clarence Williams Music Publishing Co., New York.

Recording: James P. Johnson, Brunswick 4762, January 1930, ("Early Ragtime Piano," Folkways RBF-33).

THOMAS WRIGHT (FATS) WALLER

Born: New York, New York, May 21, 1904

Died: Kansas City, Kansas, December 15, 1943

Fats was the most well-known of all of the Stride pianists. He made piano rolls, over five hundred records (mostly for RCA-Victor), had his own weekly network radio program, performed in Europe and England, was featured in such motion pictures as *Hooray for Love, King of Burlesque* and *Stormy Weather*. He began piano studies at six, played in a high school orchestra, won a talent contest playing *Carolina Shout,* whereupon he became a protégé of James P. Johnson. This relationship turned into friendship and he became a close companion, with Johnson introducing him to the world of piano rolls (QRS), records, playing at rent parties and becoming resident organist at the Lincoln Theatre in Harlem. He wrote scores to such musical comedies as *Keep Shufflin', Hot Chocolates* and *Early to Bed.* He wrote many other successful pop songs, among them *Squeeze Me, My Fate Is in Your Hands, I've Got a Feeling I'm Falling, Honeysuckle Rose, Blue Turning Grey Over You, Keepin' Out of Mischief Now, I'm Crazy 'Bout My Baby* and *Ain't Misbehavin'.* He spent most of his professional life on the road touring and playing nightclubs throughout this country. He died of pneumonia on a train to New York. In 1966 his manager, Ed Kirkeby, wrote his biography, *Ain't Misbehavin'.*

Wild Cat Blues (with Clarence Williams). September 24, 1923.
Clarence Williams Music Publishing Co., New York.
Recording: Clarence Williams' Blue Five, Okeh 4925, July, 1923.

Roll: Automatic Music Roll A-1418, May 1928, ("Thomas (Fats) Waller Vol. 2," Biograph BLP-1005Q).

Hog Maw Stomp. November 5, 1928. Unpublished.
Recording: Thomas Waller, Victor 21525, February 1927.

Gladyse. December 26, 1929. Southern Music Publishing Co., New York.
Recording: Thomas Waller, Victor V-38554, August 1929.

Valentine Stomp. December 26, 1929. Southern Music Publishing Co., New York.
Recording: Thomas Waller, Victor V-38554, March 1929.
Fats had a predilection for bass tenths and a flair for impeccable voicings. His chords seem to melt into each other. He had an ease in his swing that was incomparable, as well as the most sensitive dynamics of all the Harlem pianists. His mastery is best displayed in this rag which is highlighted in the A section by a flowing descent of eighth note triplets in the right hand —a favorite Waller device.

Harlem Fuss. December 17, 1930. Southern Music Publishing Co., New York.
Recording: "Fats & his Buddies," Victor V-38050, March 1929.

Handful of Keys. December 29, 1930. Southern Music Publishing Co., New York.
Recording: Thomas Waller, Victor V-38508, March 1929.
Waller's tour de force as a cutting contest, rent party piece, matched only by Johnson's *Carolina Shout* and Luckey Roberts' *Nothin'*.

Smashing Thirds. March 23, 1931. Southern Music Publishing Co., New York.
Recording: Thomas Waller, Victor V-38613, September 1929.

African Ripples. April 20, 1931. Joe Davis, Inc., New York.
Recording: Thomas Waller, Victor 24830, November 1934.
A section is the same as the A section of *Gladyse.*

WILLIAM HENRY JOSEPH BONAPARTE BERTHLOFF (WILLIE "THE LION") SMITH

Born: Goshen, New York, November 25, 1897

Died: New York, New York, April 18, 1973

T aught by his mother who played both organ and piano, Willie claimed to have developed his left hand by playing Bach. He started playing in Newark, New Jersey in the early teens. He joined the 350th Field Artillery in November, 1916, saw active service in France where he served with distinction and earned his nickname of "The Lion." He accompanied Mamie Smith on *Crazy Blues,* the first blues record. Throughout the twenties and early thirties, he made many recordings in bands and played nightly as a featured pianist at Pod's and Jerry's in Harlem. With James P. Johnson and Fats Waller, he was a favorite at rent parties. Famed for his red vest, a tilted derby and a cigar clenched at the side of his mouth, he had the highest opinion of himself as a pianist. He toured Europe in the late forties and fifties and appeared in major jazz festivals during the sixties and early seventies. Perhaps he was not the great pianist he thought he was, but his compositions are among the finest written, with an originality that ranks him as a leader. Of all the Harlem composers, he made the most use of bass syncopation. He was not satisfied with just varying the octave-chord accompaniment, but went on to create jagged, restless bass syncopations in more complex patterns than the other composers. In contrast to his usual *fortissimo* stride, he wrote remarkably reflective pieces (e. g. *Echo of Spring*). He won recognition as a composer from such jazz musicians as Duke Ellington, Count Basie and Dizzy Gillespie. He made a two-album set of reminiscences, singing and playing in 1968 ("The Memoirs of Willie the Lion Smith," RCA Victor LSP-6016), and wrote his autobiography with George Hoefer in 1964— *Music On My Mind.*

Keep Your Temper. September 19, 1925. Clearence Williams Music Publishing Co. New York.
Recording: Gulf Coast Seven, Columbia 14107-D, November 1925.

Finger Buster. October 15, 1934. Clarence Williams Music Publishing Co., New York.
Recordings: Willie "The Lion" Smith, Commodore 522, February 1939, ("Piano Ragtime of the Teens, Twenties & Thirties," Herwin 402). Willie "The Lion" Smith, "Original Compositions," Commodore FL 30.003, c. 1950.

Echo of Spring. April 4, 1935. Clarence Williams Music Publishing Co. New York.
Recording: Ralph Sutton, "Ragtime Piano U.S.A.," Roulette 25232, c. 1962.

In the Groove. August 18, 1936. Mills Music Inc., New York.

Sneak Away. August 21, 1937. Mills Music Inc., New York.
Recording: Willie "The Lion" Smith, "Original Compositions," Commodore FL 30.003, c. 1950.

Keep Fingering. March 11, 1938. Mills Music Inc., New York.

Cuttin' Out. Not copyrighted or published.
Recording: Willie "The Lion" Smith, (F) Vogue V-5038, December 1949, ("Willie Smith," Vogue Vol. 56 LD 693–30).

Rippling Waters. Not copyrighted or published.
Recording: Willie "The Lion" Smith, "Original Compositions," Commodore FL 30.003, c. 1950.
This is the final development in ragtime's fascination with moving waters. Hampton's pyrotechnic *Cataract Rag* was an extension of Joplin's more lyrical *Cascades,* with ascending and descending arpeggios in dramatic 32nd-note triplets (in 2/4 time). Here, Willie heightens the effect by introducing syncopated bass chords against a fast-moving, flowing treble melody in the A section.

Famous record company of Rudi Blesh and Harriet Janis

Another rag made exclusively as a piano roll

Cleveland pianist-
teacher-composer-
publisher in 1918

New Orleans composer
Irwin P. Leclere
at 84

liams entertained at the Dunbar Social Club's dance, Pythian Hall, last Monday. Williams sang, "Old Pal" and "Stolen Kisses." Tag introduced his new "Kentucky Soft Shoe Dance" and his "Piano-Jazz Buck."

LUELLA ANDERSON WINS PIANO CONTEST

Miss Luella Anderson was awarded the $200 gold medal and the title of Champion Ragtime Piano player, by the judges, at the Booker Washington Theatre, Thursday night. Miss Anderson competed against the best players in the city. In the grand final Thursday she won 8 points to Leroy Starkey's 6 and Nat Muse's 6. The scores were: Miss Anderson, time 2; variations 0, expression 2, melody 2, steadiness 2. Starkey got nothing on expression and steadiness and Muse failed on time and expression. The contest was an elimination affair and had been in progress for several weeks.

1921 ragtime piano contest reported in the *St. Louis Argus*

Rare first edition
of this popular rag

A ragtime arrangement
of this popular song

Jack Mills, publisher of the Confrey rags

The famous 1921 recording

Original cover of this masterpiece

Advertising Jack Mills Novelty rags on the back cover of his publications

Jack Robbins, New York publisher of Novelty rags

One of the greatest Novelty rags only appearing on a roll

Kansas City virtuoso Edythe Baker in 1920

The first all-ragtime LP

Lou Busch (left), Dave Jasen (center), Trebor Tichenor (right) in October, 1976

Trebor Tichenor's first LP

MISSISSIPPI VALLEY RAGTIME

Trebor Tichenor

Robert Crumb's first album design

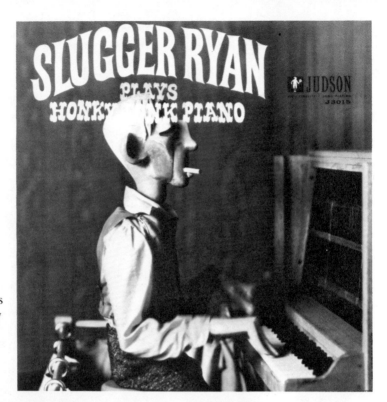

Bil Baird's
TV puppet as
performed by
Dick Hyman

Started the
ragtime revival
in 1971

One of a series of piano roll reissues on LP

THE RagTime Review

Special Issue Summer, 1965   Vol. 4 No. 3A   St. Louis, Mo. Bicentennial

GOLDENROD SHOWBOAT PRESENTS BICENTENNIAL RAGTIME MUSIC FESTIVAL ON ST. LOUIS RIVERFRONT, WEEKEND OF AUGUST 13-15

Musical Greats of the Nation Featured with ''St. Louis Ragtimers'' Band in Nite Performances Fri. & Sat., Matinee Sat., & Special ''On the Levee'' Concert Sun.; Ragtime and Classic Jazz.

Ragtime — the foot-tapping music that flourished under St. Louis leadership during the city's glorious steamboat and turn-of-the-century days — highlights a unique musical treat on the weekend of August 13th through 15th, as an official St. Louis Bicentennial public program on the levee at the Gateway Arch.

Centering appropriately about the historic St. Louis riverfront and the famed Goldenrod Showboat, the Festival of ''music of the good old days'' spotlights the authentic ragtime renditions of the nationally-known St. Louis Ragtimers, regular entertainers on the Goldenrod Showboat.

Ragtime A St. Louis Music Form

A wealth of other widely acclaimed musicians and recording artists join the festivities in a spectacular gathering of talent and virtuoso presentations of the Ragtime and classic Jazz music of that nostalgic era. Familiar old melodic favorites mix with all-time classic numbers of Ragtime music that was born and nurtured in Missouri and St. Louis on its way to national popularity.

Friday & Saturday Nights, 10:30

Aboard the air-conditioned Goldenrod Showboat, the St. Louis Ragtimers

GOLDENROD SHOWBOAT — air conditioned home of old-time melodrama, and saloon-deck haunt of St. Louis Ragtimers.

and guest artists hold forth on Friday and Saturday nights, beginning at 10:30 p.m. after the presentation of the ''Old Time Melodrama'' which runs from 8:15 to 10 p.m.

On Saturday night at 10:30, with admission $1.50, the Ragtimers and guest artists present a more intimate preview version of the wide-ranging program of Sunday afternoon on the levee.

Saturday Matinee, 2 to 5 p.m.

On Saturday afternoon at 2:00, with admission $3.00, the Ragtimers and famed musicians present a ''Concert in Ragtime'', aboard the Goldenrod. The artists vie in authentic flourishes of interpretation on old favorites, classics, and new compositions in the great old-time Ragtime musical form.

A word to the wise: since Goldenrod seating is necessarily limited, call GA 1-8675 for reservations to enjoy the special Saturday afternoon session.

Free Bicentennial Concert Sunday, Aug. 15, 3 p.m., On the Levee Climaxes Ragtime Festival

On the historic St. Louis levee beside the Goldenrod Showboat, all St. Louisans are invited to enjoy a free concert of St. Louis-centered Ragtime and other old-time music, as an official Bicentennial program in sight of the Gateway Arch and riverfront development.

The unique concert on Sunday, August 15, at 3 p.m., climaxes the Ragtime Festival with the St. Louis Ragtimers and guest artists presenting a wide range of cakewalks, ragtime, and classic jazz from a special bandstand beside the Goldenrod.

The Showboat is located just south of the Admiral landing at the foot of Washington Ave. below Eads Bridge. Parking is available on the levee and at the riverfront lot on Washington just south of Eads Bridge above the levee. As with other outdoor levee entertainments, small folding chairs or blankets for sitting are recommended.

Pioneer publication solely devoted to ragtime in the early 1960s

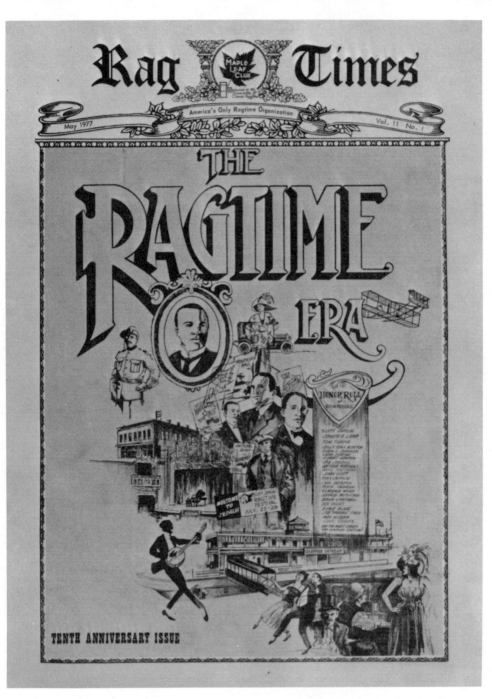

Journal of the Maple Leaf Club, the only ragtime organization in the
United States

THE RAGTIMER

PUBLISHED BY

Ragtime Society

DEDICATED TO THE
PRESERVATION OF
CLASSICAL RAGTIME

The newsletter of The Ragtime Society, a Canadian group

Dave Jasen (left) and Eubie Blake (right), 93, play a duet in 1976.

8

Jelly Roll Morton

J elly Roll Morton was a unique figure in American music. Everything he did was sparked with originality. He created a style of playing which could encompass other individual jazzmen's styles and retain his own conception. He could also take a published piano rag and transform it into "Jelly Roll" style. His sound reflected his upbringing in cosmopolitan New Orleans, where folk music from Africa, the West Indies, Portugal, Spain, France, England and Italy abounded, mixed with the blues and the syncopated sounds of ragtime. Two fine examples of this transformation exist on phonograph records. One is his version of Joplin's *Maple Leaf Rag* ("They All Played the Maple Leaf Rag," Herwin 401) and the other is a swinging version of Joplin's *Original Rags* ("Black & White Piano Ragtime," Biograph BLP-12047).

Of all the ragtime composers, Morton had many more diverse moods in his works than anyone else. His use of sixths in the left hand, an old Midwestern ragtime device, provided uncommon voicings which lent a touch of the unusual and thereby created greater interest for the listener. Morton was also the first ragtimer to consider the audience and to insure continued interest in his performances by creating unexpected rhythmic patterns within a performance and by continually improvising the same section of a tune over and over. However, unlike later jazzmen, Morton's variations were carefully built upon each section in the rag.

He had definite ideas about his music and was the most articulate ragtimer and jazzman of his time. There was nothing he did, either as composer or performer, which he could not explain. Nothing was haphazard or accidental. Every musical device he used was well thought out and deliberately done.

He achieved his distinctive piano sound by trying not to sound like a typical pianist. His idea was to imitate an entire jazz band; his extraordinary left hand not only kept a steady rhythm, like a tuba or string bass, but also incorporated the counterpoint of a trombone. His right hand alternated the clear cut melody line as played by the trumpet with the embellishments and flourishes of the clarinet. To complete the band, Morton in performance usually had a drumstick placed in his inner left shoe to beat against his bench or chair while playing.

There exists a large body of recorded work, all available now on LP, which clearly illustrates the magnitude of Morton's understanding of music and the wide scope of his interpretations. Especially interesting are the alternate takes of a tune which show just how creative he was as a performer. No less interesting is listening to the same rag recorded years apart. Morton matured musically as he got older, bringing new meaning and a fresh understanding to his older rags.

Since Morton didn't write down his rags the way he played them, and since most of them were never published during his lifetime, copyright dates for these numbers tell us little. It really made no difference if he composed a rag in 1906, recorded it in 1923 and had it published a year or ten years later. That rag could not have been written by anyone else at any time because Morton's entire musical outlook was original and unique.

With the Novelty and Stride stages of ragtime, Morton combined his composition development with his performing style, giving a uniformity to his entire work. It can be said that everything Morton played was his own creation—if not in melody-harmony-rhythm, then in interpretation. More than anyone else, Morton embodies ragtime—an original American art form—as it was conceived in performance.

FERDINAND JOSEPH LA MENTHE (JELLY ROLL MORTON)

Born: Gulfport, Louisiana, September 20, 1885

Died: Los Angeles, California, July 10, 1941

B rought to New Orleans as a child to live with his grand-mother, Morton first learned guitar and then, at age ten, learned to play the piano at St. Joseph's Catholic School. In 1902, at age seventeen, he played in the district known as Storyville and became one of the top "professors," earning a minimum of one hundred dollars a night. From 1904 on, beginning with the St. Louis World's Fair, he traveled around the country, having a good time, picking up local musical styles, playing pool, hustling for women, singing, appearing in vaudeville as part of a comedy team and playing piano. He met and won the admiration of Artie Matthews in St. Louis in 1911, and impressed budding musicians in New York the same year. He then went to Chicago where he led his own band until 1915, moved to San Francisco and Los Angeles where he attended the Exposition, ran a club, and then moved on to Vancouver, Alaska, Wyoming, Denver, frequented bars in Tia Juana and San Diego and returned to Chicago in 1923 where he made his first records. He became staff arranger and composer for the Melrose Brothers Music Company. He organized the Red Hot Peppers (one of the greatest jazz bands of all time) for the Victor Talking Machine Company and made a series of outstanding recordings. In 1928 he came to New York City, where he organized other bands for touring the East and Midwest. Morton made more recordings, accompanied singers, played in revues and entered the cosmetic business to sell a hair preparation. He settled in Washington, D.C. at the end of 1936 and worked a dive variously called Blue Moon Inn, Music Box and Jungle Inn. From May through July, 1938, he made an extraordinary series of recordings for the Folk Music Archive of the Library of Congress, talking, playing and singing—an autobiography on disc, from which Alan Lomax wrote the best biography of Morton, *Mister Jelly Roll* (published by Duell, Sloan and Pearce, 1950). The recordings have been issued in several editions, the most recent appearing in eight volumes on the Swedish label, Classic Jazz Masters (CJM 2-9). With the help of Roy Carew, he formed the Tempo Music Publishing Company to issue his songs and instrumental numbers. Looking for a comeback, he stayed in New York City from late 1938 until 1940, when he made his last recordings—both solo and with a band—and appeared on radio shows. Late in 1940 he made a final move to Los Angeles where he became chronically ill and died without making his dreamed-of comeback.

Bert Williams. June 29, 1948. Unpublished.
Recording: Jelly Roll Morton, Circle JM-45, (Classic Jazz Master CJM-8).
This was originally titled *Pacific Rag* but, when the great comedian expressed appreciation, it was changed to honor him.

Chicago Breakdown. January 12, 1926. Melrose Bros. Music Co., Chicago.
Recordings: Louis Armstrong & his Hot Seven, Columbia 36376, May 1927, ("The Genius of Louis Armstrong," Columbia G-30416). Don Ewell, "Free 'n Easy," Good Time Jazz S-10046, June 1957. Jelly Roll Morton (as *Stratford Hunch*), Gennett 5590, June 9, 1924, ("Jelly Roll Morton/The 1923–24 Piano Solos," Fountain FJ 104).
Roll: Jelly Roll Morton, Vocalstyle 50485, September 1924, ("Blues and Stomps from Rare Piano Rolls," Biograph BLP-1004Q).
This is also known as *Stratford Hunch,* the only difference being an introduction to *Hunch.*

The Finger Breaker. November 23, 1942. Unpublished.
Recording: Jelly Roll Morton, Jazz Man 12, December 1938.
A stomp taken at breakneck speed in the spirit of the Harlem cutting contest pieces, but in Jelly Roll style. It is derived in

part from *Frog-I-More Rag.* He transforms the basic syncopated pattern of ascending chromatic harmonies into a more complex Novelty rag style exchange between the bass and treble:

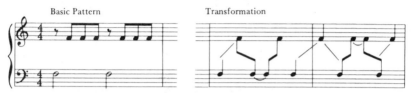

The climax of the performance comes with quick register jumps up and down the keyboard, a favorite device of Classic rag composer James Scott, here employed more dramatically with a riff-like feeling.

Frances. January 10, 1931. Unpublished.
Recording: Jelly Roll Morton, Victor V-38627, July 1929, ("Vol. 5," [F] RCA 741.054).
Also known as *Fat Frances.*

Freakish. September 28, 1929. Unpublished.
Recordings: Jelly Roll Morton, Victor 27565, July 1929. Jelly Roll Morton, Circle JM-71, (Classic Jazz Master CJM-8).
A masterful blend of Morton's style with a series of ninth chords characteristic of Novelty writing.

Frog-I-More Rag. May 15, 1918. Unpublished.
Recordings: Jelly Roll Morton, Steiner-Davis 103, April 1924, ("Jelly Roll Morton/The 1923–24 Piano Solos," Fountain FJ 104). Jelly Roll Morton, Vocalion 1019, April 1926, ("Piano Ragtime of the Teens, Twenties & Thirties," Herwin 402).
Research by Mike Montgomery tends to support the view that Morton appropriated the opening section from a pianist-contortionist named Froggie Moore. In the early twenties, Morton turned the trio into the popular song, *Sweetheart of Mine.*

Grandpa's Spells. August 20, 1923. Melrose Bros. Music Co., Chicago.
Recordings: Jelly Roll Morton, Gennett 5218, July 1923, ("Jelly

Roll Morton/The 1923–24 Piano Solos," Fountain FJ
104). Jelly Roll Morton & the Red Hot Peppers, Victor
20431, December 1926, ("Vol. 2," [F] RCA 730.605).

Roll: Jelly Roll Morton, Vocalstyle 50487, ("Blues and Stomps
from Rare Piano Rolls," Biograph BLP-1004Q).

A Morton classic and probably his favorite cutting contest
piece. In the Peppers recording he arranged sparkling breaks
for sections A and B. In the piano score, the trio opens with
instructions to "Crash-Strike bass open-handed." The "spell"
here alternates with a flowing lyrical line, providing marvelous
contrast.

Kansas City Stomp. August 20, 1923. Melrose Bros. Music
Co., Chicago.

Recordings: Jelly Roll Morton, Gennett 5218, July 1923, ("Jelly
Roll Morton/The 1923–24 Piano Solos," Fountain FJ
104). Jelly Roll Morton, Circle JM 18/19, May 1938,
("Piano Ragtime of the Teens, Twenties & Thirties," Her-
win 402). Jelly Roll Morton & his Red Hot Peppers, Victor
V-38010, June 1928, ("Vol. 4," [F] RCA 741.040).

Named after a bar in Tia Juana, this has a tricky introduction
which is a favorite syncopated waltz figure repeated four times:

When done with a band, it is usually done with clarinet, trumpet, trombone and tuba. Thus the feeling of a basic duple
meter is suspended until the fourth measure. The trio alternates beautifully sustained chords with a ragged phrasing.

King Porter Stomp. December 6, 1924. Melrose Bros. Music
Co., Chicago.

Recordings: Jelly Roll Morton, Gennett 5289, July 1923, ("Jelly
Roll Morton/The 1923–24 Piano Solos," Fountain FJ
104). Jelly Roll Morton, Vocalion 1020, April 1926,
("Early Ragtime Piano," Folkway RBF-33). Jelly Roll Morton, Circle JM 23/73, May 1938, ("Piano Ragtime of the

Teens, Twenties & Thirties," Herwin 402). Jelly Roll Morton, General 4005, December 1939, ("Late Ragtime Piano," Folkways RBF-34).

Roll: Jelly Roll Morton, Vocalstyle 50480, ("Blues and Stomps from Rare Piano Rolls," Biograph BLP-1004Q).

Probably Morton's earliest "stomp," he named it after a "marvelous pianist from Florida," Porter King. There is a legend that Morton consulted Joplin about it after he had finished it, and that Joplin returned it with the comment that it needed no improvement. Although Morton only recorded it as a piano solo, it was Fletcher Henderson's arrangement that established Benny Goodman's orchestra and gave new life to the rag in the middle thirties. The B section uses the Joplinesque broken-chord pattern but, in typical Jelly Roll fashion, breaks away from A with a syncopation on a rest:

The trio is a floating folk strain, recalled by St. Louis ragtime pianist Charles Thompson, as "the Rush-On"—a musical interlude used by local pianists in contests between the tunes. The final section of variations is built on a favorite progression that Morton used in at least one other stomp *(Hyena Stomp)*.

The Naked Dance. December 20, 1939. Tempo Music Publishing Co., Washington, D.C.

Recordings: Jelly Roll Morton, Circle JM 85, ("Classic Jazz Master CJM-3). Jelly Roll Morton, General 4002, December 1939.

This was written by Morton after Roy Carew recalled to him a "ratty strain" that Tony Jackson and other Storyville professors used to accompany the dances of the upstairs girls in the "houses." It is Morton's most haunting and exotic recollection of Storyville. The later 1939 version evokes a sensuous mood which he achieved again only in his best syncopated tangos such as *Creepy Feeling*.

The Pearls. August 20, 1923. Melrose Bros. Music Co., Chicago.

Recordings: Jelly Roll Morton, Gennett 5323, July 1923, ("Jelly Roll Morton/The 1923–24 Piano Solos," Fountain FJ 104). Jelly Roll Morton, Vocalion 1020, April 1926. Jelly Roll Morton, Circle JM 41/42, May 1938, (Classic Jazz Master CJM-8). Jelly Roll Morton, Swaggie S-1213, (1938). Jelly Roll Morton & His Red Hot Peppers, Victor 20948, June 1927, ("Vol. 4," [F] RCA 741.040).

The A section is an adventurous harmonic conception, sparked by an effective use of the lower VI chord (E flat seventh in the key of G here). The 32-measure trio is one of Morton's most original strains, despite its reliance in the first few measures on the pop blues song, *Go Back Where You Stayed Last Night.* In the key of C, he creates a pedal-tone effect with G in the bass with repeated patterns of first C-G, then D-G. Over this he created a fascinating treble: a lyrical, constantly moving melodic line, with great invention.

Pep. January 10, 1931. Unpublished.

Recordings: Jelly Roll Morton, Victor V-38627, July 8, 1929, ("Vol. 5," [F] RCA 741.054). Jelly Roll Morton, Circle JM 43, (Classic Jazz Master CJM-8).

Perfect Rag. Not copyrighted or published.

Recording: Jelly Roll Morton, Gennett 5486, June 1924, ("Jelly Roll Morton/The 1923–24 Piano Solos," Fountain FJ 104).

In this recording Morton treats us to his adaptation of the ragtime formula demonstrating the positive effects in performing improvisations. Section A is laid out in typical ragtime fashion. B, however, is a series of breaks on a circle-of-fifths, but a different break is used each time. C is a lyrical trio typical to ragtime, repeated almost without variation. Instead of a D strain, Morton climaxes the rag with a brilliantly worked out variation of C which he plays and then repeats. An inspired and most creative transformation of an older ragtime formula.

❧9❧

The Ragtime Revival 1941-1978

S hortly after Morton's death, interest in ragtime was renewed, first by musicians, then by critics and listeners— people dissatisfied with the contemporary big band swing sounds who yearned for the older forms of American popular music.

The spread of ragtime from the 1940s on was mainly accomplished with the vital help of the record industry. Lu Watters' Yerba Buena Jazz Band was formed in 1941 in San Francisco, and they made their first recordings by the end of that year. Their local fans were vociferous and loyal, but it wasn't until they made some records that they influenced countless pianists and other young traditional jazz bands. Their repertoire included piano rags, many discovered by the trombonist Turk Murphy. As their pianist Wally Rose recalled, in their set of first recordings, their version of Botsford's *Black and White Rag* sold well enough to pay for the entire recording venture. Radio stations picked up their records and played them over and over. The original sound the band created was perfect for the rags which were being rediscovered. Wally had to adapt the rags to his conditions, which included a heavy rhythm section (banjo, tuba and drums), so he had to thicken them so he could be heard in the clubs. As a result, his versions have a unique and satisfying sound. All of his recordings with the band are available on Good Time Jazz (12001, 12002, 12003, 12007, 12024), Homespun (101, 102, 103, 104, 105, 106) and Fairmont (101, 102).

During the forties two major jazz magazines published the

majority of articles concerning ragtime—*The Record Changer* and *Jazz Journal*. The former was started in 1942 in Virginia, and the latter began publication in 1949 in London. With rags appearing on records, the critics now had something to pick apart. The critical wrangling led to chapters on ragtime being included in the jazz histories which came out during this decade. Because the writers of the jazz histories were the same ones writing the articles on ragtime for the magazines, their comments on ragtime were terribly uninformed and often wrong. All of them placed ragtime as jazz's antecedent and looked upon ragtime as the beginning of jazz. Their assumption in linking ragtime with jazz bands was logical (from their viewpoint) because most ragtime was being played in the forties within traditional jazz bands—either by the bands in toto, or else, as in the case of the Yerba Buena Jazz Band, by the piano with full rhythm accompaniment. At the end of the forties, the ragtime-jazz association was further cemented by jazz pianists such as Don Ewell, Ralph Sutton, Marvin Ash, Paul Lingle and Dick Wellstood, all of whom made piano ragtime recordings in a jazzy, swingy manner.

The Dixieland bands, wanting variety in their repertoire, and in imitation of the Yerba Buena Jazz Band, included rags not only in their club dates but for their recording sessions as well. The outstanding bands of that time were Pete Daily and his Chicagoans, Pee Wee Hunt and his orchestra (actually five men), and the great playing-for-kicks band from the Walt Disney studio, The Firehouse Five Plus Two.

The importance of the jazz magazines to the ragtime revival is apparent by the many articles devoted to the subject. Another stimulus came from the record reviews given to ragtime recordings. The ragtime movement was helped by so many jazzmen playing and recording rags. In publications sympathetic to ragtime, oldtimers started reminiscing in print about the days when ragtime was new. And not only were these people being given opportunities to write about the old days, but some discovered even older ragtime composers and performers. New companies were formed to record these pioneers, rather late in their lives. One consideration in evaluating these recordings is that, even though many years had passed, the pioneer composer-performers were playing the rags in their original manner. Their playing shows that they retained the original flavor and optimism of ragtime's happily infectious sounds. They put their creations permanently onto disc enabling future generations to hear their ideas and styles. Luckey Roberts, Euday Bowman, James P. Johnson and Charles Thompson were among those pioneers who recorded during this decade—some for the first time. And, Jelly Roll Morton's fabled set for the Library of Congress was made available in a limited collector's edition during the late forties. "Piano Ragtime of the Forties," (Herwin 403) makes many of the best of these recordings available on LP.

The fifties was the most creative and active period for piano ragtime since ragtime's early era of explosive popularity. There were significant differences in both the sound of the piano and in the players. Thanks to the publication in 1950 of *Mister Jelly Roll,* Morton's autobiography, and *They All Played Ragtime* (a social history and the first book devoted entirely to ragtime), Riverside Records' recordings of ragtime piano rolls, and Capitol Records' promotion of ragtime from the piano concept as well as dixieland jazz band interpretations, ragtime was once again a popular music form, not only in America but now all over the world. This was no flash-in-the-pan popularity, but rather a steady development which increased with the years. More ragtime was recorded during this decade by more people than during any other decade in history. And, it was ragtime of the widest variety, the entire spectrum from Folk to Novelty. It was more than a revival. Rags were being newly composed, published and recorded. They were bright, fresh rags which evoked the golden age of ragtime while utilizing more modern harmonies.

This was an age when jazzmen continued to play rags, giving them a performer's swing which was not found in their printed form. They added a new dimension to the music which attracted more fans. Professional studio musicians were pressed into service by the large recording companies to satisfy the demand for "honky tonk" music. This was the pop music from the 1890s through the 1920s played on slightly out-of-tune pianos with a tinny sound, recalling the old saloon days. But when these professional musicians (Bill Krenz, Lou Busch, Sid Nierman, Ray Turner, Billy Rowland, Buddy Weed and Dick Hyman) recorded, usually with rhythm sections, they also recorded real rags, building up the weaker ones by clever new arrangements. They also composed their own rags.

It was also a time when pseudonyms masked these professional musicians (e.g. Joe "Fingers" Carr, Knuckles O'Toole, Pete Handy), and it is a mistake to dismiss them without studying their sparkling originality, for they added significantly to ragtime's ever-growing repertoire. Their musical tastes and skill created a highly polished series of performances which has not been equalled since. A sampling may be found on "Piano Ragtime of the Fifties," (Herwin 404).

The major jazz magazine established during the fifties was *Record Research,* devoted to the art of discography. A series of rollographies was presented by piano roll scholar Mike Montgomery, which coincided with renewed interest in new player pianos and the QRS Company's release of rolls of reissued Classic ragtime from their vast catalog.

The first all-ragtime long-playing disc came from Capitol Records, whose phenomenally successful late-forties recording of Pee Wee Hunt's version of *12th Street Rag* prompted that company under the brilliant leadership of James Conkling to go all out promoting ragtime. They recorded and developed such groups as Pete Daily, Nappy Lamare, the aforementioned Pee Wee Hunt, Chuck Thomas, and Red Nichols' Five Pennies, and transformed the outstanding arranger-conductor-pianist-composer, Lou Busch, into the most well known international favorite—Joe "Fingers" Carr.

That first all-ragtime LP was incorrectly called "Honky Tonk Piano," (Capitol H-188), but its cover made a lasting impression. The LP featured three fine pianists who grew up during the teens and twenties and well remembered the old ragtime performances. Marvin Ash was a jazzman who had played in bands and soloed throughout the West and Midwest. Ray Turner, born in St. Joseph, Missouri, played with Paul Whiteman's orchestra and became the film industry's greatest pianist, playing entire scores for the imaginative life stories of great composers which Hollywood indulged in throughout the forties and fifties. He had a prodigious technique and tremendous affection for the Novelty rags which he recorded for the album. The third member of this truly epoch-making LP was none other than Lou Busch who, in addition to creating a unique overall ragtime sound, composed an original rag for this album. At this time he adopted his world-famous pseudonym, Joe "Fingers" Carr, under which he recorded a greater number of rags—most for the first time—than anybody up to his time. He also composed more original rags than anyone since the original ragtime years.

The fifties also saw the rise of the ragtime entertainers. Coming from the South and Southwest, their forte was playing in clubs away from the major musical centers and building an incredible following. Del Wood came to prominence from her native Nashville, with her recording of *Down Yonder*. This led to her appearance on the *Grand Old Opry* network radio show and her marvelous composition, *Ragtime Melody*. Johnny Maddox made the first 78 rpm recording for the Dot Record Company in his hometown of Gallatin, Tennessee. His 10" LP, "Authentic Ragtime," (Dot DLP-102), was filled with the down-home flavor of the pioneers like Brun Campbell, because Maddox was taught by his great-aunt who had lived and performed in the ragtime era. Bob Darch, from Detroit, left the Army and started playing and singing ragtime solos and syncopated songs in Alaska and throughout the West. Passing through Colorado, he influenced another like-minded actor-turned-entertainer, Max Morath, who developed an appreciation for the entire age. Morath developed his love of theater and music and combined them doing stage shows, with appropriate scenery, costumes, song-slides and authentic stories and jokes from the turn of the century. He had the first television series devoted to ragtime over the educational stations at the end of the fifties.

In the sixties the first modern-day journal dedicated to ragtime, *The Ragtime Review,* was established (edited by Russell Cassidy and Trebor Jay Tichenor). This publication featured the first serious attempt at analyzing Classic rags and contributing articles exhibiting first-class scholarship. The *Review* was quickly joined by *The Ragtimer,* the journal of the Canadian-based Ragtime Society, the first organization devoted to the appreciation of ragtime. The Society was the first to reprint the long forgotten rags, and *The Ragtimer* kept readers informed of ragtime activities around the world, reviewed recordings of ragtime and reprinted the early articles on ragtime. Later, the Society started a recording company to produce albums by contemporary pianists performing ragtime. It also initiated in 1964 a "bash," an annual get-together in Toronto during a weekend usually in late October or early November. This enabled the membership to join together in a meeting of good fellowship, listening, talking and playing ragtime. It is one of the major ragtime events each year.

In 1967 Dick Zimmerman started the Maple Leaf Club for ragtime fans on the West Coast, holding an all-day meeting once every two months. He issues a bimonthly journal called *The Rag Times.* In addition to describing the meetings and reviewing recordings, publications and news stories pertaining to ragtime, he also published for the first time a sheet music version of the sensational discovery of Joplin's *Silver Swan Rag.* Dave Bourne's Dawn of the Century Ragtime Orchestra (Archane AR-601, 602) was composed of members who attended the bimonthly meetings. It was probably the best of the ragtime orchestras, playing authentic arrangements from the ragtime age.

In the early sixties, John W. "Knocky" Parker was the first to record the complete works of Scott Joplin and James Scott, mostly omitting the repeats and improvising on the sections. Later in the decade he made four albums called "The Golden Treasury of Ragtime"—a chronological gathering from 1895–1913. Most of those rags had never been recorded previously.

It was a time when only one jazzman, a modern jazz pianist at that, recorded an album of rags. Hank Jones, a versatile musician, became intrigued with ragtime and produced an incredibly understanding series of ragtime performances with taste and great skill ("This is Ragtime Now," ABC-Paramount 496) in 1964.

In St. Louis, "the cradle of ragtime," a trio was formed comprising Trebor Jay Tichenor on piano, Al Stricker on banjo and Don Franz on tuba—The St. Louis Ragtimers. As their popularity grew from playing at Gaslight Square, they added cornetist Bill Mason and finally clarinetist Glen Meyer. Their unusual repertoire is based on Trebor Jay Tichenor's vast resources in ragtime piano rolls and music sheets. Since 1965, the Ragtimers have been hosts at the annual National Ragtime Festival aboard the Goldenrod Showboat, a registered historic landmark, and the largest showboat ever built. Usually taking place in mid-June, the Festival lasts an entire week and features the best of the active ragtime pianists.

The sixties saw the surfacing of composer-pianists who came to ragtime in the late forties and early fifties, growing up with the recordings of the past, collecting sheet music and piano rolls, interviewing pioneer ragtime composers, performers and publishers. Recording for small, specialist LP labels, Dave Jasen, Trebor Tichenor, Tom Shea, Charlie Rasch, John Arpin and Donald Ashwander were promoted throughout the world and appeared at the St. Louis Ragtime Festival and at the Ragtime Society's Ragtime Bash.

In the seventies an unprecedented awareness of Scott Joplin arose through recordings by Joshua Rifkin, who played the Joplin rags in a classical music manner (Nonesuch H-71248, 71264, 71305). He influenced an entirely new audience—students of classical music, studying in conservatories and universities.

The next big event was the publication by the New York Public Library of a two-volume set of *The Collected Works of Scott Joplin,* meticulously edited by Vera Brodsky Lawrence. It is the definitive edition of Joplin's works and it prompted the staging of Joplin's folk opera, *Treemonisha,* which had its Broadway premiere in 1975, the world premiere having taken place in Atlanta, Georgia in January of 1972.

The explosion in the ragtime world came with the motion picture, *The Sting* (Universal Studios, 1974), which used six Joplin rags as background music. The arrangements were orchestrated by Marvin Hamlisch, who also played piano on the soundtrack. His version of *The Entertainer* put that 1902 Joplin rag on top of the Hit Parade and made it the number one recording for 1974. It was a genuine pop hit and millions of people around the world became conscious of Classic ragtime.

The Joplin rage was further stimulated by the first complete recording of Joplin's works done by Dick Zimmerman (Murray Hill 931079). Its success spurred RCA to ask Dick Hyman to record the piano works for their classical Red Seal label (RCA CRL5-1106).

The seventies produced significant activities designed to insure the posterity of ragtime performances on record and piano roll through their issuance on long-playing albums for record companies who specialized in jazz and ragtime. The first of the reissues coincided with the Lawrence edition of Joplin's works and was, appropriately, an album devoted to Joplin's *Maple Leaf Rag* ("They All Played the Maple Leaf Rag," Herwin 401), performed by the greatest ragtime exponents over a sixty-year span. Biograph, Folkways, Eubie Blake Music and Yazoo, as well as Herwin, have produced the finest ragtime reissues on LP.

Publications have been an important part of the ragtime scene in the 1970s. First came Jasen's ragtime discography for 78 rpm discs called *Recorded Ragtime* (Archon, 1973). Then came Schafer and Riedel's *The Art of Ragtime* (Louisiana State University Press, 1973), and then Terry Waldo's fine ragtime history, *This Is Ragtime* (Hawthorne, 1976). Quality folios of reprinted ragtime sheet music complemented the reissued recordings. The finest of these was issued by Dover ("Classic Piano Rags," 0–486–20469–3 and "Ragtime Rarities," 0–486–23157–7), the Charles Hanson folio, "A Tribute to Scott Joplin and the Giants of Ragtime" (R049), and "The Big 3" ("100 Greatest Ragtime Hits," Vol. 1-B3-3262; Vol. 2-B3-3263).

To climax thirty-five years of the ragtime revival, a bicentennial concert was staged at the C. W. Post Center of Long Island University in Brookville, Long Island, New York, on October 30, 1976. It was called "Rags to Riches" and featured the greatest collection of ragtime stylists on the same stage in one evening, the first such gathering since Mike Bernard won the National Ragtime Piano Contest at Tammany Hall on January 23, 1900. This ragtime spectacular included Joe "Fingers" Carr (who came out of retirement to perform—his first engagement on the East Coast), Neville Dickie (making his debut in the United States), Bob Seeley, the St. Louis Ragtimers, Dick

Wellstood, Dick Hyman and Dave Jasen. The concert was a huge success, and *New York Times* critic John S. Wilson's headline for the review stated, "Ragtime Program With 7 on the Piano Hits Its Stride Well."

LOUIS FERDINAND BUSCH

Born: Louisville, Kentucky, July 18, 1910

T he family name was Bush, but he added the *c* because he thought it looked good. He took private piano lessons, starting at the age of nine, and left high school and home at sixteen to tour with Clyde McCoy and other local bands. With no formal training, he became an arranger as well as pianist for Henry Busse, Leo Reisman, Horace Heidt, Vincent Lopez, George Olsen and Hal Kemp. He married vocalist Janet Blair and settled in Los Angeles. In December of 1941 he was Lena Horne's accompanist. He joined the Army in 1942 and served for the duration of the war. He went to work for Capitol Transcription Service in 1946 and became musical director for Peter Lind Hayes and Mary Healy. From May 1949, he was an artist and repertoire executive for Capitol Records. He and his second wife, singer Margaret Whiting, have one daughter. Busch created the ragtime pseudonym Joe "Fingers" Carr in April 1950, and became the best known ragtime pianist worldwide through his more than thirty-six singles and fourteen albums. He created an atmosphere for ragtime which highlighted the ebullient, rollicking aspects of this happy music. His carefully thought-out arrangements and inspired performances encouraged many of the leading ragtimers of today. In 1958 he went to Warner Bros. Records as producer-artist, where he made five albums as Joe "Fingers" Carr. In 1960 he went to Dot Records where he performed on three albums. He became Allan Sherman's musical director, arranger, composer and conductor. Among his compositions are *Roller Coaster* (used as the closing theme in television's long-running panel show, "What's My Line"), *Ivory Rag,* which became the first segment in the ragtime medley, *The Crazy Otto,* and Allan Sherman's big hit, *Hello Mudduh, Hello Fadduh.* As Lou Busch, he made a lovely mood album called "Lazy Rhapsody" (Capitol T-1072), in which he was arranger, conductor and featured pianist. Not only did he create memorable arrangements of 1920s hits and a body of clever rags, but he recorded more published rags than anyone else, and, of them, many were recorded for the first time. He was a major rediscoverer of ragtime at a time when no one else was looking.

Baked Alaska. November 23, 1959. Unpublished.
Recording: Joe "Fingers" Carr, "The World's Greatest Ragtime Piano Player," Warner Bros. W-1386.

Barky Roll Stomp. December 12, 1955. Unpublished.
Recording: Joe "Fingers" Carr, Capitol 3201.

Boogie Woogie Rag. September 2, 1952. Unpublished.
Recording: Joe "Fingers" Carr, Capitol 2187, July 14, 1952.

Carr's Hop. March 5, 1952. Chatsworth Music Inc., New York.
Folio: Bar Room Piano Solos.
Recording: Joe "Fingers" Carr, "Bar Room Piano," Capitol T-280.

Doo Wacky Rag. May 31, 1956. Unpublished.
Recording: Joe "Fingers" Carr, Capitol 2359.

Fingers Medley. Not copyrighted or published.
Recording: Joe "Fingers" Carr, Capitol 3883.

Finicky Fingers. March 5, 1952. Chatsworth Music Inc., New York.
Folio: Bar Room Piano Solos.

Fourth Man Rag (as written by Dick Hamilton and Jill Leland). Not copyrighted or published.
Recording: Pee Wee Hunt & Orch., Capitol 1091, April 1950.

Hook and Ladder Rag. May 31, 1956. Unpublished.
Recording: Joe "Fingers" Carr & his Ragtime Band, "Fireman's Ball," Capitol T-527.

Hot Potatoes. February 27, 1958. Unpublished.
Recording: Joe "Fingers" Carr, Capitol 3883.

Ironfingers Rag (with Alvino Rey). June 20, 1960. Unpublished.
Recording: Joe "Fingers" Carr & Ira Ironstrings, "Together For the Last Time . . . Volume 1," Warner Bros. W-1389.

Looney Louie. February 27, 1958. Unpublished.
Recording: Joe "Fingers" Carr, Capitol 3883.

Piano Picker Rag. October 24, 1966. Unpublished.
Recording: Joe "Fingers" Carr, "And the Bluegrass Jug Band," Dot DLP 25767.

Piccadilly Rag. May 31, 1956. Unpublished.
Recording: Joe "Fingers" Carr, Capitol 2834, August 1953.

Raggedy-Ann Rag. March 5, 1952. Chatsworth Music Inc., New York.
Folio: Bar Room Piano Solos.
Recording: Joe "Fingers" Carr & his Ragtime Band," Capitol T-443.

Rapscallion Rag. March 5, 1952. Chatsworth Music Inc., New York.
Folio: Bar Room Piano Solos.

Recording: Joe "Fingers" Carr, "Bar Room Piano," Capitol T-280.

Rattlesnake Rag (with Eddie Hanson). December 29, 1952. Chatsworth Music Inc., New York.
Recording: Joe "Fingers" Carr, Capitol 2257, July 14, 1952.

Tin Pan Rag. March 5, 1952. Chatsworth Music Inc., New York.
Folio: Bar Room Piano Solos.
Recording: Joe "Fingers" Carr, Warner Bros. 5149.

Two Dollar Rag. Not copyrighted or published.
Recordings: Professor Lou Busch, Capitol 15436 ("Honky Tonk Piano," Capitol T-188). Joe "Fingers" Carr, Capitol 3883.

Waltz in Ragtime. March 5, 1952. Chatsworth Music Inc., New York.
Folio: Bar Room Piano Solos.
Recording: Joe "Fingers" Carr, "Bar Room Piano," Capitol T-280.

WILLIAM FRED KRENZ
Born: Rock Island, Illinois, February 23, 1899

Krenz became interested in music and started taking piano lessons when he was eight years old. At thirteen he was a member of a piano-violin duo on a Mississippi riverboat and, for the next ten years, he was part of a minstrel show. He toured with Paul Biese Orchestra, recorded with the Jean Goldkette and Ray Miller orchestras, appeared at the Trianon Ballroom with Arnold Johnson's orchestra and conducted his own orchestras at many Chicago hotels and night clubs. He was staff pianist and composer for the extraordinarily popular ABC radio show "Breakfast Club" from 1933–62 when he retired. In the mid-thirties, he composed six Novelty rags. In the fifties he composed and published rags in the Popular ragtime tradition. He is one of the great ragtime pianists.

Anniversary Rag (with Eddie Ballantine). July 7, 1958. Will Rossiter, Chicago.

Barber Shop Rag. January 19, 1953. Mills Music Inc., New York.

Calliope Rag (with Eddie Ballantine). September 15, 1959. Will Rossiter, Chicago.

Marita. December 14, 1934. M. M. Cole Publishing Co., Chicago.
Recording: Bill Krenz, Cole Records 90500 (45 rpm).

Mud Cat Rag. November 24, 1953. Mills Music Inc., New York.

Nickelodeon Rag (with Sammy Gallop). July 21, 1953. Mills Music Inc., New York.

Oh! Willie, Play That Thing. May 23, 1952. Mills Music Inc., New York.
Recording: Bill Krenz, MGM 11264, June 1952, ("Oh Willie, Play That Thing," MGM E-184) (10").

Pianola Rag. December 29, 1953. Mills Music Inc., New York.

Poodle Rag. August 12, 1954. Mills Music Inc., New York.
Recording: Bill Krenz, "Oh Willie, Play That Thing," MGM E-184 (10"), ("Piano Ragtime of the Fifties," Herwin 404).

Ramblin' Rag. July 11, 1952. Mills Music Inc., New York.
Recording: Bill Krenz, Coral 9–61248 (45 rpm), June 1954, ("Piano Ragtime of the Fifties," Herwin 404).

Rochelle. December 15, 1934. M. M. Cole Publishing Co., Chicago.

Showboat Rag (with Tommy Filas). November 24, 1953. Mills Music Inc., New York.

Sophisticated Rhythm. January 22, 1935. M. M. Cole Publishing Co., Chicago.

Yvonnette. February 1, 1935. M. M. Cole Publishing Co., Chicago.

Zephyr. February 12, 1935. M. M. Cole Publishing Co., Chicago.

RICHARD ROVEN HYMAN
Born: New York, New York, March 8, 1927

Hyman was thoroughly trained in the classics by his famed uncle Anton Rovinsky. Later he studied with Teddy Wilson. He spent a year in the Navy and then two years at Columbia University. He made his professional debut in 1948 and has played with such diverse musicians as Tony Scott, Red Norvo, Victor Lombardo, Benny Goodman and Mundell Lowe. During the mid-fifties he recorded ragtime under a variety of pseudonyms (Knuckles O'Toole, Willie "The Rock" Knox, Slugger Ryan), and composed several rags under other aliases (J. Gaines, Jack Schwartz, Arthur Charleston). In the seventies, he recorded examples of practically every type of rag. His biggest ragtime project has been the five-disc set of Scott Joplin rags, including a wonderful series of improvisations for RCA.

New Orleans Rag. Not copyrighted or published.
Recording: Willie "The Rock" Knox, Waldorf Music Hall MH 33–147 (10"), ("Piano Ragtime of the Fifties," Herwin 404).

The Old Professor. 1955. Hollis Music Inc., New York.
Recording: Dick Hyman.

Ragtime Razz Matazz (as J. Gaines). Not copyrighted or published.
Recording: Knuckles O'Toole, "Plays the Greatest All Time Ragtime Hits," Grand Award GA 33–373.

Ragtime Revelation (as J. Gaines). Not copyrighted or published.
Recording: Knuckles O'Toole, "Plays the Greatest All Time Ragtime Hits," Grand Award GA 33–373.

Ragtime Fantasy for Piano & Orchestra. March 15, 1976. Eastlake Music, Inc., New York.
This is a marvelous synthesis of ragtime highlights of Scott Joplin, Jelly Roll Morton, Eubie Blake, James P. Johnson, Zez Confrey—in a delightfully original manner. By far, the most ambitious use of ragtime materials, it is artfully done. The piece, commissioned by the Austin Symphony Society and performed by the Austin Symphony Orchestra with the composer at the piano on January 30, 1976, is suitable for ballet.

DAVID ALAN JASEN
Born: New York, New York, December 16, 1937

Jasen began picking out tunes on the piano at age two. Dr. Kurt List recorded his early efforts. At six, he auditioned for Mme. Isabella Vangerrova to take theory and classical piano lessons. He studied with Helen Shafranek for eleven years. During this time he discovered ragtime and purchased recordings because sheet music wasn't available. Having relative pitch enabled him to learn rags from recordings. He started composing his own rags. With the appearance of the Joe "Fingers" Carr recordings, he imitated Carr and learned how to arrange a rag for performance. He earned a Bachelor of Arts degree from the American University in Communication Arts. He met humorist P. G. Wodehouse and became his official biographer and bibliographer. Jasen has the most extensive archive of Wodehousiana in the world. From 1959–66 he was supervisor of network news videotape for the Columbia Broadcasting System. He obtained a Master of Science degree in Library Science from Long Island University and is an Associate Professor in the School of the Arts at C. W. Post Center where he is Director of Communication Arts. He married Susan Pomerantz in 1963 and they have one son, Raymond Douglas. He is author of *Recorded Ragtime* (Archon, 1973), the pioneer ragtime discography, and has the largest collection of ragtime on records and research materials on ragtime. Jasen is a producer of ragtime collections on LP in the seventies, writer of articles on ragtime, and cited by others in scholarly journals, doctoral dissertations, master's theses, liner notes and specialist books and articles. He is editor of "100 Greatest Ragtime Hits" (The Big 3), and has appeared in leading ragtime and jazz festivals in the United States, England and Europe. His lecture-concerts are in great demand, especially on college campuses. He hosts a weekly half-hour radio program, "Ragtime and Riverboat Jazz," and produced, hosted and performed at the ragtime concert, "Rags to Riches," at C. W. Post on October 30, 1976. *New York Times* jazz critic John S. Wilson said of him, "Ragtime is still vital today wherever Dave Jasen happens to be."

Dave's Rag. 1978.
Folio: "100 Greatest Ragtime Hits," Vol. 2, The Big 3, New York (B3–3263), 1978.
Recordings: Dave Jasen, "Creative Ragtime," Euphonic ESR-1206, July 1966. Dave Jasen, "Fingerbustin' Ragtime," Blue Goose 3001, March 1972.
Composed in 1964.

Everybody's Rag (with Alonzo Yancey). Not copyrighted or published.
Recording: Dave Jasen, "Fingerbustin' Ragtime," Blue Goose 3001, March 1972.
Composed 1968.

Festival Rag. 1978.
Folio: "100 Greatest Ragtime Hits," Vol. 2, The Big 3, New York, B3–3263, 1978.
Recordings: Dave Jasen, "Creative Ragtime," Euphonic ESR-1206, July 1966. Dave Jasen, "Fingerbustin' Ragtime," Blue Goose 3001, March 1972.
Composed in 1959.

London Rag. 1978.
Folio: "100 Greatest Ragtime Hits," Vol. 2, The Big 3, New York, 1978.
Recording: Dave Jasen, "Fingerbustin' Ragtime," Blue Goose 3001, March 1972.
Composed in 1961.

Macadamian Scuffle. Not copyrighted or published.
Recording: Dave Jasen, "Rip-Roarin' Ragtime," Folkways FG-3561, June 17, 1977.
Composed for this recording in June 1977.

Make Believe Rag. 1978.
Recording: Dave Jasen, "Fingerbustin' Ragtime," Blue Goose 3001, March 1972.
Composed in 1969.

Nobody's Rag. 1978.
Folio: "100 Greatest Ragtime Hits," Vol. 2, The Big 3, New York, 1978.
Recording: Dave Jasen, "Rompin' Stompin' Ragtime," Blue Goose 3002, April 1974.
Composed in 1974.

Piano Roll Jazz Rag. July 25, 1955. Unpublished.

The Player Piano Rag. Not copyrighted or published.
Composed August, 1954.

Qwindo's Rag. 1978.
Folio: "100 Greatest Ragtime Hits," Vol. 2, The Big 3, New York, 1978.
Recording: Dave Jasen, "Fingerbustin' Ragtime," Blue Goose 3001, March 1972.
Composed in 1970 for Qwindo's Window, a theatrical ballet company.

Raymond's Rag. 1978.
Folio: "100 Greatest Ragtime Hits," Vol. 2, The Big 3, New York, 1978.
Recording: Dave Jasen, "Fingerbustin' Ragtime," Blue Goose 3001, March 1972.
Composed in 1966.

Shoe String Rag. 1978.

Folio: "100 Greatest Ragtime Hits," Vol. 2, The Big 3, New York, 1978.

Recording: Dave Jasen, "Rompin' Stompin' Ragtime," Blue Goose 3002, April 1974.

Composed in 1973 for Lew Wiggin, then editor of The Shoe String Press (publisher of Archon Books).

Somebody's Rag. Not copyrighted or published.

Recording: Dave Jasen, "Rip-Roarin' Ragtime," Folkways FG-3561, June 1977.

Composed May, 1976.

Susan's Rag. 1978.

Folio: "100 Greatest Ragtime Hits," Vol. 2, The Big 3, New York, 1978.

Recordings: Dave Jasen, "Creative Ragtime," Euphonic ESR-1206, July 1966. Dave Jasen, "Fingerbustin' Ragtime," Blue Goose 3001, March 1972.

Composed in 1962.

That American Ragtime Dance. 1978.

Folio: "100 Greatest Ragtime Hits," Vol. 2, The Big 3, New York, 1978.

Recording: Dave Jasen, "Fingerbustin' Ragtime," Blue Goose 3001, March 1972.

Composed in 1971.

Two Reel Rag. July 25, 1955. Unpublished.

TREBOR JAY TICHENOR
Born: St. Louis, Missouri, January 28,
    1940

T rebor was named by his father, who inverted his own
name (Robert) into Trebor. He first heard Novelty rags
and popular music played by his mother, whose band—Letty's
Collegiate Syncopators—was active in the St. Louis area in the
thirties. He began taking piano lessons at age five with John
Gross, and studied with Bernell Fiegler until age thirteen,
when he discovered ragtime through recordings by Lou Busch.
He began collecting ragtime piano rolls and sheet music and
learned to play rags. He was influenced during contacts with
Dr. Hubert S. Pruett, whose pioneer collection of sheet music
and rolls stimulated Tichenor's own collecting efforts. He
resumed classical piano studies for two more years with Gross,
at his father's suggestion. In 1958 he graduated, cum laude,
from St. Louis Country Day School, and received an A.B. degree from Washington University (St. Louis) in 1963. He heard
Ragtime Bob Darch perform in Joplin, Mo. in 1959. Tichenor
met ragtime pianists Knocky Parker and Pete Clute in 1960 and
they inspired him to become a professional performer. He
began composing his own rags in the folk idiom in 1961. Also
in 1961, in collaboration with the late Russ Cassidy, he formed
the *Ragtime Review,* the first regular publication devoted exclusively to ragtime since Axel Christensen's earlier magazine of
the same name appeared in 1915. He helped form and played
in a four-piece band, the St. Louis Ragtimers, in 1961, and
played with this group in St. Louis' Gaslight Square (at the
Natchez Queen and at Bustle and Bowes). He has remained
with the group ever since. The Ragtimers have appeared on the
Goldenrod Showboat continuously since 1965. He owns the

largest private collection of ragtime piano rolls (including Pruett's collection) in the country, and has an authoritative library of original ragtime sheet music. He married Jeanette Taft Jordan in 1966 and they have two children, Virginia and Andrew. His weekly radio program called "Ragophile," heard in St. Louis, is the oldest show of its kind in the nation. He has appeared in concerts in California, Missouri, Toronto and New York, and was seen with the Ragtimers on the "Today Show" "Salute to Missouri" in January 1976. He teaches ragtime history at Washington University, and collaborated with collector/piano roll historian Mike Montgomery to produce six definitive LPs (on the Biograph label) of the piano roll music of Scott Joplin and James Scott. Tichenor has recorded two record albums of piano solos and appears on five additional LPs with the St. Louis Ragtimers. He has contributed ragtime articles to magazines and furnished original sheet music to several publishers for reprint projects during the seventies. He edited and selected the rags for two major folios for Dover Publications.

Big Ben—A Rag for Ben Conroy. Not copyrighted or published.
Composed in 1974.

Boom Town Echoes—A Gold Camp Fracas. Not copyrighted or published.
Recording: Trebor Tichenor, "King of Folk Ragtime," Dirty Shame 2001, 1973.
Composed in 1961.

Bucksnort Stomp—An Arkansas Hell-Raiser. Not copyrighted or published.
Recording: The St. Louis Ragtimers, "The St. Louis Ragtimers," Vol. 2, Audiophile Records AB-81.
Composed in 1963.

Chestnut Valley Rag. "They All Played Ragtime," Oak Publications, New York City, 1966, 3rd edition.
Recordings: Trebor Jay Tichenor, "They All Play Ragtime,"

Jazzology JCE-52. Trebor Jay Tichenor, "The St. Louis Ragtimers," Vol. 2, Audiophile Records AB-81.
Composed in 1961.

Cottonwood Rag. Not copyrighted or published.
Composed in 1973.

Days Beyond Recall. Not copyrighted or published.
Composed in 1962.

Goldenrod Stomp. Not copyrighted or published.
Recording: Trebor Tichenor, "The St. Louis Ragtimers, Vol. 5," Audiophile AP-122, March 1977.
Composed in 1967, revised in 1977.

Hickory Smoked Rag. Not copyrighted or published.
Composed in 1976.

It's a Long Way Back Home. Not copyrighted or published.
Recording: Trebor Jay Tichenor, "Mississippi Valley Ragtime," Scroll LSCR-102, March 1966.

The Last Cake Walk. Not copyrighted or published.
Composed in 1973.

The Last Trip Down From Hannibal. Not copyrighted or published.
Recording: Trebor Tichenor, "King of Folk Ragtime," Dirty Shame 2001, 1973.

Market St. Rag—A Rosebud Club Revelry. Not copyrighted or published.
Composed in 1967, revised in 1977.

The Mississippi Valley Frolic. Not copyrighted or published.
Recording: Trebor Jay Tichenor, "Mississippi Valley Ragtime," Scroll LSCR-102, March 1966.
Composed in 1962, revised in 1966.

Missouri Autumn Rag. Not copyrighted or published.
Roll: Classics of Ragtime 0147.
Composed in 1963.

A Missouri Breeze—Ragtime Two Step. Not copyrighted or
 published.
Roll: Classics of Ragtime 0086.
Composed in 1962.

Missouri Rambler. Not copyrighted or published.
Composed in 1962.

Old Levee Days. Not copyrighted or published.
Roll: Classics of Ragtime 0136.
Composed in 1962.

Olive St. Rag—A Gaslight Square Delight. Not copyrighted
 or published.
Composed in 1961.

Ozark Rag. Not copyrighted or published.
Composed in 1962.

Pierce City Rag. Not copyrighted or published.
Roll: Classics of Ragtime 0087.
Composed in 1961.

Ragtime in the Hollow. Not copyrighted or published.
Recording: Trebor Tichenor, "King of Folk Ragtime," Dirty
 Shame 2001, 1973.
Composed in 1965, revised in 1973.

St. Louis Days. Not copyrighted or published.
Composed in 1970.

Sappington Memories. Not copyrighted or published.
Composed in 1970.

The Show-Me Rag—A Missouri Defiance.
Folio: The Ragtime Current, Edward B. Marks Music Corp., New York, 1977.
Recording: Trebor Jay Tichenor, "Mississippi Valley Ragtime," Scroll LSCR-102, March 1966.

Wine Room Rag. Not copyrighted or published. Composed in 1977.

THOMAS WILLIAM SHEA
Born: Mattoon, Illinois, November 14, 1931

S hea studied piano as a child for seven years. He became interested in ragtime about 1960 and learned the *Maple Leaf Rag* from *They All Played Ragtime*. He found a collection of rags on a piano roll album and learned some by ear, then started composing his own rags. He went to the St. Louis Ragtime Festival starting in 1962 and met many contemporary performers as well as Jim Kinnear, Secretary of the Ragtime Society, who wanted to publish Shea's originals. He became the Detroit editor for *The Ragtimer*, wrote articles, edited submissions by others, coined the title "Sounds Familiar" for columnist Roger Hankins, interviewed surviving members of early bands and recorded two albums for the Society. He founded Mother's Boys with clarinetist Walt Gower, a traditional jazz band which recorded for Audiophile. In 1970 he moved to North Carolina and now plays with the Carolina Foot Warmers, which was organized in 1974. He is married to Margaret Shea and they have two daughters, Robin and Julie. He is an executive with a pharmaceutical company.

Black Mike's Curse. Not copyrighted or published.
Recording: Tom Shea, "Classic & Modern Rags," Ragtime Society Records RSR-1, May 1963.

Brun Campbell Express. "They All Played Ragtime," Oak Publications, New York, 1966, 3rd edition.
Recordings: Tom Shea, "They All Played Ragtime," Jazzology JCE-52. Tom Shea, "Prairie Ragtime," Ragtime Society Records RSR-2, August 1964.

Corinthian Rag. Not copyrighted or published.
Recording: Tom Shea, "Prairie Ragtime," Ragtime Society Records RSR-2, August 1964.

Hasty Pudding. Not copyrighted or published.
Recording: Tom Shea, "Classic & Modern Rags," Ragtime Society Records RSR-1, May 1963.

Johnny Walker Rag. Not copyrighted or published.
Recording: Tom Shea, "Classic & Modern Rags," Ragtime Society Records RSR-1, May 1963.

Oliver Road Rag. Not copyrighted or published.
Recording: Tom Shea, "Prairie Ragtime," Ragtime Society Records RSR-2, August 1964.

Pegtown Patrol. Not copyrighted or published.
Recording: Tom Shea, "Prairie Ragtime," Ragtime Society Records RSR-2, August 1964.

Prairie Queen. June 28, 1963. Ragtime Society, Ontario, Canada.
Recording: Tom Shea, "Classic & Modern Rags," Ragtime Society Records RSR-1, May 1963.

R.F.D. Not copyrighted or published.
Recording: Tom Shea, "Prairie Ragtime," Ragtime Society Records RSR-2, August 1964.

Rosebud Rag. Not copyrighted or published.
Recording: Tom Shea, "Prairie Ragtime," Ragtime Society Records RSR-2, August 1964.

Spasm Rag. March 21, 1963. The Ragtime Society, Ontario, Canada.
Recording: Tom Shea, "Classic & Modern Rags," Ragtime Society Records RSR-1, May 1963.

The Storyville Sport. Not copyrighted or published.
Recording: Tom Shea, "Classic & Modern Rags," Ragtime Society Records RSR-1, May 1963.

Trillium Rag. "Max Morath's Guide to Ragtime," Hollis Music, Inc., New York, 1964.
Recording: Tom Shea, "Prairie Ragtime," Ragtime Society Records RSR-2, August 1964.

Venial Sin. Not copyrighted or published.
Recording: Tom Shea, "Classic & Modern Rags," Ragtime Society Records RSR-1, May 1963.

DONALD ASHWANDER

Born: Birmingham, Alabama, July 17, 1929

A most unusual man, whose Southern heritage is very much a part of his musical life, Ashwander has worked for the NBC-TV network, been a seaman and composed ballet music and music for advertisements. For the past ten years he has been the musical director, performer, composer and actor with The Paper Bag Players, a most creative children's theater, with costumes and scenery made from paper bags. His contemporary rags, mostly written between 1965 and 1970, extend the scope of ragtime. His performing style is unusual and his particular bounciness has attracted other contemporary players. He is a thoughtful, sensitive musician with great technique and charm.

Astor Place Rag Waltz.
Folio: The Ragtime Current, Edward B. Marks Music Corp., New York, 1977.
Recording: Donald Ashwander, "Ragtime: A New View," Jazzology JCE-71, 1970.

Business in Town. "They All Played Ragtime," Oak Publications, New York, 1966, 3rd edition.
Recording: Donald Ashwander, "They All Play Ragtime," Jazzology JCE-52.

Cascade Plunge. Not copyrighted or published.
Recording: Donald Ashwander, "Turnips," Upstairs UPST-1. Composed in 1973.

Empty Porches. Not copyrighted or published.
Recording: Donald Ashwander, "Ragtime: A New View," Jazzology JCE-71, 1970.
Composed in 1969.

Friday Night. "They All Played Ragtime," Oak Publications, New York, 1966, 3rd edition.
Folio: The Ragtime Current, Edward B. Marks Music Corp., New York, 1977.
Recording: Donald Ashwander, "They All Play Ragtime," Jazzology JCE-52.

Harlem River Houseboat Rag. Not copyrighted or published.
Recording: Donald Ashwander, "Ragtime: A New View," Jazzology JCE-71, 1970.
Composed in 1966.

Late Hours Rag. Not copyrighted or published.
Recording: Donald Ashwander, "Ragtime: A New View," Jazzology JCE-71, 1970.
Composed in 1966.

Mobile Carnival Rag Tango. Not copyrighted or published.
Recording: Donald Ashwander, "Ragtime: A New View," Jazzology JCE-71, 1970.
Composed in 1966.

Moon Walk. Not copyrighted or published.
Recording: Donald Ashwander, "Ragtime: A New View," Jazzology JCE-71, 1970.
Composed in 1969.

Peacock Colors. Not copyrighted or published.
Recording: Donald Ashwander, "Ragtime: A New View," Jazzology JCE-71, 1970.
Composed in 1967.

The Ragtime Pierrot. Not copyrighted or published.
Recording: Donald Ashwander, "Ragtime: A New View," Jazzology JCE-71, 1970.
Composed in 1965.

Sea Oats. Not copyrighted or published.
Recording: Donald Ashwander, "Ragtime: A New View," Jazzology JCE-71, 1970.
Composed in 1966.

Upstairs Rag. Not copyrighted or published.
Recording: Donald Ashwander, "Ragtime: A New View," Jazzology JCE-71, 1970.
Composed in 1966.

Voices, Voices. Not copyrighted or published.
Recording: Donald Ashwander, "Ragtime: A New View," Jazzology JCE-71, 1970.
Composed in 1966.

Waterloo Rag. Not copyrighted or published.
Recording: Donald Ashwander, "Turnips," Upstairs UPST-1, 1973.
Composed in 1973.

The Winter Fields. Not copyrighted or published.
Recording: Donald Ashwander, "Ragtime: A New View," Jazzology JCE-71, 1970.

WILLIAM ELDEN BOLCOM

Born: Seattle, Washington, May 26, 1938

Bolcom studied composition and piano beginning at age five. He entered the University of Washington at age eleven, and continued the study of classical music until he received a Doctor of Musical Arts degree from Stanford University. With Arnold Weinstein he wrote in 1963 an award-winning opera for actors called *Dynamite Tonite.* He became interested in ragtime in 1967 and started composing it. Recordings followed in 1971. He married singer Joan Morris with whom he gives concerts and makes records.

Brass Knuckles (with William Albright). Not copyrighted or published.
Recording: William Bolcom, "Heliotrope Bouquet," Nonesuch H-71257, 1971.

California Porcupine - Grand Rag Fantasy. May 24, 1971. Unpublished.
Recording: William Bolcom, "Bolcom Plays His Own Rags," Jazzology JCE-72, 1971.

Garden of Eden: Rag Suite. May 24, 1971. Unpublished.
Recording: William Bolcom, "Bolcom Plays His Own Rags," Jazzology JCE-72, 1971.

Glad Rag. May 24, 1971. Unpublished.
Recording: William Bolcom, "Bolcom Plays His Own Rags," Jazzology JCE-72, 1971.

Graceful Ghost. May 24, 1971. Edward B. Marks Music Corp., New York.

Recording: William Bolcom, "Heliotrope Bouquet," Nonesuch H-71257, 1971.

Seabiscuits Rag. May 24, 1971. Edward B. Marks Music Corp., New York.

Recording: William Bolcom, "Heliotrope Bouquet," Nonesuch H-71257, 1971.

APPENDIX

|———————————|

Other Important
Ragtime Composers

Alpert, Pauline (w)*
    b: New York, New York, December 27, 1900
Alter, Louis (w)
    b: Haverhill, Massachussetts, June 18, 1902
Arden, Victor (pseudonym of Lewis John Fuiks) (w)
    b: Wenona, Illinois, March 8, 1893
    d: New York, New York, July 31, 1962
Armstrong, Harry (w)
    b: Somerville, Massachussetts, July 22, 1879
    d: Bronx, New York, February 28, 1951
Baker, Edythe Ruth (w)
    b: Kansas City, Missouri, August 3, 1895
    d: Wurtsboro, New York, November 22, 1965
Bernard, Mike (pseudonym of Mike Barnett) (w)
    b: New York, New York, March 17, 1881
    d: New York, New York, June 27, 1936
Blaufuss, Walter E. (w)
    b: Milwaukee, Wisconsin, July 26, 1883
    d: Chicago, Illinois, August 24, 1945
Briers, Larry T. (w)
    b: Virginia, December 25, 1892
    d: Columbus, Ohio, October 9, 1946
Brown, Al W. (w)
    b: Cleveland, Ohio, January 3, 1884
    d: New York, New York, November 27, 1924

———————————————————————

*The *w* refers to white and *b*, when it appears, refers to black.

Brown, Nacio Herb (w)
>b: Deming, New Mexico, February 22, 1896
>d: San Francisco, California, September 28, 1964

Carroll, Adam (w)
>b: Philadelphia, Pennsylvania, March 19, 1897
>d: New York, New York, February 28, 1974

Claypoole, Edward B. (w)
>b: Baltimore, Maryland, December 20, 1883
>d: Baltimore, Maryland, January 16, 1952

Cohan, George Michael (w)
>b: Providence, Rhode Island, July 3, 1878
>d: New York, New York, November 5, 1942

Cooke, Charles L. (b)
>b: Louisville, Kentucky, September 3, 1891
>d: Wurtsboro, New York, December 25, 1958

Crump, Jesse (b)
>b: Paris, Texas, 1906

Dabney, Ford T. (b)
>b: Washington, D.C., March 15, 1883
>d: New York, New York, June 21, 1958

Daly, Joseph Michael (w)
>b: Boston, Massachussetts, February 7, 1883
>d: New York, New York, June 16, 1968

De Rienzo, Silvio (w)
>b: New York, New York, October 6, 1909

Europe, James Reese (b)
>b: Mobile, Alabama, February 22, 1881
>d: Boston, Massachussetts, May 9, 1919

Fazioli, Billy (w)
>b: Frosolone, Italy, October 27, 1898
>d: New York, New York, May 4, 1924

Franklin, Malvin M. (w)
>b: Atlanta, Georgia, August 24, 1889

Ginsberg, Sol (pseudonym: Violinsky) (w)
>b: Kiev, Russia, July 4, 1885
>d: Binghamton, New York, May 5, 1963

Gold, Joe (w)
>b: New York, New York, November 20, 1894

Goold, Sam (w)
    b: Philadelphia, Pennsylvania, January 29, 1893
    d: Philadelphia, Pennsylvania, January 14, 1931
Greer, Jesse (w)
    b: New York, New York, August 26, 1896
    d: Columbia, Connecticut, October 3, 1970
Grofe, Ferde (w)
    b: New York, New York, March 27, 1892
    d: Santa Monica, California, April 3, 1972
Gumble, Albert (w)
    b: North Vernon, Indiana, September 10, 1883
    d: New York, New York, November 30, 1946
Guttenberger, Ferdinand Alexander (w)
    b: Macon, Georgia, November 29, 1888
    d: Macon, Georgia, October 1, 1945
Hager, Fred (w)
    b: Pennsylvania, December 31, 1874
    d: Dunedin, Florida, March 31, 1958
Hampton, Robert (b)
    b: Tuscumbia, Alabama, August 10, 1890
    d: Los Angeles, California, September 25, 1945
Hoffman, Max (w)
    b: Gnesen, Poland, December 8, 1873
    d: Hollywood, California, May 21, 1963
Hoffman, Robert George (w)
    b: South, Alabama, September 19, 1878
    d: New Orleans, Louisiana, December 8, 1964
Ingraham, Herbert (w)
    b: Aurora, Illinois, January 7, 1883
    d: Saranac Lake, New York, August 24, 1910
James, Billy (w)
    b: Philadelphia, Pennsylvania, July 3, 1895
    d: Philadelphia, Pennsylvania, November 18, 1965
Johnson, Arnold (w)
    b: Chicago, Illinois, March 23, 1893
    d: St. Petersburg, Florida, July 15, 1975
Jones, Clarence W. (b)
    b: Wilmington, Ohio, August 15, 1889
    d: New York, New York, June 1, 1949

Kaufman, Mel B. (w)
    b: Newark, New Jersey, April 23, 1879
    d: New York, New York, February 21, 1932
Kelly, Edward Harry (w)
    b: Kansas City, Missouri, July 11, 1879
    d: Kansas City, Missouri, April 15, 1955
Klickman, Frank Henri (w)
    b: Chicago, Illinois, February 4, 1885
    d: New York, New York, June 25, 1966
Lampe, J. Bodewalt (pseudonym: Ribe Danmark) (w)
    b: Ribe, Denmark, November 8, 1869
    d: New York, New York, May 26, 1929
Lange, Arthur (w)
    b: Philadelphia, Pennsylvania, April 16, 1889
    d: Washington, D.C., December 7, 1956
Lange, Henry (w)
    b: Toledo, Ohio, July 20, 1895
Lapham, Claude Erastus (w)
    b: Kansas, November 13, 1890
    d: Los Angeles, California, May 10, 1957
Leclere, Irwin Percy (w)
    b: New Orleans, Louisiana, February 21, 1891
Lenzberg, Julius (w)
    b: Baltimore, Maryland, January 3, 1878
    d: Orlando, Florida, April 24, 1956
Morgan, Carey (w)
    b: Brownsburg, Indiana, December 25, 1885
    d: Pittsburgh, Pennsylvania, January 6, 1960
Morris, Melville (w)
    b: New York, New York, October 5, 1888
Muir, Lewis F. (pseudonym of Louis Frank Meuer) (w)
    b: New York, New York, May 30, 1883
    d: New York, New York, December 3, 1915
Niebergall, Julia Lee (w)
    b: Indianapolis, Indiana, February 15, 1886
    d: Indianapolis, Indiana, October 19, 1968
Olman, Abe (w)
    b: Cincinnati, Ohio, December 20, 1888

Perry, Sam A. (w)
    b: Russia, March 28, 1884
    d: Los Angeles, California, November 1, 1936
Polla, William C. (pseudonym: W. C. Powell) (w)
    b: New York, New York, August 12, 1876
    d: New York, New York, November 4, 1939
Pollack, Lew (w)
    b: New York, New York, June 16, 1895
    d: Hollywood, California, January 18, 1946
Pollock, Muriel (w)
    b: Kingsbridge, New York, January 21, 1900
    d: Hollywood, California, May 25, 1971
Ringleben, Justin (w)
    b: New York state, June 28, 1876
    d: Miami, Florida, December 25, 1962
Robison, Willard (w)
    b: Shelbina, Missouri, September 18, 1894
    d: New York, New York, June 24, 1968
Rose, Fred (w)
    b: Evansville, Indiana, August 24, 1897
    d: Nashville, Tennessee, December 1, 1954
Ruby, Harry (w)
    b: New York, New York, January 27, 1895
    d: Beverly Hills, California, February 23, 1974
Russell, Sydney King (w)
    b: New York, New York, November 29, 1898
    d: Palm Beach, Florida, November 28, 1976
Schwartz, Jean (w)
    b: Budapest, Hungary, November 4, 1878
    d: Sherman Oaks, California, November 30, 1956
Shapiro, Ted (w)
    b: New York, New York, October 31, 1899
Shepherd, Adaline (w)
    b: Algona, Iowa, August 19, 1885
    d: Milwaukee, Wisconsin, March 12, 1950
Sinatra, Ray (w)
    b: Gergenti, Sicily, November 1, 1904
Snyder, Ted (w)
    b: Freeport, Illinois, August 15, 1881

d: Woodland Hills, California, July 16, 1965

Stark, Etilmon Justus (pseudonym: Bud Manchester) (w)
    b: Gosport, Indiana, 1868

Sweatman, Wilbur C. (b)
    b: Brunswick, Missouri, February 7, 1882
    d: New York, New York, March 9, 1961

Thomas, Harry (pseudonym of Reginald Thomas
        Broughton) (w)
    b: Briston, England, March 24, 1890
    d: Halifax, Nova Scotia, July 11, 1941

Van Alstyne, Egbert Anson (w)
    b: Chicago, Illinois, March 5, 1882
    d: Chicago, Illinois, July 9, 1951

Vodery, Will H. (b)
    b: Philadelphia, Pennsylvania, October 8, 1885
    d: New York, New York, November 18, 1951

Wadsworth, Frank Wheeler (w)
    b: Illinois, March 27, 1890
    d: Evanston, Illinois, June 5, 1954

Wenrich, Percy (w)
    b: Joplin, Missouri, January 23, 1880
    d: New York, New York, March 17, 1952

Williams, Clarence (b)
    b: Plaquemin, Louisiana, October 8, 1898
    d: Jamaica, New York, November 6, 1965

Wirges, William F. (w)
    b: Buffalo, New York, June 26, 1894
    d: East Norwich, New York, September 28, 1971

INDEX

Busch, Louis F., 159, 262, 263, 267–70, 278
Business in Town, 285
Buzzer Rag, 148

Cabaret Rag, 155
Cabbage Leaf Rag, 56
Cactus Rag, 172, 202
Cake Walk in the Sky, The, 14, 32
Calico Rag, 202
California Porcupine, 288
California Sunshine, 171, 178
Calliope Rag (Krenz and Ballantine), 271
Calliope Rag (Scott), 121
Cammack, Jerry, 212
Campbell, S. Brun, 6, 21, 24, 25, 52–55, 56, 65, 78, 80, 105, 151, 152, 263
Campbell Cakewalk, 53
Canadian Brass, 91
Canadian Capers, 202
Canned Corn Rag, 174
Cannon, Hughie, 12
Cannon Ball, 65, 158
Caprice Rag, 243
Car-Barlick-Acid, 23, 66
Carew, Roy, 254, 257
Carolina Balmoral, 243
Carolina Fox Trot, 243
Carolina Shout, 202, 243, 248
Carr, Joe "Fingers," 127, 157, 159, 167, 175, 205, 209, 211, 262, 263, 266–70, 274
Carr's Hop, 268
Carroll, Adam, 234, 237, 291
Carter, Buddy, 26
Cascade Plunge, 285
Cascades, The, 81, 84, 87, 92, 97, 120, 133, 250
Casey, Conroy, 102, 187
Cassidy, Russell, 263, 278
Castle, Irene and Vernon, 144
Castle House Rag, 203
Cataract Rag, 172, 183, 203, 250
Cat's Pajamas, The, 179
Century Prize, 110
Certain Party, A, 158
Champagne Rag, 125
Chapman, Chris, 41
Chapman, James and Leroy Smith, 70
Charleston Rag, 190, 192
Chasin' the Chippies, 130
Chasing the Fox, 234
Chatterbox Rag, 141
Chauvin, Louis, 54, 78, 83, 101–103
Checkerboard (Tierney), 154
Checkerboard Rag (Jimerson), 203

Chestnut Street in the 90s, 25, 54, 55
Chestnut Valley Rag, 279
Chevy Chase, The, 191
Chicago Breakdown, 254
Chicago Tickle, 155
Chicken Chowder, 66
Chills and Fever, 48
Chimes, 159, 166
Chow-Chow Rag, 159
Christensen, Axel, 6, 135, 278
Chromatic Capers, 177
Chromatic Chords, 51
Chromatic Rag, 203
Chrysanthemum, The, 18, 48, 86
Classic Piano Rags, 266
Claypoole, Ed, 172, 200, 209, 234, 238, 291
Cleopatra Rag, 127
Climax Rag, 117, 119
Cloud Kisser, 43
Clover Club, 204
Clover Leaf Rag, 159
Clute, Pete, 278
Coaxing the Piano, 219
Cobb, George L., 172, 174–77
Cohan, George M., 166, 291
Cohen, Charles, 167
Cohen, Henry, 202
Cole Smoak, 66
Collected Works of Scott Joplin, The, 265
Colonial Glide, 180
Colorado Blues, 50
Columbia Orch., 75
Confare, Thomas R., 65, 158
Confrey, Zez, 22, 210, 214–21, 223, 228, 238, 273
Connors, Babe, 28
Contentment Rag, 87, 126
Conway's Band, 179, 189, 206
Cook, Harry L., 72
Cook, J. Lawrence, 168
Cooke, Charles L., 201, 210, 211, 291
Coon Band Contest, 16
Coon from the Moon, 12
Cooper, Rob, 26
Copeland, Les, 13, 55–58
Corinthian Rag, 283
Cota, El, 140
Cotton Bolls, 37
Cotton Patch, A, 47, 66
Cotton Time, 67
Cottontail Rag, 124, 130
Cottonwood Rag, 280
Country Club, 97
Cozad, Irene, 40, 67
Crab Apples, 159

Index

Index

Rendezvous Rag, 55
Reser, Harry, 235
Rey, Alvino, 269
Rhapsody in Ragtime, 194
Rhapsody Rag, 178
Rhythmic Fantasy, 237
Rialto Ripples Rag, 209
Rifkin, Joshua, 98, 265
Rigamarole Rag, 167
Ring, Justin, 235, 294
Rio De Janeiro, 237
Ripples of the Nile, 188, 189
Rippling Waters, 250
Rita, 153
Riverside Rag, 167
Robardina Rag, 106
Robbins Music Corp., 215, 227, 231–33, 235–38
Roberts, C. Luckey, 41, 172, 187–90, 222, 240, 261
Roberts, Jay, 26, 159
Roberts, Robert S., 19, 27
Robinson, J. Russel, 67, 69, 150–53
Robison, Willard, 237, 238, 294
Rochelle, 272
Rocky Mountain Fox, 56, 58
Rodemich, Gene & Orch., 75, 238
Rooster Rag, 183, 210
Rose, Al, 26
Rose, Fred, 233, 294
Rose, Wally, 29, 30, 54, 86, 88, 94, 96, 99, 126, 128, 141, 164, 181, 184, 188, 203, 210, 212, 259
Rose Leaf Rag, 94
Rosebud Bar, 28, 102
Rosebud Rag, 284
Rosenfeld, Monroe, 90
Rossborough, Patricia, 223
Rossiter, Harold, 39, 204
Rossiter, Will, 23, 31–33, 39, 42, 67, 72, 91, 92, 163, 174, 175, 176, 205, 225, 236, 271
Roustabout Rag, 5, 19
Rowland, Billy, 262
Roy, Harry, Band, 43
Royal Flush, 141
Rubber Plant Rag, 174
Rubens, Paul, 18
Rubies and Pearls, 155
Rubinstein, Anton, 43
Ruby, Harry, 238, 294
Rufenreddy, 197, 223
Russell, Sydney K., 171, 212, 294
Russian Rag, 172, 175, 176
Ryan, Slugger, 272

S.O.S., 210
Sailing Along Over the Keys, 238
St. John, Clarence, 66
St. Louis Days, 281
St. Louis Globe-Democrat, 90
St. Louis Palladium, 28, 71, 102–103
St. Louis Post-Dispatch, 77, 84
St. Louis Rag, 32, 34, 85
St. Louis Ragtimers, 32, 47, 92, 264–66, 278, 279, 280
St. Louis Tickle, 14, 47, 194
Saltman, Phil, 237
Sapho Rag, 150, 151
Sappington Memories, 281
Sarabresole, Paul, 5, 19
Satisfied, 46
Saunders, Otis, 52, 85
Say When, 175
Scandalous Thompson, 22, 40, 114
Scheu, Archie W., 167
Schutt, Arthur, 221, 231–33
Schwartz, Jean, 138, 158, 166, 169, 294
Schwartz, Phil, 159
Scott, James, 32, 40, 62, 79–81, 88, 111–21, 123, 124, 156, 173, 184, 255, 264, 279
Scott Joplin's New Rag, 85, 99
Scoutin' Around, 245
Sea Oats, 287
Seabiscuits Rag, 289
Seaman, Bernie & Marvin Smolev, 227
Search Light Rag, 93, 94
Seeley, Bob, 266
Seminary Music Co., 95, 96, 97, 98, 138
Sensation Rag (Lamb), 124
Sensation Rag (ODJB), 26
Settle, L. Edgar, 75
Severin, E. Philip, 69
Seymour, Cy, 68, 71, 140, 159
Shamrock Rag, 51
Shapiro, Ted, 234, 237, 294
Shattinger Music Co., 19, 88
Shave 'em Dry, 210
Shayne, J. H., 26
Shea, Tom, 26, 265, 282–84
Shepherd, Adaline, 71, 294
Shimmie Shoes, 199
Shoe String Rag, 277
Shootin' the Chutes, 238
Shovel Fish, The, 72
Showboat Rag, 272
Show-Me Rag, The, 282
Shy and Sly, 41, 189
Sieff, Saul, 234
Silhouette, 227
Silks and Rags, 9